WITHDRAWN

W. H. HUDSON

A PORTRAIT

HUDSON LETTERS

LETTERS WRITTEN TO
MORLEY ROBERTS
BY
W. H. HUDSON
DURING THE LAST 35 YEARS

LETTERS WRITTEN TO
EDWARD GARNETT
1901–1922

E. P. DUTTON & CO.

W. H. HUDSON

A PORTRAIT

BY

MORLEY ROBERTS

NEW YORK
E. P. DUTTON AND COMPANY
681 FIFTH AVENUE

This first American Edition of *W. H. Hudson: A Portrait* is limited to 1550 copies of which only 1500 are for sale.

Printed in the United States of America

W. H. HUDSON
A PORTRAIT

IN MEMORIAM

THERE are great sculptors who have wrought in bronze
Huge human figures, inchoate and bound
Within a fire-fused prison, yet alive,
So living that the eye of him who views
The amorphous block of metal makes to move
Those uncarved limbs the furnace seemed to drown:

Or, in some mass of marble showed the earth
Breeding her children: here a curve or hand,
The round of a woman's breast, or childish limbs,
Until the marble grows a translucent veil,
And ages, still expectant, wait the birth
Of beauty, or high power, or buried thought,
In some far-distant type of unknown man.

Come now with me, O sculptor; take your tools,
And view this cliff-side sheer above the sea,
Behind its lofty verge the tender green
Of ancient pastures and high lonely downs,
And carve me such a memory of my friend.
If soon upon the dawn-affronting rock
I find a shape, unshaped, of one who sits
Gigantic with its feet in lifting seas,
His brows gorse-crowned with chaplets of live gold,
And in the rock, rude-carved, an open hand,
Rough as the work of one to whom the steel
And carver's hammer come as new-found toys,
While in that hand a bird nests and that bird
Mothers her children, I shall know my friend
And his memorial in his native earth.

CONTENTS

CHAPTER I

CHAPTER II

CHAPTER III

CONTENTS

CONTENTS

CONTENTS xi

CHAPTER XVIII

W. H. HUDSON: A PORTRAIT

CHAPTER I

The mystery of Hudson—His brother Albert—The difficulties of Hudson's character—A biography impossible—Special difficulties in this case—Part of a
letter on these—Hudson's own monument—*Far
Away and Long Ago*—Death and Richard Jefferies—
The effect of his early illness—Blank pages of his
life—His parents—They migrate from Massachusetts
—His brothers—Effect of Darwin—Death of his
parents—Why he never re-visited South America—
Italians and bird-collectors—"The house that died"
—Dates that are irrelevant.

MANY years before *Far Away and Long Ago* was written
Hudson told me that, when he went on board the steamer
by which he came to England, his younger brother said
to him wistfully, "Of all the people I have ever known
you are the only one I do not know."

To reach any vision whatever of a human being who
even then baffled eyes which had seen him grow up into
full manhood is not a task for the intellect, but, if it
comes at all, a gift to long-lasting affection and comradeship. To reckon up Hudson in intellectual terms
would be a vain task. To build him from his books,
self-revealing as they may be, would give much but
leave more unsaid. There was something in his character
which forbade him to abandon his soul to others. He

kept it in a strong secret place, as those fabled giants in ancient myths keep theirs. For many years I felt just as his brother felt, and even when at last it seemed possible to pierce at rare moments his inscrutable reserve, it was often my thought that any new seeming comprehension of him was rather some fresh failure in me than any real increase of understanding.

There may come an hour when someone with courage will essay a complete biography. It is part of the gift of time to us that a portrait, if only done ably, at last satisfies the generation which knew not the man portrayed. Even to old folk who once "saw Shelley plain," and yet grow forgetful of the man's infinite variety, the portrait may serve. I cannot draw such a picture, for to do it implies the labour of seeking knowledge I neither possess nor desire to attain. I shall speak as simply as possible of the man I knew. And here I must for once, and once only, protest against the opinion that anything of worth may be written dealing with rich and intimate human relationships in which the writer himself can be withdrawn into the shadows of the background. It has been said that with every brush-mark the portrait-painter limns himself. Yet he can in one way stand outside, and every self-revelation ends in oblivion at last save for the historian and critic. It is not so with the writer if he lived with the man of whom he speaks. He cannot attain the colder objectivity of those who never heard the man's voice or laughter, those who never provoked answers to a thousand questions and never sat for long hours under the friendly eager inquisition of one who sought as freely for knowledge as he gave it. If, therefore, in this story I shall at any time seem over-prominent, it will not, I trust, be from any egoism, which always faded in his presence, or for want of care to remove all that is not needful. Truly I write only for those who loved the man: to them only I make such excuses, being sure that if what is put down is true and gives some light, though it were but the dim illumination of a glow-worm husk, they will forgive the failures in which some critics seek their daily bread.

Perhaps I may put down here part of a letter I wrote to one of Hudson's friends, who urged me to do this book, or perhaps one she hoped for rather than expected to receive.

"You want me to write. I shall try to do so. But the task is an impossible one. I haven't even a framework. And he was a mystery. And yet so often crystal-clear. A jester and so serious: so fierce a critic and so ardent for his friends: so savage and so gentle: a caged hawk and a reed-bunting singing by a river!

"How can one care for dates when he would have none of them, rarely putting them in letters? He hated the passing years. To catch him is like catching the song of birds for a book. There are words on the page and the thrush is still in the garden and the nightingale in the woodland. But I won't draw him as an ideal, and am likely to anger those who would have him a disembodied spirit of his Downs and not a 'reality.' You shall even see him eat at Whiteley's! I have just lately taken notes to try and save some jests of his or some savagery, a gust of laughter or some rare tenderness: even some causeless irritation which was funny to behold, a little passing whirlwind."

Of a certainty it is hard to write of him. And what is the use? Who can build a monument to a friend?

That Hudson raised his own monument we know. I saw him build it. The foundation was well and truly laid, and each year's labour added to his power and insight. His books will be remembered when many, though not ignoble in their origin and aim, have died at last. This sketch can only hope to endure so far as it draws life from his veins, and if it serves the purpose of sending but a few to the spring and fountain of his spirit, some or even one of those may carry on the tradition he delivered, a tradition which he himself took over from the nobler schools of English naturalists. For such loved man no less because of their devotion to knowledge and their desire to preserve from destruction man's kindred among animals and birds.

Some day a biographer will take the story of his early life and, having killed and skinned it, will boil it down into two chapters as if it were a carcase to be rendered for fat. Better far to let the book speak for itself: the supreme record in all literature of a boy's life and experience. We see him passionate for life and perpetuation, suffering and yet full of joys unknown to most, perhaps known to none other in such fullness. There is a book of Richard Jefferies which once came home to him, *The Story of My Heart*. What appealed in it was the element of vision, and at first the wild clamorous appeal for "life, more life." Yet in this painful desire of poor Jefferies there was something almost hysterical. The book was the work of a sick man and a weak one who wished to live and knew he could not. In spite of all the ailments dating from the time he had rheumatic fever, the effects of which killed him in the end, Hudson was so utterly active and strong that Jefferies' cries seemed at last to him as disturbing as those of a sick man complaining in the next room. They reminded him of death and the end. So of later years he rarely spoke of *The Story,* and when he could not look forward, or feared to look, he went back to the pampa and re-lived those tremendous days with his four brothers, his beloved mother and father. Illness did not destroy him: rather did it make him what he was. In health so powerful a man's energy would have thrust him into the nearest work: it would have been his duty to seek a "career," and a career might, it almost certainly would, have destroyed him as a great naturalist and a great writer. His disaster set him free, though at first he knew it not, from the common duties and obligation binding the children of a poor man. They said he was to die and, like the dying guanaco, he sought desolate places and thereby was healed for a long life and prepared for duties that none knew of, not even himself. How truly he was what he thought in *Far Away and Long Ago* none shall determine. Clear though the vision, and it is clear and bright as a living dream, he saw it through the atmosphere of over sixty years, and most consciously made it as beautiful as he felt it to be true.

None seems to know much of his life from the date of the last chapter of his youthful autobiography till I came to meet him in 1880. Yet he suffered many things till he was twenty-nine, when England, that was to be his England, called him too imperiously to be resisted. Nowadays we speak little of "England": people put themselves down as "British." I even hear of a Scottish clamour against "English" literature. But Hudson, conscious of the red earth from which his ancestors sprang, loved the word itself as he loved the soil. He cared little to remember that his parents came from another country. He went back to his ancient stock.

During many years I heard at times something about Hudson's people, and always understood that his father, Daniel Hudson, was an Englishman born in Exeter. But it appears from what I have learnt recently that it was his grandfather who came from Clyst Hyden, nine miles north-east of that city, which Hudson sometimes called his "natal city." Daniel Hudson himself was born in Marblehead, Massachusetts, in 1804. He married Catherine Kimble, a true American from Maine, descended from a traditional "Pilgrim Father." Her family were said to possess a Bible brought out in the *Mayflower,* which appears to have been much burdened with Bibles. Hudson's father married young, and was severely hurt when running along a tier of barrels in a brewery, and also, as I believe, while handling a heavy baulk of timber. It was the state of health which resulted from these accidents and threatened tuberculosis which led him to emigrate with his wife from the harsh northern climate of his birth to the sub-tropical Argentine. Their voyage, owing to calms, was prolonged to more than three months. They were one of the very first American families to settle in the early Rio de la Plata State of Buenos Aires. It was many years after their marriage and three or four after their arrival in South America that their children were born. There were four sons, of whom W. H. Hudson was the third, and also two daughters. Hudson's date of birth was the 4th of August, 1841.

His eldest brother, Daniel, whose gift of Darwin's *Origin of Species* had the remarkable effect on him which he describes in *Far Away and Long Ago,* was six years his senior. His youngest brother was Albert Merriam Hudson, and about the name Merriam I shall have something to say later. It is to his son, Hudson's nephew, that I owe some of these facts. The youngest of the family, Mary, was Hudson's favourite, and her death in his old age was a great shock to him.

Daniel Hudson, who farmed sheep during the whole of his Argentine life, died in 1868, aged eighty-four. Catherine Hudson died eight years before him. A year later Hudson sailed for England, which he never left again save for a short visit to Scotland and, I think, one to Ireland. England was not only the country of his adoption, but the land, and the only land, for which he felt passionate love. Yet once he said to me, "Perhaps I may say that my life ended when I left South America." He seemed to feel so greatly the death of his father and mother that their going was a kind of death to him. But he made a new birth in the country of the nightingale, whose song has brought many from Western countries, and little by little the pampa of his native soil became a dreamland, so beautiful in memory that he could not bear the thought of the changes time and ruthless immigrants had wrought there. This was why he said to me that he did not want to re-visit the land of his birth, which was overrun by aliens of that race in Europe which is most pitiless to birds, so that in their own Italy it was but in the deep recesses of the few remaining woodlands, or among her mountains, that the forms of life remained which could glorify by their music desolate places and make out of them, even if it were but for a little time, something to remember and be glad for. Now he knew that none of his birds could live—such a spot as Quilmes would have lost its natural life and become the haunt of those who cared nothing for natural beauty but to destroy it. They, too, were bird-collectors: they killed to eat as these others killed to make mummies in glass cases, by which they acquired glory.

For it was at Quilmes, some ten miles from the nascent city of Buenos Aires, and but a short distance from the brick-red waters of the river Plate, that Hudson was born in the house named *Los Veinte-cinco Ombues,* or The Twenty-five Ombu Trees, "the house that died."

Here I may say that so far as dates are concerned I have more or less done with them. For dates Hudson cared nothing. Indeed he abhorred them. They counted up the years. They were gravestones. They marked out the days remaining. Rarely would he use them. Not one in ten of his letters is dated. The pure and passionate biographer may lament the loss of fixed hours and days and years but, as I have said, this is not, and cannot be, a biography. So nothing more need be written of the early days he has himself described and little, indeed, of the period between his first great illness and the time I met him, when he was thirty-nine.

CHAPTER II

His life "ended" when he left the pampa—The Gran
Chaco and Patagonia—Banda Oriental—His refusal
to think or speak of the past—How impossible it
seemed to write of him—His letters—Many lost—
The common biography a thing to avoid—Hudson's
last book—Art and energy—A new art needed—A
big portrait impossible—The method of many
sketches—What is known before 1869—He lands in
Southampton—"The smell of England"—Life in
London—Chester Waters' secretary—A genealogist
at home—Visit to John Gould—Satiric sketch of
Humming-Bird Gould by Hudson—Another blank
period—He marries Emily Wingrave in 1876—I meet
him in Bayswater—What is a great man?—The
question of his age—His failings—Date of his birth—
Yet he was for ever "of no age at all."

I HAVE said he told me that his real life ended at twenty-
nine, when he left the pampa.

On those barren or grassy plains, burrowed by the
vizcacho, haunted by the carancho as it sought for dead
or dying beasts, among horses and wild cattle and wilder
men, more bloodthirsty than the puma, that *amigo del
Cristiano,* the active life granted to him by fate had
been passed. To leave the borders of the Gran Chaco,
the plains of Patagonia, and the scattered *estancias* of
his own wide homeland for the close and ordered life
of England was in a way a kind of death. Events that
can be marshalled and arrayed ceased with him for a
time. Though but little is known of his life till he came

9

to England, yet from fifteen to twenty-nine he wandered
and travelled beyond the Rio Negro southward, to Banda
Oriental across the wide waters of the La Plata, and
westward over the pampa.   Someone yet living may work
out an itinerary and chronology, part guess-work and
yet likely, but from twenty-nine to thirty-nine I find no
landmark but his marriage and a few signs here and
there in things half forgotten.   What his first years in
England were like I never asked: it was not easy to
live in the "dark backward and abysm of time" with
Hudson.   He lived in the hour whose air he breathed
and in the days to come.   And even when I followed his
career, that humble struggle not for fame but for daily
bread and for sufficient ease to rush sometimes into the
country away from the alien roar of town, there is scarce
a chart to guide one but some odd letters and the slowly
increasing scroll of his books.   Since it was never in my
mind for an instant during forty years that I should
ever write of him, it is easy to understand that one lived
with him for the day and hour and never for a long
time even preserved his letters.   Then, too, if my own
wilder life, in some ways parallel with his own, also
ended at the age of twenty-nine, three years of that
period were spent in America, and in that long adventure
we wrote to each other but rarely.   So now I have few
letters of his but those written after 1896.   I speak of
these things, not by way of excuse for refusing to write
a laboured biography, a thing always hateful, but to
give some reason for the lack of dates and the like which
many look for, for there are some who cannot grasp a
period of history without an apparatus.   Yet it may be
best that I remember little, since a cloud of inconsiderable

facts might destroy the picture. Never was a more mysterious man than Hudson. And never one so plain. A bold antinomy but true, and anything that clarified his mystery till it became a thing of dated hours and days would be a lie, though any sketch that at the turn of a swift moment limned him as less than simple would be as false. So, therefore, taking advantage of my very want of knowledge and of forgetfulness, the dateless story put down here, with some days or hours drawn with care, may more represent him than any story of his life which possesses the dangerous advantages of petty detail.

In the very last chapter of his last piece of work, which I helped to put into order, as the end had not received his final revision, Hudson analysed art into the free energy of man and of the animals that flowered in music, dancing and ornament, and again into the childlike cry of the creative artist—"Come and see!" In thinking of him now it seems that this gives some clue as to the way his picture should be drawn, this book be written. In the same chapter he speaks of the inevitable dissatisfactions of art and how the artist for ever yearns for some better way of expression. This is true, but as one cannot transcend art, which is best when it is simple, even deliberately so, it seems best to put him down with as much power of simplicity as may be possible, without any sophistication or any attempt to paint one great portrait. Taking it for granted, as I do, that this is beyond my power, perhaps in the end sketch upon sketch may almost stand for the skilfully ordered planes of some true and deep likeness. The painter is not for ever concentred on the character of such as sit to him, but builds as he may, and only at last pulls the thing together in order that character and likeness may be one. So, if here and now simple aspects are taken, careless for the moment of the rest, a portrait may be the issue, and I can at last say, not with any exultation but with the faith and loyalty of a friend, "Come now and see him, as I did." For many, perhaps, the picture will fail, not for lack of good will in the painter but because they caught something of his multitudinous personality which escaped him, some smile, it may be, which was one wave of the unnumbered miles of the floods of ocean.

Of Hudson's early life he has, indeed, left an incomparable record. None who cared to look at this book will have failed to read it. It cannot be summarised or pounded into pemmican. As he remembered his childhood with passion on that sick-bed in Cornwall, so he put it down, a living, breathing record, simple, direct, absolutely truthful as he felt it, a great gallery of impressions of life on the pampa in the 'forties, a pampa now denuded of its old glory, marked out by wire fences, harried by strange immigrants, with bird and puma and even the wild gaucho gone, replaced by tamer peons. After that record ends nothing is known of Hudson's career till the period came of which he wrote in *Idle Days in Patagonia*. He was twenty-three when he first saw the waters of the Rio Negro in that "Land of the Big Feet." The sixth chapter of that book was first written as an article for some dead London magazine, and in its earliest form was called "The Settler's Recompense." Though I knew already that Hudson, whatever his literary fate might be in England, was by nature a writer, that sketch of the pioneer whose joy was in the fight and never in the victory which always eluded him, told me that he was a genius.

Good as it is now in the book, it was, if I am not mistaken, better when alone, because I found it so fresh, so moving, and so true a picture of life which was not something wholly unknown to me. When he gave it into my hands I sat by him and read it, and held my breath, for the passion of his words communicated his own emotions. But not once in our long comradeship did either give out all he felt. Hudson's "Good!" was a certificate of honour. One asked no more. What I said I cannot remember, but I know it was something like "This will do." Though I was so much younger he never seemed to notice it. Therefore I ignored the difference in our ages and spoke as his equal, though I had then written nothing fit —shall I say?—for condonation. Now again after Patagonia the curtain fell, and only rose once more when he bade his brother Albert good-bye in Buenos Aires and sailed for Southampton. It may be that without his beloved parents life seemed unendurable. None understood him. And England, which had printed little things of his and had made him a Corresponding Member of the Zoological Society, called to him and his English blood. He never said a word as to the "why" of his departure from the Argentine.

Thus at the age of twenty-eight or twenty-nine he trod the soil of England, the land of his dreams. He came to it in the month of May. He said the light seemed wonderful. England was "a land of the morning." As he repeated the whole story to me when we were at Penzance two years before his death I can remember his very words. He said: "As soon as I landed I made up my mind not to go to London as most of the others did, but got a room and walked about Southampton. And suddenly I smelt England! I asked myself what so strange a smell could be. It was sweet, and yet there was, as it were, a touch of sourness in it, and it seemed warm and fat and strong and pervading and yet elusive. And I said, 'Why, this is the typical smell of England,' and I went up one street and down another, and sometimes I lost it, or only smelt it faintly, and then again it came in heavy puffs, and though so strange to me I found it very attractive. But it was only long afterwards that I knew it was the smell of a brewery!"

He laughed and added cynically, "Perhaps that would please the apostles of beer!"

Later I hope to give more or less in his own words what happened that day and the next, but after that time I know little of what happened to him, how he lived or starved when at last he reached London. He had some friends in England whom he stayed with first, for in 1908 he wrote to me from Malmesbury: "I came on here to-day and am dawdling about the Abbey, and climbing to the roof to-day saw five miles away the very tall and very thin spire of Telbury Church. A place of memories for me: it was there I went first on coming to England on a visit to the family of a South American friend of mine, a very fine fellow who took to drink and went to the dogs." Then again there shows a spot of light, for once he gave me a long account of his becoming secretary to an archæologist, Chester Waters, who made a somewhat precarious living by discovering, perhaps concocting, genealogies for Americans who were ready to pay for ancestors real or spurious. This man employed Hudson to look up pedigrees and the like, not that he could afford a secretary, but because he was unable to leave his house, as he was besieged by creditors and catchpolls. At times food was introduced by means of cords lowered from upper windows, and often Hudson could not get into the house because he would have been followed by bailiffs. It was sometimes as difficult for him to leave it. As may be imagined, his salary was always in arrears and he and his employer had periodical combats about money. Waters used to say, "It is no use asking me for money. I haven't any." When Hudson insisted, Waters at last with the greatest reluctance produced half-a-crown, say, and subsided groaning into his particular branch of fiction. It seems that his wife and daughter stood this life for a long time, but finally could bear it no longer and fled. Hudson, after an exceptionally severe battle about money, flung a handful of papers in Waters's face and retired penniless and defeated.

It was before this that Hudson called on Gould, the rather pretentious and unscientific ornithologist who dealt with the *Trochilidæ* or Humming Birds, to whom he had an introduction. Gould had some internal trouble which afflicted him with pains he cared not to hide. A satiric sketch of the meeting he had with Gould was published much later by Hudson, but I cannot trace the magazine in which it was printed. Nor do I remember its title. To some necrologist of letters this hint may serve to set him burrowing among magazines that died in the 'eighties. That Gould should regard Hudson as some astounding intruder who dared to believe he knew anything of birds, and should be intensely rude between groans, was a joke that did not pass unavenged. Gould was sketched under another name as a naturalist particularly interested in monkeys, and his habit of breaking off conversation to groan, and perhaps to roll on the carpet, was, I think, brilliantly, if somewhat brutally, taken off. It was, however, Hudson's belief that he had as little real illness as he had manners. In later life Hudson much disliked being reminded of Gould and the story he wrote about him. When I spoke of it in 1920 he betrayed the irritation he always felt if anything recalled to him his time of bitterest poverty and stress. It is indeed due to this that I, or others, know so little of his life between 1869 and 1876. He never willingly went back to the past if it was in any way painful or humiliating. To enjoy the present hour to the full, and look forward to the coming day with eager anticipation, was his conscious philosophy, as it is the unconscious philosophy of a happy boy. I know he was often wretched during that long blank period. If he had been happy he would have told me of it and thus regained something of ancient joy, just as the evening primrose and its delicate odours recalled things of beauty to him when he leant out of the lattice window of some cottage and remembered his youth.

But whether he spoke or was silent I knew in those days that I had made a friend for life, and often when with him I wondered whether others would ever discover that this immigrant of English blood from a far strange country had something akin to greatness in him, even though in his deep simplicity he himself did not suspect it.

I have heard of some few who thought little of Hudson: even of one who, when his friends wished to build some monument to him less enduring than his own work, urged that there were "others" when they exalted Hudson, as if the height of one mountain detracted from that

of its neighbour. Some, too, have sneered at those occasional, if rare, failures which are found even in the most
perfect styles: failures, in Hudson's case, almost always
due to his having been bilingual in his youth. Those who
do not see his greatness, though it may defy analysis, are
not to be envied. What, indeed, is a great man? Is the
word to be confined to conquerors? Hudson conquered
the English tongue and made of it an instrument of
rarest music. Or to artists? What else was he but an
artist whose pictures of the wildest or most homely
English life convey more than any painting, and are
themselves poems? To those who alter the destinies of
men as philosophers and politicians? Then he has
altered the whole outlook of thousands and taught them
mercy, pity, love and beautiful words. There is, too, a
greatness in character alone. Who cares now for what
Dr. Johnson wrote? What he said and how he said it
and his ways of thought, his indignations and endured
miseries and his kindness, surpass his poems and laboured
prose as much as his personality surpassed that of him
who drew his picture. Different as they were, it is hard
to think of one who carried such weight as Johnson if it
be not Hudson. But Hudson swamped his company, not
by words, but by his presence: where he stood was the
centre of the picture: all looked to him, with surprise and
expectancy. Yet it was not with clubs or the ferocity of
Dr. Johnson's conversation that he conquered: it was his
aspect, and his height, and his bowed big head, and his
eagle-like look, and that beauty "with the quality of
strangeness" of which he often spoke, that marked him
out from others as though of a rarer species, even a
genus of man who stood solitary and yet in all things

human. How much of this it is possible to convey I, at
least, shall never be able to judge, but though nothing
can be conveyed but mere words, my bankruptcy in power
to draw him can only convince me that it does but need
greater powers to accomplish a great portrait of one
truly great.

Something more must needs be said of his age, not
that it is important in itself, but because there was some
conflict between me and others, who assumed that they
might rely with confidence on passages in *Far Away and
Long Ago* from which they made deductions which could
be disputed. Hence in the late collected edition of his
works is found the legend *"natus circa* 1846." Now it
is true that Hudson made some statements in his early
autobiography as to dates in the life of Rosas, the dic-
tator of the Argentine, which justify this. He speaks
of being in Buenos Aires as a boy of six, "on the eve"
of the fall of the tyrant at the hands of his rebellious
general the savage Urquiza. But I am not writing in
order to conceal the curious little flaws or failings of
Hudson's character. He hated to grow old: he loved
life: the years were passing bells: he could not endure
that others should know how old he was. To have them
think he was younger than his true age helped him to live
and to hope to live longer yet. The fear of death was
always in him: death had been hateful to him since
Margarita, that beautiful girl of the pampa, a nurse in his
father's house, had put life behind her. When the hopes
of religion and its consolations passed as she had passed
and grew cold, he hated death still more, so that "in my
worst time I could always feel it was better to be than not
to be." Thus he speaks at the very end of *Far Away and*

Long Ago, and there were times he said so to me. He
felt strangely young and was young to the last. To
assume that he was older angered him. He fairly shouted
at one friend, "I'm as young as you," when his seniority
was implied. Therefore I never reminded him consciously that when we met I was twenty-two and he
thirty-nine. If in late years I ever touched on such a
contrast by accident he was disturbed and changed the
subject quickly. I, therefore, take it for granted that the
passages in *Far Away and Long Ago* were a deliberate
mystification. I knew that he was born on August 4th,
which is St. Dominic's Day in the Catholic calendar, for
he told me that the native women round about his home
implored his mother to name him after the saint, as a
saint's name might give the poor Protestant child a
chance of salvation, and, though she refused to do so, they
persisted all the same in calling him Dominic. To discover definitely what the truth was I had his marriage
certificate with Emily Wingrave searched for, but the
dates given for the wedding were so far from the truth
that it looked at first as if they had never been married
at all. Mrs. Hudson's nephew, Horace Wingrave, at last
found that the ceremony took place in 1876, and in the
certificate his age was given as thirty-six, which made the
year of his birth 1840. This, however, has been corrected
by Hubert Hudson, his nephew, who searched the records
for me, and found Hudson's birth put down in the books
of the First Methodist Episcopal (American) Church of
Buenos Aires as August 4th, 1841. It is, therefore,
certain that he was eighty-one when he died, not seventy-
five or six. Nothing more need be said of this. Many
people will understand it, since he had not attained such

years as to make him proud of longevity. A favourite story of his was one of a man who declared with senile exultation that he was over a hundred. When his granddaughter said that he was only just over ninety, the old man squeaked pettishly, "Presently you'll make me out no age at arl!" Hudson wished to be "no age at all," that is the truth of it.

It was in the late summer of 1880 that I first met him. He was then living at 11 Leinster Square, Bayswater.

CHAPTER III

IT happened in 1880 that I went to see a friend who then lived in a Bayswater boarding-house, kept by a Mrs. Hudson. It was late summer and darkness was falling as I entered the square. When I rang the bell the door was opened to me by a stranger, whom I could see but dimly against the light of the inner-hall lamp. Yet, even then I saw something highly impressive in the tall, gaunt figure of the man who spoke to me, and as soon as I got him in a full light I felt that I was in the presence of a big but very friendly personality. His great stature, the breadth of his shoulders, the thoughtful stoop of his head, as though he for ever leant to hear what lesser folk had to say, and the keen, kindly glance of his eyes made up someone worthy of Rembrandt's powers of portraiture. Very soon I learnt to know that in every look, in every casual word, he gave out a sense of unconscious

21

power, and among those who surrounded him he seemed an exile, an eagle among canaries. Many will wish to know something more of his look than they gain from photographs and sketches, even from the powerful black-and-white summary of Rothenstein, whose artistic brevity of expression leaves very much to the imagination. I shall try to put down not only the impression he made on me that first evening, but such others as well, both here and later, as may, perhaps, make some composite drawing.

Assuredly there never was a more remarkable-looking man. In the street he was as noticeable and as much noted as if he had been an inhabitant of another planet. Types like his are occasionally to be found in England. But pure types are rare. His height was about six feet three inches when he stood upright, which he rarely did. He wore a short-cropped beard and an untrimmed moustache: his hair in his youth was dark brown and in later years grizzled. His eyes were more or less hazel and deeply set, with heavy brow ridges and well-marked eyebrows: his nose, large and prominent and by no means symmetrical. His complexion was sallow, and his ears, though well-formed, as large in proportion as his hands and feet. As much might be said of thousands. But it was Hudson's whole aspect that showed the man. It marked him with a rare stamp. It was at once kindly and formidable. He looked like a half-tamed hawk which at any moment might take to the skies and return no more to those earth-bound creatures with whom he had made his temporary home. His sight was keen: his curiosity insatiable. As he walked the street he observed everything and everybody. Had he been a draughtsman he could have drawn them from

memory. He was as much the field-naturalist in London
as in the country. In town, for beasts and birds he sub-
stituted the whole race of man. This gave him his air
of interested armed detachment. People were interesting
savages. He examined new acquaintances curiously, and
put them by for future observation if they displayed characteristics out of the common. If not he let them go
as he might have released some usual bird which he had
taken for a rarity. So when some of his friends said to
him, "Come and see us?" he asked, "Who will be there?"
quite unconscious that he was showing some lack of
interest in his hosts. "If So-and-so is coming I'll come."
And So-and-so was assuredly either some rare bird or
one whose species Hudson had not determined. In
later years he assumed with perfect unconsciousness certain privileges. It was as if he said, "I come from
Jupiter and can't explain myself to you, but if you will
take me as I am, that's all right." It is true that he was
sometimes irritable, but everyone recognised that this was
due to his health, not his nature. He loved laughter: it
was like a human song to him, the note of happiness;
and when he cackled in return his whole face laughed.
As for the people he turned down, they were often enough
such as the world esteems interesting or notable. I could
name a score of well-known people that Hudson had met
and even learnt to know, for whom he had not the least
use. They were mostly "serious-minded" persons, that
is, those whose humour is not deep, those who are amaz-
ingly sure they have the capacity to run the world if only
fools would stand aside and give them a chance: those
with grievances or huge self-conceit, cheap-jacks in the
literary arena, buffoons in life or art, self-advertisers,

mountebanks, and such as Dutch-auction their great ideas
in a failing market, or sell gilt brass to fools. Hudson
took to those who knew their work and did it quietly.
A man who would pack up and go to the end of the
world to rule a wild kingdom with such a cane as Gordon
carried, without letting *The Times* know all about it, appealed to him more than those who can scarcely go to
Brighton without public uproar. The fanatical sacerdo-
talist, the prude, and the Puritan were bores, and, though
less offensive than the merely bloodthirsty "sportsman,"
scarcely to be endured without rudeness. Like so many
men of science, though primarily he was no pure votary
of science, he kept his eye on the ancient eternal drama
of evolution and scorned those who were as ready as the
cheap politician to offer cures for the world's ills at a
moment's notice and at six shillings the box. He turned
away from these to men who loved art and quietness, or
faced the world unfeverishly and found loneliness better
than the dust and ashes of public life as it is lived to-day.
If any wise man had stood with him under a penthouse
sheltering from the rain, he might have found all this in
Hudson and gone away saying, as Johnson affirmed anyone in such circumstances would have said of Burke,
"This, sir, is a remarkable man." Hudson's every look
spoke of his nature and he offered his hand to all with
insight. It is scarcely a wonder that men and women and
children looked at him as he went by and ignored those
who were with him.

No, it is not possible to draw Hudson as I saw him
first. This sketch must remain as an ineffectual composite, pleasing only to those who can use and transcend it.

Our big portrait painters never painted him and thereby missed a chance for immortality. He will be remembered when they and most of their sitters are dead dust. Though many photographs of him are good and often better than good, none will ever see again Hudson's brooding smile, suffused with humour, nor catch the light in him which warmed and illuminated his talk. His power and size, the roundness of his skull, its shape and index, showed there was much in him of Beaker ancestry, those powerful men with round skulls and big noses, whose round (or long) barrows with drinking beakers in them are found from Torquay to Caithness, men whose descendants are still strong, men who "get there," who do things, and are not born to be hewers of wood and drawers of water, slaves of common service. At times he seemed some ancient Pan who loved the withering leaves in ancient woods of autumn (he loved to move in the golden fallen beech leaves of late October or November), and as he sat and watched the birds one wondered why they did not come to him as the wild creatures of the Galapagos came to his congener Darwin. With good health he would have been a marvel of strength. At eighty he had still muscles that some youths might have envied, but they were always loose and gave a certain wild looseness to his frame which made him seem a little awkward as he flopped across the road like a winged eagle, or ran, as he would in late years in spite of warnings, to catch and board an omnibus as it went full speed in a crowded London street.

I have heard of some who say he had no humour: they would say the sun had no light, a thrush no song: that the weald of Kent was barren of apples, that the Downs were mud flats. It bubbled in him: not only in his writings. Who wrote *Manuel, also called the Fox*? to name but one masterpiece any great humourist might have gloried in. Because he was also a seer and possessed melancholy as all great men do: because his spirit, his best and noblest reactions to his beloved earth, was kin to the spirits of the remembered past, such men cannot see the springs of laughter in him. But his laughter was sometimes savage, as bitter as gall, and his tongue a sword, as his pen was when he stabbed the murderers of birds: dealers in plumage, wearers of feathers, accessories of murderers, and worse than they, since they hired slayers to decorate their empty heads. Had some great painter avoided Hebrews and their offspring, or newspaper kings, or barons with bought titles, and saved his own soul by giving us Hudson as he was, a little of his various outward character might have been rescued. Yet one fears the thought is vain. There's no such painter: we cannot get Rembrandt from his tomb, and Rembrandt has no brother living who could find higher inspiration in a poor great man than in a monstrous fee or sordid knighthood.

If I speak of his appearance and personality as I see it now, when his youth, or what remained of it, has been overlaid by the memory of him in old age, it should be remembered that he was never old, nor ever showed it save by a slowly growing greyness of his hair, once so brown in colour and always curiously wiry in character. A painter often paints over and over again upon his first impression and yet retains much of that when the portrait is finished. So now it seems to me that Hudson at eighty was still the Hudson of thirty-nine, who took me into his house and soon afterwards to his friendship. Then I never troubled to inquire why he did so. It was all so natural. I was but twenty-two and he seventeen years older, and yet age never came in with us.

To think of Hudson merely *in* a boarding-house seems an absurdity, nay, even a cruelty, as it is to pen eagles in cages; but to have to contemplate him, if not as the keeper of such a place, as the husband of one who was, seems beyond all words. The house is still there to look at, the big house he hated and would not hear spoken of, just as a man out of prison may hate to hear a word of it, and when I passed through the square in after years it had the effect of making me think I, too, had been in jail and had there met someone who affected all my life. Till I entered that boarding-house I had never been in one and knew nothing of the genus of boarding-house habitués—I ought to say species, perhaps, for there are few specific differences among them, though aliens of brighter plumage alight for a time where they are and then fly away. They might be conceived to breed among themselves all the world over and to be barren if mated to any of the outside world. They are ghosts so often, or half-dead, widows, grass-widows, people waiting Micawber-like for something to turn up that never does turn up. Too many of them seem to lack spirit or enterprise, and drift from day to day, growing more and more bloodless, less and less ambitious, till to die is but to change lodgings, impermanent for permanent ones, where no more weekly bills can be presented to them. It was not always at No. 11 so bad as that, but take it all in all the differences did not count, and there sat Hudson, dark, sombre, or suddenly glowing, bitter or humorous, a condor in a little Zoo, with Emily his wife at the other end of the long table. But for the fact that she sang divinely and had a beautiful look of kindness, she might otherwise have been wholly of the type that sits in such places and does very well. That kindness of hers led, no doubt, to bad debts. Given the average poverty-stricken or "close-hauled" haunter of such houses, how could such not take advantage of weakness and become more and more parasitic? A good woman she was and gentle, and to her Hudson was as some great bronze god is to a worshipper. Or it may be she regarded him as a bird half-tamed who might yet fly away. But she loved him and bore with his irritability, which sometimes broke out and was perhaps not mitigated by an unholy passion he had at that time for the juice of a squeezed lemon, which he took in the belief it somehow did him good. He would get up from dinner with obvious relief and go to the sideboard to squeeze and drink the juice pure, and then come out with me into the Square if it was fine, and there we sat till it was ten or more, talking of the Argentine and Australia and the long plains of Patagonia, or the sea. Sometimes we read verse to each other, and I know it was a relief to him to come across someone who had a passion for literature and hoped, it might be, to do something some day not unworthy. And little by little it came to me that here was not only a very strange but a very big man. Impressive he was from the very start, but even then I had met those who carried, as it seemed, all the marks of character, and yet upon trial appeared to have nothing in them and were but squeezed lemons with the juice gone. Did I not say that it was only when I read *The Settler's Recompense* that I knew my instincts were

right? From that hour I never varied in my opinion.
Whether anyone else knew it or not, I knew he was a big
man. Here I may say, for it is the exact truth, that this
impression never affected in any way the very simple,
straightforward terms on which we met. Late in life to
meet a big man, one really such and not easy to measure,
is a great event and apt, perhaps, to make some shy or
nervous. For we learn little by little that if "good men
are scarce," as Juvenal remarked baldly, great men are
still scarcer, but when I was young I believed they were
to be found with ease. The papers said so, and they say
so now weekly, even daily. So to meet one at last was
nothing strange, though to find him the titular head of
a west of London boarding-house was something at which
to raise one's eyebrows and then to smile and roar out-
right and afterwards to lament over, almost to weep for.
Soon I saw the ambition in him and the artistic fervour
which he hid always even to the end, for he was not one
to exalt his artistic temperament, but rather to conceal it,
as something, if not disgraceful in itself, shamed by the
vulgar uses to which the words and the thing itself were
put. The artist in him was what kept him caged. Civilisation had hold of him, and his child-nature came out as
he wished to sing, to express himself among some who
could appreciate him if he could but do well. For were
there not those who had written the books which he loved,
and was this not the England which had produced all
English literature? Surely he might hope to be heard, if
he sang aright. So all artists think, and Hudson waited
for thirty years to hear the sound of late applause. A
good thing, maybe, for it sent him more and more to
Nature, which led him on the highest path and opened

the skies to him. With early success he might have been
"a literary man" instead of a philosopher, a man of
letters, and the very essence of a great naturalist.

Even in those early days our discussions foreshadowed
those which came afterwards. They were, indeed, the
same in nature, though they differed in scope from some
of the more profound talks we had at times in the last few
years of his life. In one thing he was happy, the manner
of his going, but not less happy for those who remember
him was the fact that to the last hours of his life his
intellect burned brightly and his interests were unabated.
As in those later days he interrogated me upon special
points in science, so in the early days he drew from me
what knowledge I might possess of the birds and beasts
of the strangely isolated Austral continent. Much he
knew of marsupials and monotremes, of echidna and
platypus and kangaroo, but here was one who had beheld
the wild echidna in the forests of the Upper Murray, who
had watched the platypus swimming in the flood of the
Lachlan, who had nursed the "dinged joey" of a kangaroo rat into tameness, and had visions of the thousand
coloured, screaming, whistling birds of the sombre scented
bush. In both our memories were trees which birds
turned into living changing jewels, mine a leafless dead
gum on which red or green parrots and paroquets made
chorus and transmuted its white deadness into sudden
glory; while his were peach trees, wonderful in blossom,
with paroquets who stripped the twigs for perches and
made him wrathful and yet full of wonder. For long
hours he and I sat on that bench in the garden of the
Square while he told me of the pampa, of the gaucho, of
the horses and cattle, of tricks with the lazo, of the game

El Pato of which he speaks in that wonderful *El Ombú,*
while I tried to repay him with tales of the wide salt-bush
plains of the Lachlan Back-Blocks, of the myriad sheep
and cattle, of the emus and the snakes, of kangaroos,
trap-door spiders and iguanas and horned lizards. As all
who have been born in, or have at last been subdued to,
the fascination of great plains greatly love them, so the
reviving memory of his own open spaces delighted him.
He spoke of long rides by night, and how when galloping he sometimes lay back with his head almost on the
horse's crupper and stared upwards into the starry southern sky, feeling divorced from earth and translated into
a new ethereal world, while still his horse carried him
deeper into dim wastes far from home. With what was,
perhaps, a harder grip on what we call "reality" and a
less spiritual outlook, I yet recognise, even then, what the
earth was to him and in what way it must be transfigured
by his emotion. To be with Nature and yet to avoid
her cruder moments, to be with man and to forget all
about him save that he was a wild creature of the earth's
various fertility, seemed characteristic of Hudson from
the first. One would think, in the words of nurses, that
as soon as he was born "he sat up and took notice." He
never ceased to take it. He lamented my lack of detail.
Why hadn't I made notes? He had to put up with my
being no naturalist, but worked me for such values as
my memories might contain. Now I am glad I never
thought of writing about him till so late. Such a notion
would have spoiled our comradeship. Yet if I could but
have a record of the hours spent in that garden with the
plains before us and the boarding-house forgotten! Then,
too, we talked of England, of which he had so far seen

little. The Downs even in those early days had not become a passion with him: he knew not the spire of Salisbury, or Bustard Down, or the western country away
to far Cornwall. As it happened, I could tell him of
much that he did not know, since as a child I had been
moved from one county to another. He was ready to
love all England where there were cottages and woodlands and birds.

Now it seems sometimes not a little hard, for those
who know nothing but England—and, perhaps, little
enough of that—to grasp the fact that Hudson was not
an Englishman. He who was born at Quilmes, within a
walk of the waters of the river La Plata, the so-called
"Silver Sea," was not naturalised in this country until
June 5, 1900, when he had already been in England for
thirty years. I believe I was one of those who signed
his naturalisation papers, but have only a dim memory
of doing so. He had a reluctance to admit that he was
not English by birth, and he never referred again to
having been technically an alien, but there were so many
things we never talked of or touched upon. Why is it
that I never "wound like a serpent" into the inquiry as
to whether he had ever had a great passion, perhaps for
someone like Dolores in *The Purple Land,* and, being
disappointed by fate or maybe death afterwards, became
one who loved lightly and passed on to other flowers? I
suppose that it was not only that he betrayed his everlasting reluctance to re-tread a sad and ancient path, but
that he was always and presently, here and now, so amaz-
ingly interesting. There have been hours when I went
to him primed with questions and subjects and straight-
way forgot them all as he talked, never with any inten-

tion of display, as widely as his native pampa, and in every word suggested other things to come. One sees in *A Hind in Richmond Park* how this lasted in him. Should one go to beg a penny of a man who without asking gives a king's ransom from his perennial purse of Fortunatus? Perhaps this was why in all our long years I never said, "Are you a naturalised Englishman?" or "When were you married?" One might ask ninety men such questions out of sheer boredom, to change a weary subject, it may be to break up a barren flow of words, but none but a fool was ever weary or bored in Hudson's presence. He dominated the room so easily, not by the loud screaming of some parrot of a man, but by his easily flowing song. And as to his not being an Englishman— there never was a better! Many thousands of years ago his brachycephalic ancestors, with their big bodies and big noses and a power of domination, landed on our eastern shores. His own grave is on their coasts, at Worthing, and what does it matter if he first drew breath in the Argentine under the shade of ombú trees, to the sound of trampling horse and lowing cattle? Yet that he was so bred up among an Indian Spanish race gave him qualities and made him more than an Englishman, never less. This was always his home. I think he saw as much when he read White's *Selborne,* and never did he truly regret smelling out England that day he landed in Southampton, never truly regretted remaining in it, and therefore never re-treading the pampa which yet lived in his memory. Folks sometimes spoke of him as if he had travelled from England, not to it, but assuredly when he came to it he came home. If he had not been naturalised, what need was there to be made an Englishman by a piece of stamped signed paper from the Home Office at a fee of so many pounds? His blood was almost wholly English in its sources; and he paid all his life back to England, which he loved so greatly. I could imagine him replying if I had asked, "Did you ever have a great passion, Hudson?" "Yes, a very great one that mastered me as sounds and scents and the colour of flowers and the blue of night skies and the thunder of trampling horses and the cry of ten thousand crested screamers by Lake Chascomus had done, and it drew me from where I was born and carried me as a great wind might bear some migrant to the north, to England, England, the dear great lady of my desire."

But I must go back to No. 11 in Leinster Square, Bayswater, to which the nearest Chascomus is the Round Pond in Kensington Gardens.

During that first year and the after years till 1884, when I went to Texas, it became a settled thing that dinner at No. 11 was there for me whenever I cared to come. A week rarely passed without my going. It is not fair to say that all the inhabitants of that house were of the boarding-house type, for some were at times Englishmen from abroad, engineers and planters and so forth, and some from South America who came, perhaps, because Hudson spoke Spanish. The table was not without its charm for all its ancient widows and dodderers, and one or two of the younger of us kept it lively, a thing for which Emily Hudson, who slowly became a real friend of mine, was truly grateful. She knew the difficulties and the discontents of folks with memories and without stomachs and with as scanty a purse as their cup of bitterness was full. But for me the time was after dinner, when Hudson and I walked or sat in the Square gardens when it was summer and renewed our long talks about birds and animals and their habits and customs which he desired to explain. This led me a little towards zoology and biology, and so to Darwin and others, and it happened that in this way Hudson discovered in me something of a capacity for inventing explanations and offering hypotheses free of charge. Though Hudson talked so easily and freely on all subjects which he knew or had thought out, his processes of mind had a certain stateliness of motion, I cannot call it slowness, when he dealt with the unknown or unclassified phenomena of life, whether they were those connected with birds or animals or that strangest animal, man. Finding one who was already deeply interested in many of his own subjects, though then with but a smattering of science, who possessed a lively and specious gift of explanation, Hudson took to using this and, discovering that he could slay any of my hypotheses without my taking their death as a tragedy, he made at times full employment for me. This led to long-continued discussions, postponed time after time and yet renewed once more, and in not a few of his books I come across passages which suggest past hours to me, for if I could not supply him with an explanation, I did sometimes help him to one. So we argued about the ways of cattle and wild horses, and why the guanaco has a Valley of Death toward which it escapes as the shadow of death comes down. Traces of these talks may, perhaps, be found in *The Naturalist of La Plata,* for he was then working out much of the matter that composed it. But of that book I shall speak a little more in detail when I come more closely to his general work. Yet how shall I recall the long days when we "tired the sun with talking and sent him down the sky"? But it was not then that I spent whole days with him. Those were to come, when much had happened to both. "Make notes: memory is no good," said Hudson, and disproved it in *Far Away and Long Ago*. Now some of those *Noctes Ambrosianæ* are almost more to me than the few hours when sad premonitions set me making some record of his last days. Yet all detail of those early times is lost in incommunicable impressions. But if I had kept a record or a diary, this book might have been a heavy labour of mere compilation and by no means what I would fain make it, something that is faintly tinged with the after-glow. I shall speak no more of No. 11. It still stands in Leinster Square. There are trees in the garden that sheltered him, under which, as evening fell, I sometimes recited things to him which I trusted were poetry, and he read to me *The London Sparrow,* his only essay in blank verse, which therefore to me has a beauty not wholly its own, although it is beautiful. It seems as if ghosts now sat beneath the branches of those trees.

CHAPTER IV

Hudson's few friends—Hudson and Gissing—I go to America, 1884—Correspondence—Emily Hudson's failure—Southwick Crescent and Ravenscourt Park —Poverty—The Parsee—My return in 1886—40 St. Luke's Road—The house "Illimani"—Emily Hudson —Her age and voice—A strange mating—How he came to marry—Mrs. Hudson teaches singing—Hudson's taste in music—Gissing and barrel-organs—A list of songs—Hours to remember—Emily Hudson's simple character—The house of destiny.

With, perhaps, the exception of Mrs. Hubbard, sister of Sebastian Evans, the poet, and Mrs. Philips, two ladies to whom he was devoted as a son, Hudson at that time was acquainted with few who were devoted to literature. He spent his time with books when poverty shut out the country and kept him in London. To meet any who shared his passion for letters as enduring in him as his love of wild life and wild animals, was something that stimulated him, even as his enthusiasm stirred them. So it came about that I brought him and Gissing together, and though two more different beings never perhaps existed, Gissing's book-love was mated with Hudson's, and both of them when together roused in me a half-slain love of learning. Of Latin and Greek Hudson knew not a word; his only foreign tongue was Spanish. This incited Gissing to learn it and thereby satisfy an ancient desire to read *Don Quixote* in the original, an ambition,

37

whether achieved or not, that comes some time to all
true men of letters. These two met fairly often and
sometimes wrote to each other. Whether Hudson's
letters to him are in existence I cannot say. Hudson in
his fury to destroy, so that no letters to him should remain, no doubt burnt Gissing's with thousands of others
and whole volumes and masses of notes. They often ex-
changed their books in later days, and Gissing found in
Hudson's something alien, strange and yet soothing. For
Hudson the other writer's books were a pain: they recalled poverty and stress in the past and foreshadowed it
in the future. Gissing's perpetual bitter humour about
Marylebone Workhouse was never comforting: he more
than half believed in it as his destiny. And Hudson,
though he said nothing of it, had suffered and was
to suffer again. As for me, not yet, if ever, a man of
letters, these were my two great friends. Small wonder,
then, that they should draw me in the end into that whirl-
pool in which so many drown or are cast ashore like useless chips, and lie forgotten. Yet I know they together
made life tolerable for me: too tolerable, perhaps, for
otherwise I might have shaken the dust of London from
my feet before I did and gained one freedom at the loss
of another. There is no need to say why I did go at last
in 1884 and sailed with poor health, little money, and
little hope westward across the Atlantic.

Of the years that followed I have written: let the
record stand or fall. I should not speak of that book
here were it not that but for Hudson and Gissing it would
not have existed. While I was away in Texas, California,
British Columbia and many other parts of North
America, I wrote when I could to them both. They

answered sometimes: I have no letter of theirs to show.
A wanderer cannot keep them. I have lighted camp-
fires with letters of both these men. Such might now be
valuable, more valuable than dollar bills, but there are
seasons when a man may light a fire with bonds or title-
deeds, if he has them. I heard, therefore, at intervals on
the Texan plateau or in Oregon or the Rockies of Hudson's fate and Gissing's doubtful progress. Gissing's
Demos I picked up for twenty-five cents in Santa Rosa
in California. Of Hudson I knew that No. 11 had failed
and that he and his wife Emily had migrated for a time
to a house in Southwick Crescent in which she strove to
repair misfortune while he wrote. And then I knew that
she failed again: they were in lodgings in Ravenscourt
Park and practically starving. "One week we lived on a
tin of cocoa and milk," said Hudson to me grimly when
I came back to England. But he seldom spoke of that
time. He would not re-tread paths of misery. But Emily
Hudson, heavy and getting old, with her hair and skin
faded, trudged about teaching girls without voices and
temperaments to howl opera, and those without music to
beat a wretched piano, while Hudson sat at home and
wrote what was mostly rejected. Though he so seldom
spoke of these times, he said in a letter written to me long
years afterwards: "When I had not a penny and almost
went down on my knees to editors, publishers, and literary
agents, I couldn't even get a civil word, and of ten or
perhaps twenty MSS. sent, nine or nineteen would come
back. And now when I don't want the beastly money
and care nothing for fame and am sick and tired of the
whole thing, they actually come and beg a book or article
from me!" The one piece of humour that came out of

this wretched time was after all tragic. In the same
house there lived a Parsee married to an English wife
who had many children, incurable laziness, a fool's love
for bad novels, and glorious hair that fell below her knees.
For this, it seems, her husband married her. He worshipped it as he worshipped the sun. And one day she
came down with her hair cut close. She said she could
no longer be troubled with it. I believe Hudson prevented
murder, but told this lady what he thought of her. She
retired in tears and read more novels, while the poor
Parsee packed up the hair and put it away in his trunk.
Hudson wrote something about this incident, but destroyed it.

The worst of this life was over when I came back to
London, for they were then living at Tower House, 40
St. Luke's Road, Westbourne Park, which had been the
property of Emily's sister. She left it to Emily, and
though it was mortgaged for £1100, then almost its
full value, Hudson, by letting the lower floors for flats,
was able to keep the garret floor for himself and get a
little more from uncertain, and at times dishonest, tenants than paid the interest on the mortgage. It was here
I found them on my return.

This dull house in which he spent the greater part of
his remaining years is close to Westbourne Park Station.
For many years the neighbourhood, once a "highly re-
spectable" resort, had been decaying and everything in it
showed the mournful memory of better days. In that
house's narrow strips of garden facing two streets there
are still some stunted melancholy trees. The poverty of
Hudson and his wife prevented them from doing anything to the place they lived in save at rare intervals, and

it was, therefore, stale and gloomy outside and dim with
ancient paper and paint within. On what remained after
paying the interest on the mortgage, and on the little
Hudson made sometimes in the earlier days, supple-
mented by a few sparse fees gathered by his wife, they
managed to live, while he worked as arduously as his
health permitted. When I first saw him there they occupied the top flat, the summit of their Cordillera, their
"Illimani," as he once said grimly, and year by year it
became more of a toil to them to climb the long and
sombre stairs. In the hall, and on the stairways and land-
ings, there was no attempt at decoration: they were
barely kept clean by the tenants and the housekeeper who
occupied the great basement, which was not far from
being the most cheerful part of the big gloomy house. It
was impossible to enter without some sense of oppression,
even of rage, to think that in this grim jail was held for
the great part of the years a prisoner of genius, whose
only true home was under the open sky. As I stood on
the step week after week, a step rarely cleaned to a hos-
pitable brightness, and listened for Emily Hudson's slow
steps upon the stairs, or his which were so much quicker,
it seemed that I was calling upon a great raptorial whose
flight was quenched by iron bars. And yet, no sooner did
he smile down on me (he was my only friend who could
do that) than I forgot he was in jail. For a friend to
come, from whom he need conceal nothing, gave him, for
a little while at least, some freedom of the spirit. Now
he would be able to discuss, to argue, to lay down the law
and then take back what he said in laughter at his own
arrogance. For Mrs. Hudson, though deeply attached to
him, understood little or nothing of him or his work and

the wider reach of his big spirit. She served him humbly, though at times she resented, not without bitterness, his attraction for others. With glorious hair and a grave colour as a young woman, she had now faded into something so colourless that she became a part of the room, while Hudson year by year grew more and more the kind of man at whom strangers stare and women, young or old, smile. She was very many years older than he— though he did not know how old until she was dead— and her voice, too, was fading fast. Formerly she had been a soprano, I think it may be said of the second class, though once or twice she had been upon the stage, and had even sung with Sims Reeves and other stars. Since his death a woman wrote to me, "How could one be his lover? As well be mated to an eagle or a thunder-storm." Emily Hudson was mated to a great elemental, to put that word to nobler uses than it has been subdued to, and found the miracle as much as she could bear. She did her best to be his companion. Scarcely less than fifteen years his senior, and very heavy for her height, she went with him into the country and trudged patiently scores of miles through highways and byways. Desiring ease and comfort as she did, she yet endured gently the rough lodgings which not only suited their purse, but pleased him better than any inn. She sat on village greens while he sought for rooms with cottagers, persuading them often against all obstacles to house one the like of whom they had never seen. It would give a wrong impression if any thought he did not love her. He did, and was grateful to her for beautiful service in the past, but it is a question if it was in him to love any one woman with a great passion and thereby put himself in

chains. He looked for freedom, and that he ever took
her with him at all when there was the liberty of the open
roads and woodlands before him shows that he cared—
and cared much. He could hurt no one easily.

But how was it that he, who loved beauty so much,
came to marry her? Is not the answer simple when one
thinks that she was kind and fair and sang to him, the
big dark man from the South who was poor and lonely,
and to the eyes of one who loved him, greater than the
world yet knew? She gave the stranger a home and the
chance to prove himself. For all his faults he never forgot that, or any kindness.

Now I am glad I have only a dim memory of those
days, of the recalled hours in that sombre, untidy room
where no spark of colour showed, because after all it
was not a home for him but only his den, his deep nest
in some hollow branch, whose true home was the tree-tops
and the sky. But the woodland bear puts up with a dark
cave in winter: the tiger lies close at times.

The hour came when Emily Hudson would sing no
more. Her voice was going fast. But Hudson loved to
hear singing, and being uncritical resented her new silence.
Whether for this reason or not I cannot say, but she insisted on teaching me to sing. As a boy I had sung in
the Bedford School choir for two years and had a strong
baritone voice of wide compass, of which she believed
something could be made. So, twice a week for years
I went to Tower House and climbed "Illimani," and
presently sang, or tried to sing, to Hudson who lay on a
big sofa and listened. His tastes in song were mostly
simple, perhaps now we should call them primitive: often
he wanted the old Italian operas or English ballads of no

great merit. Yet he did not object to better or bigger things.

As he shows so plainly in the last chapter of *A Hind*, he had a native, if uncultivated, passion for music. He showed this by his very catholicity. He could enjoy very childish stuff, but at the same time loved Wagner's greatest work, especially *Die Walküre*. He knew nothing of music technically, and I suppose most musicians would hold that all his theories were wrong. They may be, but often we owe as much to those who dare to make rash hypotheses as those who pick their way timidly to some cautious induction. Truly he liked almost any kind of musical "noise," and a fairly good uncultivated voice gave him as much pleasure as the singing of a master of song. He was like Gissing, who loved barrel-organs and bribed them with hard-earned pennies as he set his window open and thereby outraged the conventional belief that all authors are driven mad by organ-grinders. When Emily sat down to the piano, Hudson used to lie on that big old couch which is now in my possession, and urge me to sing things out of the older operas, such as "Il Balen"; "La donna e mobile"; "Sulla poppa," a rowdy barcarole; Schumann's "By Celia's Arbour"; Rubinstein's "Song of the Arabian Slave"; "The Erl-König"; "Caro mio ben," a woman's song of course; "Che faro"; Hatton's setting of Davenant's "The Lark now leaves his Watery Nest"; "In questa Tomba" (Beethoven); and a number of Handel's songs from the oratorios. This is a very incomplete list, but I forget the others. Sometimes he laughed when his wife pulled me up and ragged me, and then sang to show me how to do it, and often he said, "Sing that again," and lay

back in a higher state of contentment than my own, as
Emily Hudson often gave me very plain opinions as to
my want of progress and my almost ineradicable tendency to make my own time rather than stick to that
which the composer seemed to favour. I sang no more
to him after 1902, for all my vocal ambitions perished
under the threat and shadow of long-continued ill-health.

Those hours are happy hours to remember. They
seemed to help him. And after singing came tea, when
we discussed and fought over a hundred questions about
Darwin and Wallace, questions of habit and custom, of
mimicry and protective resemblances, of migration, perpetually a mystery and a big interest for him, of variation
and structure and ornament, of dancing and singing in
birds and their relation to music and dancing in man.
And of men and women and of writers and poets and
old books, for among old books he for ever dug and
disinterred ancient fossils or forgotten worthies.   So
that high garret with its low and sloping roof seemed
no longer dull or dreary, but a little home of strange
knowledge, of speculation and enthusiasm. And mean-
while Emily Hudson went about her work with her poor
flat tread, and though she understood nothing of it all
and perhaps wondered at her man and his young friend,
she was always a homely and kindly presence, one for
whom that young man felt affection and respect, on
account of her infinite kindness, goodness, and simplicity.

There is something of the touch, the very hand of
destiny, in the way that sombre house remained the dark
background of Hudson's life. He stayed in it till Emily
Hudson was too ill to live there, too weak and old to
look after herself, and something like success came to

him, a curiously bitter success for the poor woman, which enabled her to live and be looked after at Worthing, apart from her beloved husband for the first time in her life since 1876. He hated Worthing and now took more freedom. He had to take it at last or die, and he knew it. Even then No. 40 was his "home," that gloomy, dingy tower in a faded London quarter. It was as if a peregrine nested by the cracked bell of some dreadful methodistical abortion of a chapel in the Black Country. Whatever he did, there was no getting away from it. Emily Hudson would not sell it. Like so many women she clung to property. R. L. Stevenson said to me in Apia, "It is women who want to own things, not men." It was so with her: mortgage or not the house was hers: she held on to the last, and thereby held Hudson to it even to the end. At her death it came to him, but then it seemed hardly worth while parting with it. His time was short: and after all he had "holed-up" there so many years, had lived and suffered, worked and at times played there. So some old bird might cling to his ancient nesting-place though all the world around had changed and its feeding grounds were far away. When Hudson married it was in many ways a fatal mistake. It was not that he did not love his wife, for even at the very last he wrote to her daily, but it was as though some son of the wild gods had married a dear, but too tame, creature of the earth. Emily Hudson had a beautiful nature, I know, but she could not fly. The upper heavens were not for her, and often her mate was like the wild stallion who comes down from the hills and finds a mare in hobbles and tries to take her away, and kills her at last because the poor thing's "cannot" he translates into "will not." The parallel is incomplete. Hudson was never brutal, but he had wings and she was a gentle apteryx, a brooding, singing creature of the lowland woods or bush, where he was not long content to stay. It was a hound of the chase coupled to one bred in the house, whose widest happy world was a narrow garden, a garden that was never to grow for her.

CHAPTER V

No framework for Hudson's life—The date of his books—
Chelsea in 1888—Painters and sculptors—Sterling
Lee, McCormick and Hartley—Shoreham—Chanc-
tonbury Ring—Hartley and Gissing—Hudson's
knowledge of painting—His favourite picture—
Hudson's wanderings—Sir Edward and Lady Grey—
An incident at Shoreham—In London—At the Café
Royal with Graham and Champion.

SINCE in the ordinary way no "story" is to be told of
Hudson, nothing arresting or even overwhelmingly
painful, while his final "success," or what folks call success, came almost stealthily upon him, and was as much
a warning of the end as any sunset glow, there is no
strong skeleton of events in his life to make it dramatic
and therefore easy to relate. It might be that gaps could
be more or less artfully hidden by quotations from letters
and the praise or blame of critics. So biographies and
compilations of all and any material come into existence
and perhaps serve as quarries for others. If this book
is to serve as one, I would rather they who use it should
find rough carvings as rude as eolithic art itself than
a tumulus, partly built by others, or piles of letters. As
a groundwork and a plan I have little but memory till
1920, and the long row of his books upon my shelves.

On my return from the Pacific Slope at the end of
1886 he gave me the two volumes of *The Purple Land*,
with its old title, *The Purple Land that England Lost*,

48

which had been printed and praised and a failure in 1885. The first word of praise that ever came to him was from Professor Keane. In 1887, when I dedicated my own first book to him and Gissing, he wrote, or rather got printed anonymously, *A Crystal Age*. Of these and his other books I shall say something more when I come to speak of him as a writer: noting them now but as milestones. It was in 1888 that my choice of a Chelsea backwater for a dwelling, a holing-up den, led to his meeting some in whom afterwards he took perennial interest. These were painters and sculptors, for just then many artists lived in Manresa Road and Glebe Place who have since made names for themselves, some justly and some by luck. And some have died and others are already half-forgotten in the Royal Academy, so often the half-way house to oblivion. Among the colony were J. J. Shannon, Sterling Lee, Harvard Thomas, McCormick, and Alfred Hartley, to say nothing of others. The last two became friends of his and illustrated some later books. Especially he took to Hartley, now best known to some collectors as a quiet but distinguished worker in aquatint and as an etcher. It was through him that Hudson and I took to going to Shoreham for many short and sometimes long holidays.

Shoreham in those still days, before its shingle beach was made an affront to nature and the sea by a ghastly agglomeration of hideous bungalows, greatly appealed to Hudson. The sea he always greeted by walking into the edge of the surf, there scooping up a handful of water, which he drank as some kind of ceremony which re-united him to the salt wildness of nature. But not only the sea was peculiarly grateful to him. He loved the whispering wide mud flats of the Adur, with their sandpipers at ebb tide, and that river's broad surface when the flood made and turned it into a great river which he rejoiced to see from the Downs above. They were his Downs, as one might say, at the back of the town: in those days made picturesque by an old windmill which afterwards perished by fire. Northward of the hills which shelter Shoreham from the winds of winter stretched wide grassy, barren tracts where racehorses were trained, but which were otherwise essentially lonely save for scattered shepherds and solitary farms in the folds of the hills. And over the quaint wooden bridge by old Shoreham, farther up the stream of Adur, lay Lancing College on the slopes leading over springy turf to Chanctonbury Ring. At night, when mystery touched the school's incomplete folly of an ambitious chapel, it seemed to Hudson that the ancient days returned and that, if he listened, he might hear the monks chanting where in the daytime there were many birds.

The town itself and its notable ancient church with Saxon dog-tooth ornament, its queerly named street, Raptigal, a corruption of Rope-Tackle, and its people, pleased him much, though people say he hated Sussex. Truly he hated only Chichester, a priestly cathedral town of drinking-shops. Shoreham was at any rate a clean and fairly sober town, made interesting by little shipyards and yachts building or repairing or lying at anchor. Often he accompanied me to Suter's yard and yarned with the men there, and at times went into the neighbouring studio, an old converted sail-loft, that belonged to Gogin, a friend of Samuel Butler, whose *Erewhon* was a pleasing book to Hudson, as it satirised with almost inhuman savagery the things Hudson only mocked lightly in talk.

Even in those days he was not always able to take long tramps without fatigue, but there were times we went across the bridge and up past the school and the other windmill above it, and so climbed upon the grassy sheep- and bird-haunted uplands, with a rare dew-pond, on which he speculated, and so came at last to the crown of Chanctonbury Ring. It was true that man had planted the beeches there above the old ditches, as man had planted the same trees on wilder Exmoor, but still the shadows were grateful as we lay and smoked and talked for hours of a thousand things. The country round about he knew far better than I, whose natural leanings were towards the river and the sea, so that I knew little but Beeding and Bramber and Steyning and Chanctonbury and the woods of Wiston. But he knew Cissbury well, and Findon and Poynings under the shadow of the Devil's Dyke and far beyond them.

More often, perhaps, we sat upon the ancient beach and played with the sea. Sometimes Hartley came with us and sketched, thereby leading me to try my unskilful hand at water-colours, but for the most part Hudson and I were alone, and when we were tired of talk he put a big pebble on a post of some groyne and we threw at it after the manner of boys. Then home to tea, and afterwards another walk, perhaps to the Downs, by which we could get to Bramber without using the road or the field path, which ran through tunnels and close walls among the grounds of some kind of entertainment gardens, to which few or none repaired.

Hartley also knew George Gissing and we four became close friends. Gissing dubbed the quartette the Quadrilateral, after the Italian fortresses. We were thus supposed to hold together against the world we had set out, it may be, to conquer, which looked more likely to conquer us. The world will give dead Hudson a laurel crown if it starved him till he was seventy. And no great artist can paint his portrait now. Whether the greatest could have satisfied him or anyone it is hard to say. His notions of the art of painting were at once deep and shallow. Of the springs of all art he knew much, but when it came to walking in a gallery and finding out the best he took a childlike, simple view. He was often satisfied with illustrations to his books which made my blood run cold. His favourite picture in the National Gallery was the Vision of St. Helena, for reasons I could never discover. He would pass by Rembrandt or any of the delightful naïve works of the Early Italians to moon before her. She seemed to satisfy him as a feminine type. Yet he was the man who drew Rima. In spite of all his deep simplicity he was interested in new developments. His criticism of a Vorticist even would have been fairer and more instructive than that of some hidebound Academician. The primitive always appealed to him, and a wild attempt at the new for ever recalls the old and the efforts of children. He could, however, appreciate the finished art of our forgotten ancestors, the Magdalenians, in the caves of Altamira. Had his early ambition to be a painter proved itself, what he says in the last chapter of *A Hind in Richmond Park* points to the conclusion that he might have been a great artist of the wilderness. But for all

his sight his hands failed him. He had no manual dex-
terity, and even in his wild days dreamed and mooned
and lost his whip or his knife, though to do so is a
cause of scornful reproach among the gauchos from whom
he learnt so much.

During these years (I speak of 1880 to 1892) his life
was almost without incident. Sometimes he got away
to the Downs of Sussex, and again to Hampshire and
to Wiltshire. He began to love Salisbury and the Plain,
and Stonehenge; and when I suggested that he might
like the ruder character of Cornwall he put the notion
aside as an absurdity. Sussex, Hampshire, and Wilts
were good enough for him! Now he sometimes stayed
for a little while at a cottage lent him by Lord Grey
(then Sir Edward Grey), though whether they made
acquaintance before or after the publication of *The
Naturalist in La Plata* I cannot say. For the first Lady
Grey he had a deep and chivalrous affection. Her death
was an unspeakable grief to him, though he never spoke
of it more than once or twice in many faithful years.

I have said that there was little or no incident in
Hudson's life during this time, though inwardly it was
very often tumultuous, for there can be adventures of
the spirit and of the unsatisfied passions. Yet one thing
did happen when at Shoreham in September, 1893, which
I should not mention were it not for the conviction that
Hudson not only saved my life but the life of someone
else. We went to the beach one quiet sunny morning
and sat under the shadow of a groyne, and while he read
I tried my hand at a sketch. Presently three girls passed
us with an elderly lady, and when just out of our sight
as we sat half-hidden the younger people went in bathing.

The flood was making and there was a strong easterly set along the beach. This caught the girls and drifted them from the shallow water above the groyne to the deep water below it, and presently we heard a cry for help, and looking up we saw them far beyond their depth and obviously drowning. The older woman stood wringing her hands and uttering piercing screams. Hudson could not swim and I had always been a strong swimmer, so there was nothing for me to do but to go in after them. This I did with my clothes and my hat on. The first girl was an easy matter, for she kept her head and allowed me to tow her in by her hand till Hudson, then up to his neck in the sea, was able to get hold of her. She was the daughter of Alfred Aumonier, the neglected landscape painter who never came into his own. The second girl when I reached her had been down to the bottom and was dangerous to approach and lay hold of. Somehow it was managed, and by this time a young Church of England clergyman had come to Hudson's help. It took both of them to tear away the unconscious girl's grasp of my clothes. She almost pulled Hudson over, for the sea was breaking and the shingle very bad footing. When I got out to the third girl, who had been to the bottom twice, I could not prevent her catching me round the body and we went in some fifteen yards or so under water. If Hudson had not been there neither of us would have got ashore. He was much taller than the young parson and could come out into deeper water. After that I cannot say what happened. Next day Hudson told me that I wanted to know if there were any more, and that he gasped out with his mouth full of salt water, "No, old chap, there aren't any more." He and the parson got the pair of us ashore somehow and parted us with great difficulty. Considering the condition of Hudson's heart, the fact that he could not swim a stroke, that he was as scared of a wetting as a cat, for he knew well an attack of bronchitis or pneumonia would probably kill him, he ran nearly as many risks as anyone else. I am satisfied that if he had not been very tall and strong there would have been two saved and two dead. He sent me home as soon as I recovered consciousness, and stayed in his wet things on the beach till the others were able to walk. One thing greatly amused him, and he often referred to it in later years. When he got back to our lodgings he found me grumbling because I had lost my pipe. "Oh no, you haven't," said Hudson, "I've got it." "Did you find it on the beach?" I asked. "No," said he, "I twisted it out of your teeth as you lay on the shingle. You went in with it and came out with it." And he took it out of his wet pocket. Ever after this he kept an immense interest in the "salvaged damsels," as someone called them, and was always asking for news of them, whether they were married, or at the least in such good case that they nourished no grudge against him or me or the curate whose name I regret to have forgotten.

Our times at Shoreham came but seldom. But they remain to me and I have set down what I can in one place. It is not far from that beach that Hudson lies in company with his fervent yet weaker brother of the birds, Richard Jefferies. Of his life in London about the early 'nineties one thing remains clear to me of a different company in an environment far removed from the true antiquities of the sea and shingle, the high Downs or the singing mud flats of the Adur. For in some year of that time Hudson and I had "breakfast" at the Café Royal with H. H. Champion, who brought with him Cunninghame Graham. Champion will be remembered as the one-time gunner who resigned his commission because he thought Arabi Pasha was evilly entreated by the British Government. Afterwards he became a Labour leader, ran the Dock Strike, and was indicted with Burns and Hyndman for sedition and conspiracy, but acquitted with his notable "accomplices." This day was the first on which I met Graham, though it was not the occasion on which Hudson made his acquaintance. Graham was then active in Labour politics, and not long before had had his head broken in Trafalgar Square by a policeman who had no respect for unborn books such as *Success* or the writer of *An Indian Ghost Dance*. It was a very notable head, and, for all Hudson's Conservatism, this native of Scotland, who was in essence by some miracle a veritable son of Spain, a hidalgo or "son of someone," was highly sympathetic. Did he not know Spanish and the Argentine? Had he not camped on the pampa with gauchos reckless of human life in country where "so many beautiful horses die"? We were all in some sense children of adventure and the saddle, for even the political Champion had had his times of struggle with a thousand transport mules on the barren burning rocks of the Bolan Pass leading to Afghanistan. It was a notable gathering in a place that became still more notable afterwards, and still remains, I hear, a "stamping ground" for the young bisons of the literary and artistic herds. There, long afterwards when dining with John Davidson, we ended curiously in a row with some Frenchmen, and

Davidson, much to my amazement, issued challenges for
me to the crowd. "My friend will fight you all," said
Davidson. There was no such fracas in that other meeting, though we talked for hours and drank much coffee
and smoked cigars till "breakfast" ran into tea-time over
talk of La Plata, Australia, India, and the wide plains
of Hudson's Patagonia, where he spent, perhaps, the
happiest time of his life, as only lately Graham wrote
to me. Still can I remember how brilliant, both in looks
and talk, our hidalgo was. With a burning pointed
beard and shining moustache he looked like a Velazquez
come to life, while Hudson, big and bent and smiling,
older than any, and yet ageless as he remained to the
day of his death, untouched in his spirit by greying time,
looked down on us and told us tales and laughed at
politics, and came back again to the natural life of man,
of beasts and birds. Champion was ever a good talker
and good at everything but his own affairs: the staunchest
friend and wisest and as subtle in following the devious,
crooked ways of man as any, and with his strongly
marked features and his pallid skin he made contrast
with our hollow-cheeked Hudson of the Bronze Age and
the vivid native of the North. It is impossible to decorate
or spoil after the sad manner of the anecdotal biographer
with his stale repetition of witticisms that once sparkled
and died, all that might be put down of such hours.
Is it not better to remember the spirit of youth in the
four of us than to recall mere words? What Conrad
says of "youth and the sea" is true, and that scattered
company, with Hudson gone, with Champion in far-off
Australia, with the hidalgo, alas, not quite so young as
then, and oneself half a shadow, sailed the sea of

life not ungallantly. Such moments pass and come again like some faint odour that recalls a vanished country of adventure in *Far Away and Long Ago*.

How one must needs lament for the fore-doomed biographer of any big man! Whether he knows him or not he works in the barren grooves in which true life perishes and, overcome by details and sad piles of begged or borrowed letters, builds like an Egyptian slave a pyramid to bury kings in, so that neither friend nor foe shall come at the treasure or look upon the lineaments of him who is as those "beneath the sand." I would not undertake such a task for a king's exchequer. "Time, which antiquates antiquities and hath an art to make dust of all things," may yet spare a minor monument.

CHAPTER VI

A book without a story—Hudson's reticence—Hudson and egoists—Friends and acquaintances—His courtesy—Rich and poor—A "noble"—How his character comes out slowly—His simple hedonism—Inns and hotels—Dislike of Puritans and ascetics—His unformulated philosophy—Love of life and trust in instinct —Essentially a thinker all the same—Neglect of general science—Criticism—Ruskin and a parson—Hudson bigger than his books—Art and Life—Energy and Art—Hudson's activity of mind—Never a recluse—His friends kept apart—Wednesdays at No. 40—Hudson's decoration—His world the open air—Henry James and Meredith—Some of his friends —Those "who went"—Hudson and politics—Sir Frederick Banbury and bird-snaring—Hudson a Conservative—Abuses of the ownership of land—Murderous squires and gamekeepers—The ideal squire —His tolerance of parsons—His imaginations.

THOSE who mean with courage to continue must see how hard it is to write "a life" of one who had no story. If a writer trusts wholly to his own memory and the shadows that remain, he must be damned or excused for vagueness and dim impressions as he walks in the avenues of the past with the pleasant ghost of an old companion and comrade. I say "comrade" here because it was Hudson's own word for one he knew so long and so well. And when he wrote it first in a book of his which he gave to me, I knew at what strange cost to his almost unconquerable reticence he put it down. That was his

way: he never confessed to any tenderness save, on the
rarest occasions, for the dead. In ways he was as shy
as some adolescent girl: it was much to surprise the
glance of affection he sometimes cast on those who were
his few real friends. I go back specially to those rare
days by Shoreham beach, or high above it at the Ring
of Chanctonbury, because then he had so few friends
and was not known by many even of the bird-loving
world to whom he came as a strange, semi-avian mis-
sioner and prophet of mercy. He chose friends with
difficulty: tried them and discarded most. He had, it
is true, a great capacity for friendship where there was
real sympathy, but for those in whom egoism grew rampant he presently had no use at all. For all his immense
simplicity he saw pretence or haggard vain ambition in
many who would conceal it. But truly it seems to me,
as I think of our long days together, that egoism faded
in his presence like a snow-wreath under the sun. If
it did not, then the egoist himself presently vanished
from Hudson's life, for to the truly self-centred man
egoism is his very soul and he would fain have it watered
hourly. Many departed of themselves, but of others it
might be said in the ironic phrase of one novelist, that
"They went!" This did not come from any egoism in
him, for egoism is a little thing blown big, an effort of
the small to enlarge themselves, and instead of that there
was in him often a sweetly natural way of coming down
to the level of others. So he said wrathfully, "I'm as
young as you," because he was as young, and so he
grew young as a child with a child or a boy with boys,
a man with men. With a man of eighty, such as Wilfrid
Blunt, he might have been eighty. If he liked anyone

he was his equal comrade. He hated consideration for
his years, and when in these later times his health made
him at times irritable, as a failing heart inevitably must,
so that I avoided abrupt negatives to anything he ad-
vanced, it was best to hide one's care not to rouse or
anger him. When he asked in a letter for some criticism
it was often hard to avoid, in giving a brief and com-
pressed opinion, some appearance of dogmatism, even
when I strove to avoid it, and sometimes he replied
with an indignant, half-jesting remonstrance, founded,
perhaps, rather on his native dislike of the scientific
desire to deal with any question in the driest, coldest
light and on his difficulty in dealing with anything without emotion, than on what I really put forward against
his views. But all the same he loved a stand-up fight
in argument, provided that one sought for an explanation
and not for victory. Big as he was, I say again that he
had no egoism, for personality is something so much
bigger, and a humorous cosmic pantheist, as he may be
called, had no need to puff himself with healing self-
conceit. Why was it that many more or less eminent,
or at least well-known, men remained at the best acquaintances or drifted away from him? Is not the answer
this? That men who could not face the world without
the armour of egoism against wounds found him, even
without his knowing it, ironic, critical, peculiarly mor-
dant. Some, indeed, thought him such and forgot that
he was often ill. The biggest, kindest old watch-dog,
even Argus, the dog of Odysseus, might have snapped
when kind hands touched a wound, though they sought,
it may be, to heal it. But if any such went away sorrowfully they parted with a heritage, and few there were

who went away sorrowfully. He never pleaded for anyone's love, but took love openly, returning it lavishly
but almost in secret. This was so when he was com-
paratively young, and in his noble old youthful age he
became no more open in expression or less profound in
what he hid with such sedulous care.

There were, it is true, many whom the world calls,
or would call, his friends, themselves among it, who were
but pleasant acquaintances. How, indeed, should they
know in what secret category he placed them? He had,
as so many have who come from the Spanish Americas,
more than a touch of high Spanish courtesy which is
not far from being kin to the courtesy often found in
a splendid and kindly peasantry. This perhaps gives a
key to one thing which may puzzle many. Hudson had
not a few acquaintances among those known as the aris-
tocracy, some of whom were truly noble. There are
a few who, on a casual observation, might have deemed
this a proof that he loved high rank and station. The
conclusion would be false. He found far more friends
and intense objects of interest among the poor, if they
had the qualification that attracted him among the rich
or those of high rank. The mean or servile were but
objects of pity. He understood the tyranny that is sometimes found in the countryside, but when he found some
peasant, nobly suited to his environment, a native product
of the soil he loved, and therefore "free," with thoughts
of his own and emotions unspoiled, he looked upon him
no less kindly than he looked on a stag in the heather or
some falcon on the wing. Such a man lived a natural
life and, whatever the smallness of his ambit, had real
liberty. In the middle classes and ·in those narrowed

by custom and convention till freedom was a thing of which they knew nothing, even though their chains ached and bit, such were rarely to be found. But among those who, with greater wealth and an absence of anxiety, combined a scorn of opinion with free human qualities, he could still find some finer creatures to observe with pleasure and to become friendly with. Perhaps he ranked them with the nobler cats and greater eagles if they showed high qualities and peculiar freedom. He was a naturalist of men and women. But it took some individuality, passion and humour, and sympathy with his pursuits and thoughts to secure him.

It is only now, after forty years, when he is dead, that these conclusions and such an analysis have become possible. Long years of a myriad impressions as of some complex composite portrait come out at last with clearness. For long, indeed, I could have repeated his brother's parting words. Yet now it seems that he becomes simpler for me as after a long day of mist and sun and wind and rain a landscape clears in the evening and one—

> "Views wilds and swelling floods,
> And hamlets brown and dim discovered spires."

Presently I shall have to speak of his philosophy, his plan to live in and endure the world, unchoked by vain indignations. Yet a man may have more than one philosophy, and one characteristic of Hudson's mind was his hedonism. But, like the better type of Epicurean, he found his most enduring pleasures in his reactions to the visible, tangible, sonorous, odorous world. He seemed totally indifferent to the common comforts of life which, as age increases, become necessities to most. There are many, not natives of Sybaris or Capua, to whom the lack of a hot bath spoils the day in which it is, perhaps, the only luxury. In Tower House there was no big bath: Hudson never missed it, and, rejecting propositions for its installation, used a tub. When he wandered he went to a hotel only as a last resort: he preferred a primitive inn or a cottage with the sanitation of the pampa. This was due not only to his poverty but to his search for character and variations from type. In big hotels the birds wore the same plumage and sang the same social songs, especially in the evening, when Hudson preferred to seek in some country bar or the kitchen for new plumage and new wild music. So we often squabbled about comfort. Why did I go to hotels? Comfort, eh? And he snorted almost indignantly at a man who had been over much of the world and yet at last desired a little ease.

After all there had been no baths in Quilmes or among the ombú trees, or on the far pampa, and a horse's skull had often been his most comfortable chair in the land of the gauchos, so he took his own way and was paid once in a while by some queer human rarity, or some old tale, and now one knows that he thereby got the best and gave it to us. His hedonism never leant to luxury. He had no instinct for it and he believed in and trusted his own instincts through everything. Nature knows best. He had more pity than love for Puritans and ascetics, tyrants over nature, who wished to rule with a rod of iron their own souls and the souls of others, so letting one poor instinct of restraint dominate the rest. Out of this feeling that his body and his unconscious self had found the way for him sprang his philosophy. When I wrote of him—

> "Whilst you, by Nature led, seem set apart
>   To prove the earth, man's great forgotten friend,
>   Heals and forgives and sets the captive free,"

there were two readings of this first line, and he said, "Put 'by Nature led.' " And so it stands.

I doubt if Hudson ever consciously asked himself how he looked on the universe. A man can have, must have, a philosophy even without knowing it. Philosophy is love of wisdom, and in any man it is love for his own wisdom, that is, for the method by which he has learnt to travel through the time allotted for his tramp in this universe. He has to learn and make for himself a general scheme of things, and the poor labourer with his three hundred words for all expression, and the squire, farmer, and parson as his masters, may be as much a philosopher as those who use ten thousand words, and handle time and space as Einstein handles them. Hudson, whether he thought of it or not, had a world before him which was a live world of interesting animals, of which man was, after all, the most interesting product of the earth and the whole of nature. As the *Trochilidæ* used up their energy in colour and gorgeous plumage, so the earth used hers and created man and the beasts and birds to live and breed and sing and work and die. To be weak was the only true misery. Hudson would have been the strongest man on earth if he could have had his way, and the span of Methusaleh was but poor to his enormous thirst for life. This was what dominated him. To live and exercise and indulge a powerful nature

was what he asked for.   But, being only accidentally
an "invalid" and strong enough to carry grave disabilities
for eighty years, he did not cry out for "life, more life"
in the way of poor Jefferies in *The Story of My Heart.*
Jefferies was not strong in anything, and Hudson was
weak in nothing if it were not in his fear of death.   But
death shut out forever the magnificent enjoyment of the
natural gods, the earth and sun and the fruits thereof.
We can, therefore, read the end of *Far Away and Long
Ago* and understand why in passion and pain and poverty
Hudson yet found it "better to be than not to be."   He
had energies to exhaust.   These were his gifts: he could
not bury his talents.   To enjoy the world for ever was
his philosophy.   To refuse nothing at the great hands
of Nature was a duty.   And to ask more and more yet,
and to cajole life into complaisance so that Joy sat at
the table, or by the camp-fire, in splendid loneliness which
was never loneliness at all, these too were duties.   To
be alive and to be greatly oneself, so much oneself that
one grew ever more and more by the inclusion of all
living things, and never to complain or caterwaul about
one's soul, or be humble to some deity, and thus to be
insufficient, this was his philosophy, and when it failed
him he was unhappy.   It seldom failed.

Yet there were other things than the instincts.   He
knew nothing of the brain, but regarded the instincts
it held as signposts.   New thinking in the wilderness
into which man for ever progressed (unless, indeed, he
had some day to come back to simple earth and peasant-
hood, and the friendly ox for labour) might make new
instinctive paths in which man could travel not with
doubt, but carefree and singing.   He thought this out

fully: so fully that he could listen with patience to many who held orthodox faiths and sought to convert him.

Hudson was always essentially a thinker. He knew what misapprehensions there are concerning thought. It seems to be believed that it is mere remembering. But thinking is establishing new paths in the brain; it is solving problems new to the thinker. If original in him it is thought, though a thousand knew it. Many big thinkers may often say, *Pereant, qui ante nos nostra dixerunt.* Hudson with his neglect of general science might have said that often. He was indignant when told that a sense of polarity in birds as an explanation of migration was not original. But he was always exploring even in his own mind. He sometimes rejected help. He might find things worth finding by going a new way. Yet, just as I at times appealed to him for knowledge, so he frequently came to me. He might reject my peck of beans and yet plant one and see it grow to the heavens with himself as a new Jack of the Beanstalk. Much as I was with him we never kowtowed to each other, but stood up and fought. He took no advantage of his years: I never considered my comparative youth. We formed no mutual admiration society. I was as guarded in praise as in criticism. If he liked anything I did he preferred to let me gather a favourable opinion from casual *obiter dicta,* while he often said of work I had done, "I don't like it." Once I reminded him of an American parson, a friend of mine, who made an appointment to go for a walk with Ruskin. When Ruskin saw him coming he started off uphill. They walked to the top with a hundred yards between them,

but when the American joined him Ruskin remarked,
"I don't believe in immortality." "I don't care a damn
whether you do or not," said the American; and they
went back as they had come. Of course I did care. Yet
how could I show that I did without discussion? His
views were settled. He felt himself a critic. So we
never praised each other overmuch in words. He was,
as all big men are, bigger than his books. That he was
sometimes less did not matter. A few little men, by
some monstrous birth, are delivered of things bigger than
themselves. Hudson never expressed Hudson or he might
have gone beyond any ambit. Often he did go beyond
mine, and when I resorted to pure logic he retorted either
half scornfully or in a moment's pet, that I was being
"superior." But for a man on a perpetual voyage of
discovery there never was so human a companion. His
intellectual curiosity would have kept him fresh forever.
The loss of some instinct might be lamentable, but even
after the failure of many powers there might remain
the instinct of thinking, the instinct of workmanship, an
insatiable curiosity, a lively fancy to do what was art
and yet beyond all art, an enduring satisfaction. In *A
Hind in Richmond Park* he speaks of what may replace
the arts, but asks the question without answering it. I
know what his answer would have been. He looked
for human free energy to glorify and decorate the world,
as the splendid energy of the humming-birds overflows
into colour. He built a world in *A Crystal Age* not so
wholly alien from his desires as it might seem, though
a sexless world had lost so much.

I said before this that one great reason for my knowing
so little of his early life was that he gave one no chance

to get out questions. He flowered like a magic mango plant the moment I saw him. He was full of matter. His activity of mind was amazing. In no book has he showed this as he did in *A Hind in Richmond Park*. It is as near his talk and way of moving through a world of ideas as book-words may get. It is discursive and yet connected: he kills one hare and starts a hundred, and remarks casually that he cannot pursue them. He draws rapid conclusions and thinks as he goes, as some orators think upon their feet and have long phrases and sentences ready ere the time comes for them. Yet it all came so spontaneously that the matter often seemed as new to him as to his readers. But he wrote to me, "My plan is to seem to have no plan." True to his instincts he followed himself to the last.

The notion that Hudson was in any way a recluse is as absurd as a picture of him as a "serious-minded" prophet on a mountain top. Some men decline from society as they grow old: their health fails: their interests narrow: they become peevish, garrulous of their ills, and perish almost in solitude. Through his whole life Hudson was too much interested in mankind to be alone. As he grew older and could work less there was more time for his fellows. I cannot set forth any list of his friends and acquaintances. He was apt to keep them apart: many I never met: some I heard of by mere accident: I never knew he corresponded with Edward Thomas till Thomas died. It was his custom in the old days—I speak of the early part of this century—to set apart Wednesday afternoon for such as wished to come. I seldom went on those days, but many did. The big sitting-room at No. 40 was a gloomy place. It was furnished with derelicts from boarding-houses: there was nothing beautiful in it, no gleam of brightness or spot of colour save in one glass-covered case which held his best books. In the centre of the room stood a gigantic circular settee covered with horsehair. It might have been salved from Dickens's Mugby Junction. It filled and blocked the centre of the room, a comfortless and dreadful thing of which he seemed unconscious, though its preposterous construction made my blood run cold whenever I saw it or had to sit upon it. The outdoor colours of Nature he bathed in: he cared, it seemed, as little for colour in his house as George Gissing. And Gissing sat with black and white upon dark walls and missed nothing. In Hudson's case it was not poverty which kept him from some attempt at decoration. Indoors did not matter. Some of the brightest birds live in the closest nests. To-morrow and to-morrow he would go where there was light. Truly he had no real sense of colour or decoration. Often writers make characteristic dens which reveal much. It was so with Henry James, who might have been a banker to look at, and yet his house at Rye had an artistic delicacy of choice in adornment and an atmosphere at once formal and aristocratic which recalled much of his writing. Although Meredith did not live in such a Georgian house and had less space, I remember with pleasure the room in which he sat. It had refinement and a sense of literature about it. Perhaps after all these two were essentially indoor men, and that Hudson never was or could be.

I said I could make no list of his friends. I could name some "who went," but must not. Among women he had many friends. Some wrote to me after his death.

I had never heard their names. Of her whose face he saw "fluttering" in the wind, I also knew nothing. He speaks of this in *A Hind in Richmond Park* in a long passage upon telepathy, for which he thought there was much evidence. Concerning these friends of his, or at least of those I know, I have nothing to say here. Many have spoken, or will speak, for themselves. If the meanest—

> "Has two soul sides: one to face the world with,
> One to show a woman when he loves her,"

Hudson assuredly had as many sides as he had friends. He could and would play with a child or bird or dog or cat as if he were upon their level, and then turn swiftly to things of intuition and philosophy and deep speculation without any strain or pose or affectation. And he could enjoy harmless chatter and scandal and social criticism as if he thought of little else, though at the bottom were always his sense of character and his deep curiosity as to the ways of men and women. If anything bored him it was politics, and I never knew him show the slightest interest in it save when I tried to prove that politicians and parliament represented, however feebly, the organ by which society adapted itself to a changed environment. The politician might often be a disagreeable personality, but if he stood for forces making for variation, he had a scientific side and was part of general zoology. For one politician, Sir Frederick Banbury, whom I think he never met, he had a high admiration, which was, however, not founded on his complete and amazing Conservatism, but to the fact that he put through the Act which stayed Cornish boys from catching birds with baited hooks, a horrible local custom which Hudson had lashed in his book on the Land's End.

So far as Hudson was anything in politics he was Conservative. Yet those who have read *A Shepherd's Life* will see how bitterly indignant he could be with the abuses which are too commonly connected with the ownership of land. He had seen tyranny in action. The type of Conservative landowner who was to him a noble and desirable animal to preserve, was one who preserved the peasant and preferred healthy children to many head of game: one who did not encourage the breed of game-keepers: who did not collect or destroy birds, who hated a pole-trap and an owl or a jay-murderer worse than a trespassing old woman seeking fallen firewood: one who was an ideal, kindly gentleman who thought more of humanity than of sport, who gloried in the varied life possible upon his estate and sought to increase it. It may be left to others to determine how many there are of the kind that appealed to him, as they and their fellows are displaced by rich men without the authority of an-cestry or of manners or any true culture in their veins. Such changes may, indeed, be lamented by those who are not Conservatives, since they make more for revolu-tion than the ancient rule of squire and parson.

Of parsons Hudson was very tolerant. He knew many in the southern counties, and doubtless few were ever aware that the man who loved birds believed as little as the birds themselves in immortality or the creeds and dogmas of their church. It may be, however, that some of them were better men for knowing him: he felt that, whatever their view of a divine scheme, they were com-

mitted to teach mercy, and that a few might be led to
preach and practise it for the benefit of the wild life of
their cure. Perhaps in his dreams he imagined their
converting a gamekeeper and a bird-collector. He had
a great imagination.

CHAPTER VII

Idealisation of Hudson—"Please say nothing of Mr. Hudson's faults, if he had any"—Bowdlerisation of life —The magician of the pampa a man—Painting what one sees—"Come and play!"—Serious-minded men —Hudson's variety—His simple humour—Perhaps incapable of a great passion—His affection for his wife—His great duty to inculcate mercy and kindness—Hudson and women—He belonged to himself —His real friends—Egoists and Hudson—Current morality—Puritanism—*The Purple Land*—Love of women—And Rima—Biography in England—A great natural Conservative—The "Beaker" man— Hudson and great men—The brotherhood of man and beast and bird—Hudson's real power—A great writer—His style—His power of drawing character —Hedonism and the instincts.

IF there has been, among the tenderer and more unreasoning followers of Hudson's unexpressed philosophy, an absurd, yet pathetic, idealisation of his work, the same process has been going on as regards the man himself, though in this case it has been a curiously conscious process. Directly and indirectly I have been asked to treat him as a professional photographer treats a customer and his negative: to work over any sketch or portrait and obliterate the lines, the faults, the very marks and *differentiæ* of the man. Here is a process of sanctification, and the *Advocatus Diaboli*, however friendly the advocate or the devil, is to get no chance to deny him

a seat among the saints. Not long before writing this
I was sent a letter which contained a message to me.
"Please ask Mr. Roberts to say nothing of Mr. Hudson's
faults, if he knows of any." Such worshippers would
desire to have St. Augustine's life edited by a specially
sanctified St. Bowdler. "Leave out my warts and I will
not pay you a penny," said Cromwell to Leli, or so they
tell us. There may be some who in Cromwell's
life would leave out King Charles's head. But what *are*
faults? It might be that many would esteem virtues
traits which Mrs. and Miss Bowdler would faint to hear
of. Hudson was a man, and who shall balance a man's
qualities according to the Aristotelian mean so that they
shall stand sublimely averse from extremes? Perhaps
the most perfect character in all human history of whom
we have many authentic details is Cervantes, but we
might be better pleased if he had killed a few of the
mean hounds who let him come near the fabled fate of
Otway. Perhaps the Bowdlers may be recommended to
read *The Purple Land* and ponder over some of its stories
of passion, and then go refreshed and invigorated to the
magician of the pampa and the Downs, being assured
that he is a human being, kind, jovial, full of laughter
and of those strong qualities which the thin-blooded
ascetic calls human weaknesses. If I could not write of
him as I saw him: if out of consideration for a few
who prefer ideals to reality I had to smooth his rugged
features till they were as sleek as some of Raphael's
saints: if I were forced to emasculate him for a chapel
and lighted candles, I would write nothing. I prefer to
put down Hudson as great and little, fierce and kindly,
chaste of thought yet passionate, splendid, irritable, wide

and petty, savage and gentle and vain, and as fine a whole man as ever loved work or a woman.

It is a man's failings which make him lovable: the perfect character affronts our imperfections: the throne has no place by the hearth. We may spend an hour with a saint and make it a high remembrance: for our friends we choose the sinner, one who is imperfect, not flawless and aloof. Truly, little things do not make a man less: the foothills cannot destroy the mountains, nor homes upon them diminish the glory of their peaks. I cannot go with those who think Hudson's "faults" or "failings" diminish him. They made him kindly and full of understanding, open to access without flattery or incense. Big men never seat themselves high: there was no cloud about him but his own atmosphere. He showed his failings plainly: never sought concealment for anything save his quiet affections: never claimed a high place, though he knew, none knew better at last, that he was a great artist and, maybe, a great seer. We have little men enough, whose claims are as the clamour of hungry hounds: they yap in the streets and beg from or bite passers-by. He smiled at such, having met many, but imitated them in nothing, and sought no power nor the eyes of man save when he was indignant with cruelty. Therefore I put him down as I saw him, and if I hide anything at all, it is assuredly not for fear of making him seem less than he was to all who revered him, even when they smiled.

I have said that it was not everyone, however wise or eminent, that Hudson could get on with. I have known him become friendly with those who are thought great and gradually drift away from them. He never abused them, but he was in some curious way disappointed: they had not come up to expectation: they had failed him. It took me a long time to get to the bottom of the reason or, rather, of the feeling which inspired him, but one day a woman said to me, "They won't come and play with him! That's it! What he wants is someone who will play, and play fair, and go into life and all it means with some sort of joy." But who could expect all the eminent to come and play? Some cannot: they are serious-minded, and there is nothing that may be so fatal to friendship as that. My own father had fits of serious-mindedness which inspired me with terror. He said once in a dreadful access of this form of inhumanity, "I can imagine nothing more delightful than a company of serious-minded men, in which one of them takes up and develops a subject with appropriate illustrations." I knew which the one would be, and having as a child sat through long hours of such delightful symposia, I was the more inclined to regard Hudson's growing horror of serious-minded men with charity. It was not that he could not be serious himself at times, even suddenly and disconcertingly serious, but he wanted real interludes in which everyone would play and give jest in exchange for jest, and keep thought alive and quick, so that when it was all over one had not a memory of a dismal afternoon, but a vague, bright recollection of many-coloured specks and thoughts and words to chuckle over and think upon. At sea we used to have a game called "Blind Swaps," in which we rolled up an old torn shirt, or a pair of trousers with more than its native means of entry, with the best part showing, and said, "Who'll swap?" The exchange was made, and the joke was discovering that one was lucky or unlucky. Conversation should be a game something like that: a thing of bright, quick chance and laughter. Hudson's friendship had to be paid for, and paid for in a varied diet, not always in serious-minded bread-and-cheese alone. When it was not he resented it. People had not played fair. In fact they had not played at all. Life was not a sober-sided Nonconformist chapel: he wanted colour, a touch of humour, variety. As his gauchos would have put it, he himself took raw wool and wove it beautifully and did not care to be paid for it in a subfusc piece of dull cloth. Some people had "no ear for life," as he might have said, and yet they taught the music of life and expected him to enjoy their five-finger exercises and dull moral fugues. He would have a duet at the least, and, if it were an orchestral piece, would take any instrument or a dozen one after another.

In those idealisations of Hudson as a prophet and a seer, a visionary gigantic figure on a height, which are already foreshadowed in things written about him, the one trait will be missing, the essential *differentia* of the man, his elfish, puckish humour. These adjectives I owe gratefully to one who knew him not long but well, if the keenest observation could serve. The man who loved children, so long as they were children and did not approach their sad age of reason, that is, of appropriation of other people's ready-made notions, was a child himself, and for half his time "did not care a single damn" for sober wisdom. If attacked good-humouredly he answered with vigorous humour. He saw fun wherever it was to be found, and sometimes discovered it elsewhere when it really lay in his own mind, in some

odd kink of thought. Unconscious absurdity in anyone
gave him infinite pleasure : whether it were an exhibition
of megalomania or that which always accompanies such
disorders, an extreme lack of humour, or some simple
mistake in words, into which the newspaper-reading
working classes sometimes fall. Any simple jest, when
its source of laughter was a want of humour, appealed
to him. But pornographic humour was highly distasteful
to him, as it mostly is to the healthy satisfied man of
strong passions. Love of it is a sign of increasing
incapacity, of want of natural satisfactions, or of the
morbid curiosity of adolescence.

He was faithful in proved friendship. Women knew
they could not own him, but he hated to hurt any, nor
can I believe it possible that a living creature, of whatever
sex, has a justifiable grievance against him, or views him
with any of the rancour that follows deceit or cruelty.
Often I thought him incapable of the passion which may
wreck a man. He could scarcely have understood the
poor fool who followed Manon Lescaut through hell.
Sometimes it seemed to me that this capacity had been
exhausted in his youth. If anything of high and deep
chivalrous affection remained, it was, it may be, given
with devotion and a pure heart to one dear woman who
died a tragic death.

I have spoken of what I believe to have been Hudson's
continued affection for his wife. It is impossible to
believe other than that this remained true to the end,
in spite of the fact that she died at last without him.
He wrote to her every day. In some men a letter every
day might have been a sacrifice to a sense of duty.
Hudson recognised no duties, and was free of many

obligations, or what the world esteems such while it
ignores them. He had duties to animals and birds: a
linnet in a cage was to him, as it was to Blake, worse
than a man in slavery. Human beings could cry out:
they could raise an alarm: they could revenge themselves.
The whipped horse, the Chichester owl in a stifling
kitchen: a bird struggling on a baited hook, these appealed to him most of all. Man could take care of
himself. If he ever desired to help any it was the children
of the soil, the ploughman of his native earth, the everlasting peasant who should remain when dynasties had
crumbled and the very names of nations had been obliterated. There his instincts called to him. In other matters the "stern daughter of the voice of God," in Wordsworth's mixed metaphor, left him cold. This is no
prelude to any narrative of Hudson's relations with
women. I do not know them, and if I did should regard
them as being just as unimportant as they were natural.
Endowed as he was with powerful passions, there may
have been many in his long life, as many perhaps as in
Landor's. If we spoke openly of these things thrice in
forty years or more it was as much as we ever did.
There is even some difficulty in estimating his opinion
of women. One wrote to me, "I think he looked on
them mostly as the trimmings of life: not capable of
understanding the more important aspects of anything.
Women were there to fulfil a certain important purpose."
This cannot be reconciled with all he says of his own
mother in *Far Away and Long Ago,* nor with the many
women friends for whom he had the highest regard.
As a young man he was devoted to certain old ladies:
he spoke of them with reverence and affection. For

one lady he grieved as if for a dear sister. His patent
interest in many young women, plainly existent yet without any offence, was pleasing and kindly. To every
woman that he knew intimately he was a different creature, of the same genus but a different species. He would
have resented particular appropriation: he belonged to
himself. They knew it: the deeper ancient instincts of
women revived in them. They took their share and
were fain to be content in the belief that they knew
something that others did not know. But in 1899 he
wrote to me that women had one quality only. "Men
have many qualities to attract: women but one—charm,
which is absolutely indispensable. Who has ever painted
a woman with pen in whom you recognise this elusive
character? Not Meredith nor another. When you recall
the people you know intimately, the people you have
never met and that never lived, how many women do
you find among them? Precious few: they are nearly
all men."

He was the same with men as with women. Intensely
interested in the moment of passing time, he gave himself
to a friend and the hour. That might be the end of it.
Of some he spoke, of others he said nothing. Till one
man was killed in the war I never knew he had been
a friend of Hudson's. It would not surprise me to learn
he had been acquainted with kings: they would have
passed in the procession if they had not earned his friendship. As he gave, so he required. He paid lavishly for
love and required his due in return. Women and men
had to interest him. He exhausted any single vein of
ore and left the mine. Each new acquaintance might
turn out a Patagonia. When the mists rolled away he

looked for Cordilleras, but was content with foothills if
there was to be found there some taste of wildness or
the memory-haunted scent of the evening primrose.

To say so much they may seem to imply that Hudson
was an egoist.   There are many kinds and orders of
egoists.   Never was any who required more help: never
any who was more solitary.   The meaner kind of man is
apt to console himself with the belief that he has peculiar
qualities: the nobler, and therefore the more humble,
are surprised to find others so different.   If there were
egoism in Hudson it was thus based.   If "it was bitter
at the end of life to walk alone," so it was bitter to find
mean qualities where he looked for bigness.   Those who
do so are continually thrust back upon themselves if life
does not compel them to be at last "subdued to what
they work in."   His health and his instincts for the
wild, his pursuits as a naturalist, gave him long hours
of loneliness and nourished his natural spirit.   "Solitude
in the sense of being frequently alone is necessary to the
formation of any depth of character."   This aphorism
of Mill's may help to show how Hudson became what
he was.   His character grew deeper and deeper still.
So the Colorado has cut through the Arizona plateau
and carved out the tremendous peaks and spires of the
Great Cañon.   If this be hyperbole let those say so who
never knew him.   Even in the depths of the cañon there
are homely Indian villages: birds chatter in the fragrant
groves on the verge of its painted cliffs and gorges.

Many think in their hearts that current morality has
little or nothing to do with them.   Men and women tend
in stress to regard themselves as special cases.   They
know how they are tempted and how or why they fail

or fall. They have a thousand excuses and many that they cannot or do not express. But what do they or we know of the special circumstances of others, their nature, their temperament, their pains and passions? We know nothing, and say that for them, sinners as they are, the common law should guide them, their excuses are mere words to hide their evil instincts and to extenuate judgment. Yet curiously enough the world forgives sinners of the past: they remain historic. It sees that morality is not only a creature of latitude and longitude but of time. The sin of 1900 is therefore to be condemned: that of A.D. 900 is something to examine curiously. A contemporary, perhaps, may be forgiven for outraging law if he seems a candidate for a niche in the temple of history. Even women themselves can be pardoned if their errors seem mere accidents of expressed power. Their very faults become great characteristics.

Yet speak as one may of these things, it remains true that many desire a hero, who is their hero, to remain spotless according to their own canon. This is excusable, but he who writes of him has to ask whether he is writing for the most delicate-minded and sentimental of his own age, or, in little or great measure, for posterity. It may seem a crude and rash assumption even to dream that any book can last beyond a common season. Yet if White of Selborne, the very father of field naturalists, still broods not only about the hills and woodlands of his village, but lives in literature, I cannot but think that a greater man will so outlast him that White in the end may be remembered only because of his successor's deep appreciation. If that is so, nothing written of Hudson can be idle or superfluous, and the false attribution to him of saintly and inhuman qualities will be as unwelcome to those who know humanity as the truth may now be to many who know it not, or refuse to see it in him of whom I speak.

To attribute the actions of a writer's characters to the man himself is as inept as to give him the opinions with which he endows them. George Gissing showed the little venom he possessed when discussing such a critical attitude, but after all Euripides suffered, and where he was troubled who shall escape? Yet there is an attitude of mind, a general outlook on the world of man and woman, which every writer displays whatever the care with which he would conceal it. We cannot attribute Puritanism to Fielding or Smollett: a rigid regard for ecclesiastical dignity and morals to Sterne: while the simple heart of Goldsmith could scarcely utter the thunders of the leonine Landor. These and all writers in the end discover their souls. We estimate them from the very words they thought. It may be, to escape under: they draw a hero or indict a nation and put themselves upon canvas and on trial. There are books of Hudson's from which we might not know much more than one aspect and that perhaps not a great one. Mont Blanc does not look from every quarter the mountain monarch of Western Europe: the Matterhorn itself may rear its head in clouds. But there are some passages in all of them which declare his bigness and his gentleness and a beautiful spirituality and oneness with Nature. From these alone we might with imagination almost picture a saint, one who had put humanity behind him. But then, again, there are others in which hot blood runs and youth riots and the world is very good, even the world as the thoughtless and gay-hearted might see it, with love and

joy to be had for the asking as Life lifts her magic
cornucopia and tumbles her fruits upon the fertile earth.
Can any read *The Purple Land* and not see that the ideal
picture I have so often been asked to draw of him who
wrote it would be an emasculated portrait? He wrote
with a pen, not dipped in blood, but in the deep pool of
experience: he spoke of what he knew, of the love of
horses and of women and the sunlight and the earth. In
that book Lamb was married, but he went out as a knight-
errant of the pampa, and though no kings offered their
daughters, as they do in the tales of Malory, many
daughters of the soil came and listened to strange stories.
If Hudson ever loved any woman passionately so that
others became mere shadows and eidola I know nothing
of her. That book of his youth, for it was written first
of all his books as *The History of the House of Lamb,*
most of which was destroyed, showed his nature plainly.
Some of it is mere construction, some unconvincing, but
take it altogether it gives the spirit in which he faced life
and entered life's orchard and took the fruits thereof.

He spoke intimately of women very rarely. He was
so full a man, with such innumerable diverse threads of
interest, that there was for ever something greater to talk
of than love, its follies or its pains. He was as reticent as
a maiden or as Mona Lisa, but unlike her he showed no
secrets by hiding them. It was known, it was understood,
that they were there. Indeed, he put merely pretty and
silly women in their place as much as any Sultan,
though assuredly not as any Kisler Agha. That was his
deep conservatism: women were beautiful and the more
beautiful if tender-hearted, but after all, ancillary, the
great servants of mankind. I should be misunderstood

if it were inferred that he could not reach to deep devotion, even though it was not eternal. There was no frivolity in him, none could find it. But truly I think that such great love as many men feel, and such as one might perhaps look for in him, was given wholly to the girl Rima of *Green Mansions*. If there was any secret about her, forty years of friendship never discovered it to me. Year after year I heard of the Venezuelan romance, until at last I was the one most astonished to know that it was finished. It had for so long borne all the marks of the one great story an author never ends or never even begins. Sometimes I have thought that there was a Rima, some woodland child whom the boy Hudson had loved, and then again I came back to the thought I now hold to, that she is the embodiment, but no more than that, of all his imaginations concerning the girl-woman who would have satisfied his body and his soul. If that is so, I understand how it came that he put other women in their place, for they were women who lacked the bird-like spirit of this dryad who died at last with her tree.

We cannot write biography in English or it must be published out of England. If Montaigne lived now and were an Englishman he would have to operate on his book before it could be printed save for private circulation. Though they had the ceaseless courage of Montaigne, his smiling gift of self-analysis, his acute and remorseless mind, and all men of any importance do not lack these qualities, none may speak the truth. The infection of the family biographer has overspread literature: he has become a romanticist, and his triumph is to fill two volumes with the idealism of those who purchase his pen. We need a new renaissance, a new birth of joy in instinct for

which Hudson fought all his life. Those are sadly to
seek in their estimation of him who look for him nowhere
but in passages of sheer joy in wild life, or even in the
whole field of philosophy in which he sported like a brilliant dragon-fly, seen at one moment on a flower and then
far off upon the river of life. I never knew a completer
man or one with a more humorous scorn of the fetters
forged by civilisation and that morality of which ecclesi-
astics fondly believe themselves not only the embodiment
but the originators. The youthful wildness of his spirit,
which left him for a while at the time of the illness which
determined his life's direction, returned again and in a
great sense remained to him to his last hour. Not even
his conservatism, though that was but partial, came to
him second-hand. It was born of the pampa in which he
found the capable in possession of the earth, with the
peon and the gaucho made a class subdued by greater
power of hand and brain, such as his Beaker ancestry had
doubtless made of those they conquered on the shores of
Britain. So one might say, and he would have believed
it, that his very conservatism and his leaning towards the
aristocrat, provided he neither slew nor collected birds,
was the gift of his ancient wild blood, of the very shape
of his skull, which told to the skilled eye the ancient story
of his lineage. It is said that even now the Beaker type
with its big round skull comes to the top in the heavy drift
of modern life. It makes not only occasion serve it, but
often moulds the laws to its convenience, for it has all
the marks of power. Among these is its native want of
reverence for the fetters of slaves.

There are some, and those not a few, who already
reckon Hudson a great man, and I confess that viewing

him now, not from the standpoint of intimacy and the
affection he inspired in all who really knew him, but from
a more melancholy and detached position, he seems that
to me. What, indeed, are the marks of a great man?
They must be many and various, for none is, or can be,
perfect. Yet one mark is surely common to them all,
and it is the fact that their greatness is a function of
their influence. By influence in the end we measure their
stature, and it may, therefore, seem to many that the
time is not come to measure Hudson among those to
whom the world must own its indebtedness. Yet there
are certain qualities of man which experience shows to be
of an enduring power, and if an all-embracing affection
and sympathy for living things be not one of them, then
I know not what they are or can be. No writer, man or
woman, has expressed so well as Hudson the deep essential kinship which pity and understanding reveal between
us and what men call the lower creation. In the far
future someone may truthfully declare that it was his
books, founded though they necessarily were on others,
which finally made justice possible not only between man
and man but between man and bird and beast. We speak
commonly of promoting the brotherhood of man, as if
that far-off goal were the final aim of humanity. Hudson
would have declared, and as I believe would have declared
truly, that this was but the beginning. Man can avenge
himself: with desperation and courage the victim can
bring down his oppressor. It is not so with those whom
Hudson made his chiefest care, and if the time shall at
last arrive when the beasts and birds he loved and would
have protected shall cease to pass from the face of an
emptied and desolate earth, he will have been the prophet

and great cause of their salvation. To say this is not to put in a low place his forerunners but rather to exalt them; but few, if any, can rank with him in the variety of their interests, the noble and passionate expression of their love for the "little brothers of St. Francis," and over and above all this he had the philosophic mind that ranged now with the wings of an eagle and then with the alert eagerness of a wren over the great field of the world's general and related life.

Copernicus, Kepler, and Newton changed the very look of the heavens and Leonardo da Vinci triumphed in fields other than those of war. I would rank Hudson not with them, though he changed the heavens for many, but perhaps with such as Cervantes, one of the noblest of the earth, and wholly a man from his "stumped and paupered arm" to his vigorous and pitiful mind. In other circumstances I could imagine Hudson a leader in war, and as powerful in persuasion and influence of pure character as he who gave us the ridiculed and sublime Don Quixote. If this be high praise, none who knew him will call it extravagant, for each will add some quality which seems the appanage and peculium of the great. Nor will it in any way detract from such essential rank to show that he lost no common instinct by the growth of those which are the rarest. Hudson never wholly grew up: he was child and boy and man at once, and loved laughter and little things as well as the subjects of philosophy, and found more joy in freeing a bird than in the construction of a theory. To some men simplicity seems as great a detraction from greatness as a sense of humour, and, doubtless, if I showed Hudson rejoicing at the comedy of some humorous film, to which they were superior, they would be as much shocked as if they saw Cæsar playing at cat's-cradle or Cleopatra with a lipstick. There are some who seem scarcely able to bear the thought that their hero washes his face and would die to know that he damned his dinner. What these think of Wordsworth and his illegitimate daughter would be a puzzle for a critic.

Some deny Hudson's claim to be considered a great writer. To me he seems one of the greatest. One finds the *griffe de l'aigle* not always, but never a chapter but has its marks. There are who think it better to write well about nothing than ill or not well about something. Years ago that was Professor Saintsbury's opinion, and maybe it is now. Hudson would not have agreed, but he took pains, the pains of an artist with a sense of symmetry, of true balance and its music. I said to him once, "They say you write by intuition." He laughed. Yet those who said it spoke not altogether falsely, for much of his untouched, unpolished work would have seemed perfect if later one had not seen the printed page. Though he was not in the technical sense a great poet, yet he had much of a poet's equipment. But the harmonies and the melody of prose which seem simple drew him on so that in the nobler passages he reaches real music. When he rises to passages of passionate indignation there is no loss of balance, though the lava of his rage against blood-slaughter, or the more general cruelties of much that passes for sport, burns redly or white-hot. Those who doubt whether his prose style was one forged with pain, though born of native fire, may read the elaborate, and often too elaborate, pages of *A Crystal Age*. There he used overmuch artifice: his rhythm is sought for too

openly: his balance is visibly an exercise in style: the
result is dexterous but mechanical, impressive rather for
pure skill than for the feeling he afterwards made the
master of his pages, as it was of all his actions. *A
Crystal Age* was mainly an experiment, though much of
it was felt. It showed what he, a strong man of instinct,
thought of sexless life and love. But he never loved it
and looked back upon its pages without satisfaction. To
compare it with the earlier work in *The Purple Land* is
to see that a full pen without practice or technical knowledge may surpass later work as much as a child's scrawl
may surpass a drawing done in school under the instruction of some arid master. But in *The Purple Land* he
shines in character. Those he draws from the life stand
upon their feet, or sit their horses, or squat upon a
horse's head by a pampa fire and fight and talk and love
like men.

Nothing written here is a defence of a man who needs
none. Hudson stands erect on his feet, on his own philosophy, which he never put forth and which he was much
too unself-conscious to think out. But it may be taken as
a defence of the view of life which came so naturally
to him that any theory or theology which denied it seemed
absurd, since his was a healthy, happy hedonism which
took into due regard all human instincts. He believed
that when they worked together in harmony they produced the strong type of man he desired to inherit the
earth. He did not imagine that self-sacrifice must always
be essential to the happiness of others, or that self-torture
was a recommendation to heaven. He saw that the ascetic
had an absurd pleasure in dominating himself, and that
the Puritan extended his vision to the mutilation of

others. Such desired to save their souls, that is, to secure
their own approval and misname it a god's. But Hudson
accepted life freely and rejoiced in all his energies, being
assured that a tempered regard for all man's gifts in their
due order must in the end make for the happiness of the
whole wonderful world in which he delighted.

CHAPTER VIII

An imagined diary—Hudson with us in Sussex—Woods
and flowers and birds—Man, the great animal—
Nature and the decorative instinct—Egrets' and
gulls' wings—Benjamin Moore and poison gas—
Views on vivisection—The young white owl and a
clerical jailer—Hudson will not interfere—Reasons
why—The owl freed—Hudson's health—Life and
death of big men—Writers and disease—Rheumatic
fever—Its results in Hudson—State of his heart—
Sir James Mackenzie sees Hudson—Doctor's letter,
1916—Dr. Frederick Price in 1920—Work done in the
shadow of death—Fear and courage.

If Hudson had kept a diary it would have told us the
names of places and of people mostly of no account in
the world, of humorous or tragic nobodies, dramas of a
village or some market town near a woodland or plain or
by the sea where wild geese came or herons built, such
as Selborne, or Salisbury, or Abbotsbury, or Wells in
Norfolk. In this diary that never existed I might have
come across a note of the times he stayed in my own
house in Sussex, where on a fine June night the nightin-
gales rendered sleep difficult, and made himself loved by
everyone in it for his humour and grave courtesy and
consideration for all who served him, even in the hum-
blest way. With him a walk in the woods or by fertile
hop-fields became a new thing. The chattering jays took
on brighter colours for me, the woods were more popu-

lous, since birds I thought alike he distinguished by notes
I never could remember. He knew, too, the simpler
names of wild-flowers and half approved, with some
laughter, of my dislike of picking any of them, and
my way of giving them for the moment psychological
attributes not in accordance with his own theories. Yet
such a trick of the mind pleased him, though he would
sometimes take a blossom from its stalk and show me
some peculiarity he had noted, even when I remonstrated
on his inflicting suffering on a harmless beautiful live
thing. But his mind was strangely constructed. It was
amazing to discover how far his tolerance of humanity
could go. It extended even to bird-catchers, as one sees
in *Birds in a Village* (p. 168), and was based on his way
of looking at human beings as part of a tremendous interesting animal kingdom, and by no means the least
interesting part. If I repeat this too often, it is because
it was fundamental in him. "My credentials are those of
a field naturalist who has observed men: all their actions
and mentality." So he says in the last chapter of *A
Hind in Richmond Park*. For some exceptionally strange
specimen of humanity he could even desert birds and
make as careful notes of the new peculiar creature as if
it was some fowl hitherto unobserved in England. It
was this way of thinking about men which led him to
tolerate the reasonable sportsman, if not bloody-minded
or cruel. Eagles took beasts for prey: hawks smote
down lesser birds: robins hawked for butterflies and
sparrows for crane-flies, and man snared fish or chased
deer or shot birds, even the noble wild geese. The
greatest ways of man were the ways of instinct, and instinct was the true god of man: the ancient lawgiver for

all men and animals. He felt like Whitman; for the
animals

> "do not sweat and whine about their condition,
> They do not lie awake in the dark and weep for their sins,
> They do not make me sick discussing their duty to God."

Hudson knew that the whole duty of man is to combine
consideration for all living things with consideration for
himself. Good, no doubt, to use one's fore-brain on
occasion, though by it man seemed to have achieved the
special privilege of making himself thoroughly wretched,
but instinct knew where the highest thought fumbled and
failed, and so he often went back and solaced himself
with it as he observed with calm phenomena that made
less naturally instinctive people rage. He was never
troubled by any inconsistency between this calm view of
nature, reddened with spilt blood though it might be, and
his bitterness against the decorative instinct in some hated
women. With his knowledge of the good that money
might accomplish, though sometimes he said peevishly
that he was being paid too much, as if an editor or publisher were some reckless philanthropist, a notable lapse
of his observing power, it seemed much viler for a
"civilized lady" to hire a feather-hunter or subsidise a
lying dealer than for some savage woman to strangle a
bird and tear off a wing for her matted hair, or for a poor
ignorant rascal to catch linnets for a living. I told him
once that I had seen a gull's wing in a woman's hat which
had had the upper part dipped in red dye to represent the
bloody end torn from the bird. But he had seen the
same. He never missed these things. He would rather
forgive the horrible instinct which led to such crude

adornment than its refined form seen in society and even at Court. Once I said to him, "What would you do if you were to meet in a drawing-room some woman wearing egrets?" He replied, "I do not know." The notion of what might happen made me tremble. To such he could be brutal: a vivisectionist was as nothing. I never heard him speak much of the ways of research, but he made no comment when I told him of the late Professor Benjamin Moore asking me during the war to stay and see some rats experimented on with poison gas, and of my reply that I could not bear to see such things, though I recognised their necessity. For Moore said cheerfully, "Yes, I understand: it's a matter of temperament, a matter of temperament!" But any useless cruelty, for some physiologists are cruel, would anger him beyond speech. I told him of one worker in Paris. If Hudson could have surrendered him for like experiments he would have done it. His tolerance had limits: a debauched instinct for cruelty reached and went beyond them. If it is shown that he ever spoke bitterly of vivisection, that will not surprise me. He had many standpoints: he was as variable as a spring day to the very last, and, therefore, often hard to understand.

This leads me to something that happened during the last years of his life, something so surprising and apparently so uncharacteristic of him that at first sight it seems shocking in one so easily wounded by all forms of injustice and cruelty. For if there was one thing characteristic of Hudson more than another, it was, of course, his love of animals and his intense dislike of seeing them ill-treated and imprisoned. Few who have read his scathing and almost brutally just criticism of a cathedral town in

Sussex can forget his vain efforts to free a wretched owl, caged in a hot kitchen with a glaring fire. It is, therefore, remarkable that on one occasion he deliberately and repeatedly refused to interfere with a somewhat similar, if less cruel, case. In a certain remote village a lady, a great friend of Hudson's, was asked by the clergyman's wife to bring him to the house, as she had something to show which would please him very much. It turned out that what she believed would delight him was a young white owl which had been chained for two years to one branch of a tree at the bottom of the cleric's garden. What appeared most charming to this kindly ecclesiastic and his wife was that the owl's parents actually visited their poor offspring daily. The lady believed this would afford Mr. Hudson peculiar gratification. Hudson's friend endeavoured to free her from this singular delusion and expressed her opinion with native vigour. She used every argument to induce the woman to let the bird go, and every argument was vain. She, therefore, went to Hudson and suggested that he should interfere. He promptly refused, and when pressed for his reasons would give none save that any act of his must inevitably give rise to unpleasantness. This seemed more than astounding, but I think the explanation is very simple. Hudson was then over seventy-five, and knowing perfectly well the condition of his heart, was aware how he must live, if he were to live at all. He believed, and believed rightly, that it was better for him to go on living and working for all birds and animals than to die of rage on some miserable cleric's prison lawn. If he had visited the house and found that nothing he said was of avail, I am convinced that some such disaster not only might, but

would, have occurred. But not for worlds would he have
offered such an explanation, and he and his friend actually
quarrelled about the matter for two whole weeks. Yet
this lady is not easily beaten. She had failed with the religious jailers and failed with Hudson, but the promise of
a sovereign to the policeman of a neighbouring district
made him visit the house as if armed with the terrors of
an imaginary new law which had special reference to
white owls. He found only the son at home, and so
worked on him that this youth freed the owl and was,
very properly, bitten to the bone in the process. Hudson
never afterwards referred to the incident. I have not the
least doubt that my explanation of his conduct is the right
one, for, knowing what the cardiologists thought of him,
I myself had warned him against excess of any kind,
physical or mental, and especially against anger.

Here, perhaps, may be said what remains to be said of
Hudson's health. Doomed to death as he was by ignorant physicians, who may, however, be excused for ignorance seeing how little was then known of the heart in
disease, when he was but fifteen years of age, he yet
lived till he was over eighty-one. If the life of its big men
concerns the world, it may be held that the manner and
reason of their death concern it not at all. Yet, again,
it is possible that to the interest of mere curiosity we may
add something which inspires hope in those who, like
Hudson, have been sentenced to death and bidden to pre-
pare for it untimely. Moreover, the mere curiosity is not
without its justification: all that concerns one of whom
we desire to know much can surely be excused. Such art
and purpose as there are in a sketch like this tend to the
explanation of a man, his hopes and fears, his motives, the

causes which led to his development, and in his death and
its manner, tragic or peaceful, there is possibly a solution
of many mysteries. We desire rightly to know where and
how a man was born, of what parentage and stock he was,
whence his ancestors sprang, for these things concern
true explanation and place him so that we do not wholly
depend on his work for the elucidation of his life and
progress. And death ends and crowns all. How greatly
ill-health determines men's careers and, indeed, makes
them what they are, or what they were, we see through
all history. We need not go back to Cæsar; the literary
history of England is full to those who understand its
examples. Such men as Swift and Pope, as Shelley,
Keats, and Blake, to put together classicists with great
instinctive writers, show what a factor disorder and disease may be. But for that attack of rheumatic fever, of
which Hudson speaks in *Far Away and Long Ago*, he
would not have been the man here so dimly adumbrated.
The condition in which it left his heart determined the
order and direction of his life: it liberated him from any
such career as his great natural physical strength and
energy, and the conditions of his home, might have led
or forced him to adopt. It may be that without this fever
we in England should never have known him: he might
have been an unknown engineer or one who died in ex-
ploration of new territories in the wilds of Brazil or
Venezuela. Truly it set him free for all that his nature
best fitted him, even if it also determined the manner of
his death. So for what follows I shall make no more
excuse, though I will put it as simply as possible.

The legacy left to Hudson by rheumatic fever is a common but often a very bitter one. The attack resulted in

disease of the mitral valve which lies between the left auricle and ventricle of the heart. Consequent damage to the natural passage threw more than normal work on the auricle and was to be diagnosed by a very easily recognisable murmur. In those days there was great ignorance of the disorder: doctors were accustomed to find such a sign and make a prognosis without taking into account the general condition of the patient's heart muscle. They accordingly sentenced Hudson to death. He was told, and his parents were told, that he might as well do just what he liked, since in no case could he live long. The effect of this on a youth with his imagination and his passionate love of life can be reckoned up by those who have read his work and have especially pondered on the latter chapters of his early autobiography. Yet year after year passed and he did not die. As soon as compensating muscle enabled his heart to do its work life again became possible. But always through all the earlier years of my friendship with him he was worried by what are known technically as "extra-systoles," which the laity mostly recognise by the loss of a beat in the radial pulse. They are, however, caused by an attempt of the irritated heart to begin a new contraction before the heart muscle is ready, and the result is a weak interpolated contraction not to be felt at the wrist. It was only in about 1916 that the extra work thrown upon the left auricle determined its final degeneration, so that the state was established which is now known as auricular fibrillation, a condition in which the auricular muscle fibres cease to work together and merely twitch without co-ordination. I found him in this new condition and sent him to Sir James Mackenzie, to whose work and that of Dr. T. Lewis the general recognition of this disorder by modern cardiologists is due. The pulse was now wholly irregular and very fast. The physician wrote the following letter to me: "Mr. Hudson called to-day and I found him a typical example of auricular fibrillation, so I gave him some instruction as to how to manage his heart by the use of digitalis, and I have told him to be sure to look me up from time to time as he passes, so that I can see that the digitalis is keeping a grip of his heart. Apart from that I found him a wonderfully healthy man, but as he is liable to bronchial attacks and so forth, the danger to his life depends upon them more than on the heart condition." This was written on the 28th of June, 1916. It may be that the treatment given then saved him for many years of active life. I have at least often thought so, for he was always difficult to manage, and Sir James Mackenzie possessed the qualities of authority and power which alone could earn his confidence. He was given digitalis and carefully instructed how to use it. Yet when he was alone with me he sometimes argued that the physician was wrong. His natural and often humorous combativeness came to the surface, and I was sometimes hard put to it to make him obey the directions given to him. His heart did better, he asserted, when it beat more than the doctor liked. Didn't he and his heart know best? I did not think so, but had to walk warily between alarming him and encouraging him to go his own way. When Sir James Mackenzie had left active practice, and had taken up special investigation work at St. Andrews, Hudson's condition grew somewhat worse again and I sent him to Dr. Frederick Price. Once more I had the same difficulty with him. "Price wants my heart to do only seventy beats to the minute, and I feel better when it is eighty," he urged, and I compromised on seventy-five and tried to make him keep it no higher, telling him truly that the less work his heart did the longer it was likely to live, and that it must be coddled and considered, as it might not be so anxious to carry on as he was. Without doubt if he had been left to the care of the general practitioners he would not have lived long. Their knowledge of cardiology and the scientific use of digitalis is rarely extensive, to say the least.

It may be that many will think all this as unnecessary as it is unusual in biography. Once more I reply that this is not a biography, whatever else it may be. Such details, perhaps not wholly intelligible to all, in their summed effect show in what way Hudson, the lover of life, lived for ever in the penumbra of death, and yet did splendid work with a youthful mind and spirit in spite of the shaking fears which sometimes beset him and made him write to me, "Last night I thought I should be found dead in the morning." I wondered at his putting it into words. Yet after that he wrote *A Hind in Richmond Park,* a mature book, but one essentially full of life and young in spirit and energy of thought, a book of varied powers and wide range and wisdom that was born of instinct, and yet wiser than instinct, for it sprang like a spring and grew to a river and a lake and poured out into a wonderful half-fantastic sea of philosophy. And even then he was destroying papers full of matter that he did not wish to leave behind him.

It seems to me that the young fear death least, perhaps because they cannot realise it and have not seen it. The old have seen it in action, and resent a like quiescence. Yet it is in old and young a natural fear, and for the most part they avoid it even in thought. For when they talk of it they are not touched by it: they speak as if they themselves were "notoriously immortal." It was Spinoza who said, "the free man thinks of nothing so little as death." Yet in Hudson it was a constant fear, and thereby his freedom was not perfect, great as he made it and beyond common estimates. But the hours of a man's greatest freedom from these cares or thoughts are in his boyhood, and death's own self seemed to stand by him even on the pampa when ignorant doctors prophesied his early end. To one to whom life was so great a gift of nature, who yet had no hope of any immortality, their words were as bitter as gall and remained as a cruel legacy even though many years passed and they were unfulfilled, while "a frightful fiend" trod for ever behind him. This, perhaps, was a weakness in him: yet many share it without his courage. Many, indeed, die of it, and Hudson lived and worked and drank sweet and bitter as life offered him the cup. There were times when he hoped death would come suddenly. When his wife died he wrote to a friend, "Blessed are those who die struck by lightning! That was often said by a preacher of rebellion against the Mother Country in the pre-Independence days. I believe my mother was a collateral descendant of his." Yet all the while I knew his fear of death, and as age came on it was my task, as far as lay in me, to watch and encourage him. Accident in my own life had led me to study cardiology, and such knowledge as I possessed proved useful to Hudson, for it taught me how to help him and minimise his danger and yet to send him when it proved necessary to the man who at that time knew more of heart disease than anyone in London. That his advice and authority kept Hudson alive for many years may be regarded as certain. It was some two years after this that I took Hudson to a very eminent surgeon, Mr. John Pardoe, on account of a passing ailment which gave him more worry than real trouble. After examining him the surgeon came into the waiting-room and said to me, "I can't see how the man keeps alive: his heart is the merest rubbish." Hudson was much interested in this surgeon, as he was descended from a Spanish stock, the name originally being spelt Pardo. It was not till 1920 that he needed further advice about his heart, and it was then that I arranged for him to consult Dr. Frederick Price, who saw him occasionally till his death. I need say nothing of the impression Hudson left upon these men. They were all far more gratified to know and help him than to take their fees. I had brought or sent to them someone of whom they had not seen the like. Dr. Parsons-Smith, who saw him in Dr. Price's absence on the 17th August, 1922, too late for skill or courage to save Hudson, will, I know, say the same.

CHAPTER IX

THOUGH I have not sought to distinguish the years of this long period within many landmarks, it might be possible to divide it by books and published papers and quotations from correspondence, which task I leave to those who come after. Yet I may divide his life as I saw it into the time which followed my return to England until Emily Hudson failed at last in 1913 and went to Worthing with a nurse, and that which came afterwards when he spent the winters at Penzance, to which I could so seldom accompany him. Of that earlier era I have little real record save in his letters, too many of which are undated and have to be placed in order by guesswork or by something he says of current things, of his own books, or, perhaps, of mine. It may, however, be noted that when his wife broke down he had a severe attack of gastritis which tried him badly and made him utterly unable to continue nursing her. Following this he had bronchitis, which threw a great strain on his heart. He was then advised to winter in Cornwall. If now I draw no picture of him in any special time, I must simply follow the thoughts in my own mind, which depict him with all his variety as a composite being, loving, angry, bright and gloomy, laughing and irritable, splendidly enthusiastic, and again an invalid upon a couch with a pile of books and pens and ink and paper and pencils by his bedside. Though the later days dominate those that came earlier, yet age never touched him and he seemed no older at this time than when he opened the door to me in Leinster Square. Whether I shall use many of his letters in this book I cannot now say. They may be printed separately, but, whether here or apart, they will be witnesses to his variety and speak for the truth of what is here put down. So now I may write of them without detail or long examples, for he was a good, even a great, correspondent, and in that respect, perhaps, belonged to the past. Not for him the custom of allowing letters to answer themselves: he had too much native courtesy, the courtesy he found chiefly in the highest and the lowest. He possessed the courtesy of the gaucho of the pampa or that of some hidalgo of Spain. It was, therefore, almost a patent and proof of real intimacy for him to be rude to a friend in speech or writing, and sometimes he made sly or open hits at those he loved who understood. He wrote letters freely and at length and hated to receive short ones. "I got a miserable card from you," was often his word. "Why don't you write *letters?* Yours was half a page," he would grumble. Sometimes he wrote letters of inquiry that meant labour and search among the books he himself hated to plough through. He wrote on "whiteness," "blueness," "migration," and asked for hypotheses, theories, explanations, and mostly would have none when offered. But they served for thought, for suggestion, and out of a bucket of offered chaff he sometimes picked a grain or two with a "yes, perhaps," and I knew he was as much pleased as if he had returned elaborate thanks.

Many will miss in this book a due and proper ingredient of all righteous biographies. I shall say very little of his many friends, though much might be said of them, since his sympathies and interests were as wide as the sky itself. Yet there being no such thing as consistency, I may at least speak just a little freely of one friend and make no more excuses. I said earlier that he always seemed to take to those who knew the wilds, those who had crossed mountain ranges, ridden across great plains, who had been the friends of horses and had camped beneath the stars. Such a man was Cunninghame Graham, who must bear being spoken of again. Graham is Scotch, a Graham of Gartmore, who might yet be a true son of Spain, a horseman, a swordsman, an adventurer among men and beasts and among words as well. I remember best one thing of his about a Ghost Dance. Hudson spoke of that and many other things the man had written. How should such a man "succeed"? Impossible, said Hudson, knowing that failure was often the sign of great success, as he of whom he spoke knew well enough. To Hudson, Graham was a kind of Don Quixote, a tilter at mills that ground not corn but the wind, or ground other things most cruelly. His very appearance, his youth when we

were all young, even Hudson himself, was in his favour.
What a pity we all grow grey! said Hudson. For a while
he himself darkened his hair and moustache a little. Shall
a big man have no weakness, if weakness it is to cling to
life and youth so ardently? He wished us all to stay
young with him. "You're not grey yet!" he said when
I pleaded growing scarcity of hair. When I told him
"dear Cunninghame Graham" was at last touched with
grey he lamented. He liked to get those wonderful indecipherable letters from Graham, sealed with the tiny
figure of a pony, and remembered him riding in the Row,
to all London's amazement, upon a mustang with a fine
long tail, so that the flies could be switched off where the
muscles of the ancient panniculus were atrophied. To
dock a horse was foolish, cruel robbery. Graham set a
good example and fools did not follow it. Still Hudson
spoke of Henry Salt's *Seventy Years among Savages,* and
owned grumpily that things were better now. At least
the Eton boys did not hunt a wretched fox with one pad
cut off, even if sportsmen chased hinds in young, or harried bitch otters into parturition on the banks of some wild
river. One could not say like things of Graham even if
he were worse than a Radical and had had his skull
cracked in Trafalgar Square. Graham must and will no
doubt bear being spoken of in this way, for he was part
of Hudson's life for a long time, being one who endured,
who was not tried and found wanting. That was why
he took to one he called "Arabian Lawrence." To know
the wild was to have barriers thrown down, if, indeed, the
knowledge was true and bought with pain and long days
and nights of endurance of heat or cold or other suffer-
ings that the wilderness inflicts upon its mad votaries,

whether in Eastern deserts, or the long pampa, or high plateaux, or the grey and brown Austral plains.

It is true that he knew and loved many who cared for none of these things, who were Gallios as regards them, who thought the pen finer than the weapons of hardship, and many hours at the desk more than sufficient exercise, who took books for gods and found in them their dawns, and sunsets, and deep and solitary midnights as in lone forests. Hudson used at one time to go to some literary gatherings and met there many notable men, amiable and able people, and he sat among them while they talked and, as I know, understood him little or not at all. They were intellectuals, "the intelligentsia," anything but creatures of the wild. It was hard to forgive them this, though one who worked for animals as well as for poor prisoners was taken to his heart. I always felt there was a wall between him and a score of his friends. He put his arms on it and talked to them over it, and probably they never saw the wall. He was so difficult: he asked, without a word, so much, and none knew what it was and he never told them, and it was only those who had the "something," however small it might be, who knew they held the golden key that opened his heart, though he never acknowledged affection, or so rarely that one doubted when he did whether he really meant it. "We've known one another over forty years and there's never been a cloud," said I one day. He grunted, "Hasn't there?" and that was all, as if he would throw doubt on it and have me know he would be damned if he acknowledged we had never come to words or blows. That was Hudson with men. What he was with women let women tell. He never told of them.

He was the cleanest-minded man and doubtless a true great lover. Is there any need to hide it? Who would understand him if it were hidden? It would be a lie to say he locked any big instinct in a cage. He loved beasts and men and birds and women, all but those unspeakable creatures who wore egrets' or gulls' wings as a crown of infamy. He would have seen no beauty in Aphrodite if she had worn birds' feathers, though she had come nude to him. He saw women's beauty plainly. He damned Schopenhauer, and once argued I had been reading him because I did not agree with his theory of beauty in flowers.

In this wandering story of him, in which I care for nothing but the truth as I saw it, so that it may lack or possess art or not as destiny or character will, much may seem irrelevant, but one must work as one can. So when I speak of Hudson's interests in life it may be noted where he had none. Curiously interested as he was in what masquerades as occultism, since there was, he thought, in all the mountains of lies and false deductions which were called "truth," something real to be found out, he still had for theology and the like a pure contempt. And yet he would sometimes pore over *Hibbert's Journal* and plunge in the disturbed pool of that metaphysical Siloam which seems troubled by no angel, but by some foolish devil of discord who forever muddies objective thought and wastes man's energies. However, he never pushed so far into orthodox religion as to observe it as a branch of anthropology. He rather fixed his mind on the fact that the clergy rarely preached mercy to birds and animals and cared little for fishes, unless in connection with the loaves of preferment.

And so with politics and politicians. Unless politicians could be induced to pass Plumage Bills, Acts for the preservation of birds, Hudson took no interest in them. The din of Parliament was confused shouting: it meant nothing or meant folly. His native conservatism led him rather towards the vain and vague ideal of the One Wise Ruler than to any more obvious political ends. Yet, as I said before, when I tried to show him that politics might be considered in the light of biology; that they were the processes by which the huge, undeveloped social organism adapted itself clumsily to new conditions, he did show some interest in them. But on the whole no subject appealed to him unless it touched his instincts or his general love of wide scientific thinking, though, as soon as he saw the chance of being the "field-naturalist" he speaks of in his last book, politics did not seem so futile or so impossible of comprehension as he had imagined. It was for this reason that he for ever urged me to finish a book on social physiology and pathology, and was often impatient when I urged insufficient preparation, or want of time and money. I hesitate to put down anything he said as to my capacity to deal with such subjects, but think it may be added that his chief lamentation regarding my literary life was that it took me from what he regarded as my proper vocation, that of a lecturer to all and sundry upon every abstruse subject he wished to see illuminated. This was not his humour, though it seemed not a little humorous to me, for here and there he lacked humour, and the prospect he held out to me did not appeal to my instincts or my ignorances. And the difficulty of seizing a professorial chair by force seemed insuperable, even if he recommended me to an anxious and expectant universe.

It may be said that a continued interest in anything
tends to keep a man alive. But continued interest in
poetry, especially as it changes, has always seemed to me
a sign of intellectual youth. This I myself cannot boast
of: there seems too much chaff for the wheat, even for
a grain of barley, and purposed extravagance is too often
merely a mask of incapacity, a sign of ambition without
intellect or taste or that fine respect for tradition which
preserves order, even though the pattern of thought be
altered. Yet in Hudson there was a lively passion for
many of the moderns, though many he looked on as impermanent variations which did but adorn, or perhaps
mar, the field in which they grew. To change the
metaphor, they were poor new song-birds, and from few
of them should arise an evolved species whose music made
the air of life more tuneful. Still, they were fresh unobserved birds, and the twitter of a member of the
Passeres was more to him at times than the song of a
Tennysonian nightingale or philosophic Wordsworthian
thrush. He perpetually spoke to me of new men, saying
there was something in them of newness or strangeness,
a thing he perpetually sought out and loved, if it was
not the deliberate affectation of those who say, "Come,
I will be original." I shall not here advertise many.
Advertisement will not keep them alive in authority: nor
will criticism hasten their due and orderly decay. One
poet I tried to bring to him, but John Davidson at that
time began to get haughty and strange in his neglected
pride and anger at a world which could not recognise
merit till it died in despair. But Hudson knew some of
his work, and curiously enough put, in a way, *The Ballad
of a Nun* into practice, since it was owing to his influence

that one Catholic novice refused to take the final vows and left her convent to become a nurse. Those are mistaken who think he believed happiness was not possible. Happiness was truly "not a potato," but it was the free exercise of all a man or man's nature. "I indulged my nature, all my nature," he once wrote to me. To be thus alive *was* happiness, not to make the great refusal of life with all its gifts. And there could be more than happiness as one sat content close to the earth and heard the birds and felt the touch of the warm summer air. A man could truly be blessed with ecstasy, not the ascetic ecstasy, but the full-breathed, full-blooded ecstasy of oneness with Nature—"so that seeing the sheet of blue flowers I did not walk, but just floated, floated!"

He knew more of this modern poetry than anyone I ever met. He could assimilate *Dawn in Britain,* no mean task for a man of his age. I suppose it was an adventure of Doughty's, just as *Arabia Deserta* was an adventure, and Hudson wandered in both and then took hold of the young men, even the poor fellows who wrote and died in the war and were, in the pity and passion of the hour, called genuises. He looked on their adventures and for the hour, too, loved them. As for the war I shall say little, but I know that one night when the enemy was over London and the ears of us all were deafened, and many Londoners, native and alien, took cover in the Tubes or cellars, he spent hours on the high roof of No. 40 and said it was "splendid." And yet, on other nights, when his spirit burnt low and his heart worked badly, he went to the basement, and sat silent by his kind and friendly housekeeper with his elbows on the table and his head in his hands. In one letter he wrote to me, "I had made up

my mind to fly to the roof on the first indication of a
Zeppelin coming over London, but, alas, when they
came I wasn't well and had gone to bed early, and when
the uproar began when they passed over Westbourne Park
I wouldn't get up. Then the roar of guns started and I
did get up, and went out and saw some of the excitement
in the street. Everyone had seen one Zeppelin when it
went over here and I had missed it!"

Whether in fact the airship was really overhead I cannot say, and merely note that a single Zeppelin in Middle-
sex always appeared to possess the miraculous power of
being over every head in the county at the same time.

CHAPTER X

It is not my purpose to write at length about Hudson's
work. Many have done that, and more will speak in
generations to come. So long as the glory of English
prose remains and is still cared for by its votaries, his
books will be regarded as the fruit of a period not too
rich in those classics which belong to the right line of
literature and beget, it may be, far descendants. My
thought was ever not so much the work as the man. It
will speak, but he himself will not be silent. Some things,
indeed, have already been beautifully written of him: I
cannot despise or hope to emulate them. I look through
the mist of woven words and see him smiling, pleased
yet a little scornful, sardonic and yet kindly, as great men
may be who understand humanity, and are not too bitter
that praise and ease and triumph come too late. Yet once
he quoted to me Johnson's letter to Chesterfield—"when I
am old and cannot enjoy it: when I am lonely and can-

not impart it." That was a passing mood; for none can say he was bitter. Only a few days ago I saw Chatterton's monument raised high above the grassy tombs of St. Mary Redcliffe: I shall see a monument to Hudson, who needed none. Yet he, too, starved, and yet went on courageously with little recognition save from the few who were drawn to him by his nature and not by his books.

A man may be more than his work, as some may be less. Cervantes made Don Quixote live and suffer. He wrote a great book. Yet to those who knew his history he bulks larger than his work. Nobility of character and such high courage as his surpass words, though we call them immortal till dust and oblivion cover them and their creator at the last. There are those who had and have a little golden gift better than themselves. Such a man was Sterne. Swift again never wrought to his full powers. The evil gifts of ambition frustrated and mad bitterness half destroyed him. We live now among little men. They achieve "success" and shout in the arena. Words make philosophers: rash presumption and ignorance a thinker. Literature has become posters: a poet yearns for sandwich men in the Strand. Some, it is true, are silent and do not bellow in the market-place, but who among them will survive? If I am not mistaken, few of this time but Hudson will be remembered.

As I sit and write of him who was so long my friend it is hard to get away from the memory of his presence to his books. They were truly the fruit of the tree and might be merchandise, but I had sat so long almost solitary under his branches when few marked their growth or verdure or shadow, that his books fell about me sometimes scarcely heeded. I aspire to be no critic, for the critical faculty needs continuous exercise to develop itself, but, still, perpetual contact with literature, old and new and good and poor, and much writing, not always merely for the day, gave me insight, aided by his talk, into what he meant and sometimes hardly wrote. It was this continued speech with him about his work that often made me for the moment somewhat disappointed even with his most beautiful things. Curious and even absurd as it will seem to some, this was the case with that deep and noble romance, *Green Mansions*. The book took years to write, and though I saw little of it till he sent it to me in print, yet ever and again he spoke of it, and in my mind his conception grew to a story that had all the colour he could give it, and all that which was added by my own imagination of its greatness and colour. Therefore I saw it, not as a book in which one has to come down to words and print, but as a dim, strange tale that I had been told and had dreamed of, so that it had a strangeness as of magic. It was, therefore, something at last that even he could not write, though in everything it was truly that to which he aspired and knew he could not attain. With a writer this is always so. No man writes, no painter paints, the book or picture that he sees, and so it happened that I took on at last something of his own feeling and suffered a little, as he and all writers suffer who in the end see the reality, not the vision and the dream, the picture, not the remembered sunset. I cannot now criticise the book even if I would, but I remember being repelled by the machinery with which it began. Here, again, was Hudson, that child of the southern pampa, under the strange and alien mask of some cold northerner with a ruddy complexion and blue or grey eyes, such a figure as "Smith" in *A Crystal Age,* or the blue-eyed Saxon "Lamb," who told with southern passion those wonderful tales of the Banda Oriental. It still disturbs me to see the way in which the supposed writer of the story of Rima appears to imagine that his own simple confidences justified him in demanding a like openness from one who had suffered so greatly. These figments still seem unnatural to me for all the life and vigour and beauty of the books. And yet they are nothing, and in *Green Mansions* is the very spirit of the secret Hudson whom few could or should know. Especially is it marvellous that he so caught the wonder and power of the tropic forest, for never in his life did he come near one and enter into its mysteries. The pampa of the Argentine and the grey plains and rolling country of Patagonia are practically treeless, and the biggest woodland he ever knew was in England. He had not seen palms or tree ferns or any jungle, or the forests of the Rockies, or the mighty religious groves of redwoods, some of which still remain unmurdered near the coast of California. It was from Bates and Bell and Wallace, that he drew the spirit of the woods, and he placed the story in Venezuela, which he had never seen, because its vast interior was as little known as the builders of Copan in Spanish Honduras, or those who carved Easter Island into gods. In that unknown world he dreamed of Rima, an incarnation of his desire, a strange, bird-like woman. I believe that in her discovery he found for those years a mate for the spirit and much consolation. But, like him who told the tale, he kept the ashes of his thought close to his heart. In much no book could be more tremendous and more true. He worked to make it so, even as Abel adorned the earthenware pot which held Rima's ashes. Hudson's art was great, but never, or only rarely, mechanical. His opposed contrasted figures grew out of the soil, and if Rima seems to come down from heaven, she was yet a being who sprang living from his memory of some white and lovely children, whom he had known on the pampa, some who died and some whom he saw no more as he went away wondering who those might be who had left such pale daughters by the hearth and horses' skulls of a gaucho hut. But the story of Rima is also the story of those birds and of that ancient beauty which inevitably perish at the hands of barbarians, even those gold-giving and reddened hands of the collectors whom he hated.

Of Hudson's first book I heard much from 1880 to 1884, in which year I went to America. *The Purple Land which England Lost* was printed in 1885, and I did not see it till I returned to London at the end of 1886. It was in two volumes, and is now reprinted as *The Purple Land.* These stories composed part, and a very small part, of a long book called *The History of the House of Lamb,* which Hudson destroyed. The beginning and the end of the part which he kept show signs of its origin. No book racier of South American soil exists, and scarcely a word is not characteristic of the younger Hudson. If there are two better stories of this kind than *Lock and Key and Sinners Three,* and *Manuel, also called the Fox,* I do not know them. Hudson's inbred knowledge of the gaucho and the pampa, and his being bilingual gave him unequalled opportunities of observation, and in places his humour is absolutely riotous. It is, however, essentially a book by a young man, and the tale of Dolores is a failure. He altered some of it on my recommendation, but even now the passion of it rings false. But the Maid of Yi, Candelaria, and the wife of the Juez, are wonderful studies of women good and bad. I have always considered "Manuel" the "pick of the bunch." Hudson wrote to me long after the book was published, that "when my very first book came out, and the *Saturday Review* and the *Athenæum* jumped on it as a farrago of indecent nonsense and lies, Keane [Prof. Keane] wrote a glowingly favourable review in the *Academy*. The first taste of praise I ever had." Yet in later years he was sometimes inclined to disparage the book as he disparaged *A Crystal Age*. This was printed in 1887, and was anonymous. A comparison with the later edition shows his growing sense of style and the selection of words. The word "phenomenal" in what Gissing used to call "the tea-board sense," since one firm advertised "tea of phenomenal value," was used in the first few pages of the first edition but disappeared in the second. My copy of the first edition contains some slight corrections in his handwriting. As an essay in "late decorated" prose the book is not unworthy of any young author, and although Hudson was over forty, as a writer he was still young. He thought little or nothing of the tale when he came to his full strength, and it remains after all no more than an exercise and partially successful experiment. When the second edition was printed in 1906, he wrote to me, "I care precious little about the book as a fact and don't care whether it succeeds or not." It may be noted that he followed Samuel Butler in *Erewhon* in making illness a crime, for which "Smith" was sentenced to some days of seclusion. He was a great admirer of Butler, and frequently abused and bantered me for remaining too critical of much of his biological work.

It was in *The Naturalist of La Plata* that the zoological world discovered a new observer of a very high rank, and men of letters, since some do not disdain all science, found there a new writer. None could read the end of the first chapter in which Hudson lamented the passing glory of the world, and the ceaseless destruction of its nobler ancient ornaments, without discerning that he wrote with power and a marvellous sense of the rhythm which makes English prose of the highest order akin to great poetry. In the following passage may be observed the later results of the preparation he gave to style in *A Crystal Age*:

"And, above all others, we should protect and hold sacred those types, Nature's masterpieces, which are first singled out for destruction on account of their size, or splendour, or rarity, and that false, detestable glory which is accorded to their most successful slayers. In ancient times the spirit of life shone brightest in these: and, when others that shared the earth with them were taken by death, they were left, being more worthy of perpetuation. Like immortal flowers they have drifted down to us on the ocean of time, and their strangeness and beauty ring to our imaginations a dream and a picture of that unknown world, immeasurably far removed, where man was not: and when they perish, something of gladness goes out from nature, and the sunshine loses something of its brightness."

If men of science prepared to add his name presently to the roll in which Darwin and Wallace do not disdain the humbler White of Selborne or Richard Jefferies, some writers and critics thus became aware of a new musician in words. A few, perhaps, remembered that this was the man who had achieved the rarest distinction on the tales of *The Purple Land,* and, since the authorship of *A Crystal Age* was not long a secret, one who had also exercised his natural gifts in a story which depended for its effect, even though that effect was passing, upon a more than academic mastery of rhythm. I shall make no attempt to estimate the value of *The Naturalist of La Plata.* It has gained its place and cannot be dispossessed of it. Like so many of Hudson's books, I cannot turn its pages without more than the common melancholy of those who read the work of a friend when he is dead. Every now and again I seem to catch the faint sounds of his speech about Maldonada and the puma, that *amigo del Cristiano,* for whose strange respect for humanity I can also vouch, since under other names it ranges from Patagonia to Alaska. I remember that at Shoreham we spent nights over those very problems. But for such hours I might have missed a great abiding interest in the animal world. And none knew so well as Hudson that everything we know or can know of any living creature is relevant to man, the strangest and most awful creature of them all.

Long ago I said that Hudson had built his own monument, and that I had seen him build it stone by stone, and book by book. To have seen so much and no more would still be something, a pleasant memory of the years that brought the books into being, but in some of them I have a greater share, since none used a suggestion better or more eagerly if it fitted with his thoughts. This was so with parts of the book of Hudson's which first revealed him to the little world then ready to acclaim him, though it was to be so long before he was known beyond the boundary of a narrow fairy ring on a high and lonely down. Hudson seldom mentions those by name who were intimate with him, hence not till his very last book does he ever mention me, but still it pleases me to look here and there and find, as it were, a finger-print of my own or even a footstep, and the words "a friend of mine." So in this book when I read towards the end and find the chapter about horses coming home to die, and remember that the alternative suggestion was one suggested by myself, I recall the hours when Hudson and I talked ceaselessly of such things from morning to sunset time, and then to midnight, while he used me with an amused pleasure in the swiftness with which I invented hypotheses for him to murder with a fact, after the manner of the Herbert Spencer tragedy, until, with a mass of dead explanations underfoot, he at last acknowledged that he had got a weather-proof one that would stand any sort of scientific weather. Then, again, there was the matter of the red flag and the bull. When that came up we were staying together in very simple lodgings in Shoreham, and Alfred Hartley, the artist, was with us, but that night Hartley, after listening for some hours, went off to bed and left us at it hammer and tongs, until in the end we turned to, or found, or made, the challenge theory which satisfied Hudson and stands in the book. So far as the mere suggestion of a challenge was concerned, that came from me, but it was Hudson who gave it life and set it on its feet, by showing, as I think he fails to show clearly in the book itself, that red after all in any striking isolated mass is the rarest thing in nature, especially to cattle, who live in a predominantly green world. But to me the great things are the remembered *Noctes Ambrosianæ* when Hudson bowled at me for hours, and I set up the wicket again and yet once more. It always seemed to amuse him that though I knew nothing or next to nothing of his subjects, I had yet a general capacity for explanation. He used to say I reminded him of a doctor he had read of in some forgotten romance, who at a moment's notice was on the spot with a solution of any problem, however recondite, and, like the political candidate who owned himself willing to change his opinions if the electors did not like them, was ready with another hypothesis if his hearers objected to the first one. And Hudson was almost always ready to fight any accepted orthodox opinion. After the manner, perhaps, of less distinguished field-naturalists, he professed a certain contempt for the man of science in his laboratory or working-room. He might possibly have named an osteologist a "bone-disturber," and for such ornithologists as would have been unlikely to recognise a bird on any bough, being more familiar with their skeletons and muscles than their habits and their music, he had little to say which was complimentary. It is not given to all, or even to the greatest, to be for ever wise, indulgent, and unprejudiced, and I have always believed this feeling of Hudson's was founded upon his relations with Prof. Sclater, who wrote the purely scientific portion of *Argentine Ornithology,* published in 1888. This book was always a sore subject with Hudson. Judging from his description this eminent professor lacked charm, to say the least of it, but balanced the lack by a keen regard

for royalties somewhat repugnant to a much poorer
collaborator. Without Hudson's vivid description of the
birds among which he grew up the book would have
been no more than an arranged bone-heap, a pile of
patiently sorted avian dust, a catalogue without life, or
pity, or the splendours and charm of words. Here, with
all the faults of an immature and unbalanced style, Hudson first revealed his nascent powers of description and
understanding. By the side of his colour the very
painter's colour failed: he breathed life into dead drawings which feigned to illustrate him and were themselves
illustrated by a greater artist. Of Sclater and John Gould
and a few other men, with whom he had something like
a conflict, such as Alfred Newton, he very seldom spoke.
They reminded him of disagreeable things. These he
was ever apt to bury, and to bury them deep, and he
growled if any approached their grave. Whatever the
woes of yester-year, they should not spoil a more genial
hour of grace.

If, however, Hudson felt like this about the Dryasdusts
and museum-haunters of the scientific world, those who
cannot see beyond their antennæ, it was never beyond
him to appreciate fully the nobler specimens of *Homo
sapiens,* such as Darwin and Wallace, who inspired and
always held his respect. These men were at least not
narrow: at their best they dwelt upon Pisgah and sur-
veyed the world in life and colour and motion. Hudson
rejected many of their conclusions, but owned they were
great observers as well as thinkers. If they, though
field-naturalists, did not survey the greater field of the
whole works of man, including art and philosophy, as
human activities, it was truly a pity. To Hudson, as he

has shown in *A Hind in Richmond Park*, nothing living was alien. His contempt for the smaller dusty hodmen of science was sometimes humorous: he often observed their gyrations with a not ungenial gravity of aspect. They could annoy, but were interesting when they criticised, though they were almost vinchucas, "little things that go about," biting insects of the night that he described in *The Purple Land*. He asked for vision.

One without qualifications as a naturalist cannot, perhaps, judge all his work, but its value depends immensely on the way he stood apart and cultivated his own garden, though such a method has dangers into which he ran sometimes without due caution. It is obvious that his was not wholly the scientific mind: he rarely saw things in " a dry light," but all the world, even the world of science, was coloured and irradiated by his imagination. When we discussed things within my ambit I found him at times queerly and obviously wrong, for conclusions come to even in his youth often remained obstacles to better explanations. He yielded occupied ground after battle with difficulty and withdrew, as it were, by night, so that in the morning he was found in a fresh position, entrenching it with eager passion. Later years made him, as they make us all, a little more rigid, a little less ready to shift his camp. Still on the whole he was never unreasonable for long, and but for his health we should have continued to argue as of old, in the humorous, rude way of real friends, who insult each other jocosely and are forgiven. There is nothing which keeps together those whose philosophy agrees fundamentally like continued intellectual curiosity. This burnt brightly in Hudson to the last day he lived. When poverty, ill-

health, loneliness, and an enforced town life oppressed
him sorely, he found in the motions of his restless, curious
mind perpetual consolation.

Of *Fan,* published in 1892, Hudson's one and only
novel in three volumes, little need be said. I never even
knew he was trying his hand in the full-length fiction of
the time until he gave me the printed book without an
inscription, so anxious was he to preserve anonymity.
As soon as the book was done he thought little of it,
and by no means resented free criticism. Though there
are passages in it which show the pen of a naturalist,
the book is without enough merit to keep it sweet, and
I was disturbed by learning the year before he died that
he had mentioned it to his publishers. I did everything
possible to get him to withdraw and suppress it, but
since there was some money in it for the Bird Society
he refused to do so. For the birds he cared much, for
his literary reputation nothing. I had the same struggle
with him about his early story, *Ralph Herne,* a book of
no value save for the picture of yellow fever in Buenos
Aires, which he sold in America, and even went so far
as to offer to re-write it for him, an offer he considered
but finally refused. He owed his knowledge of the
epidemic to his sister, to whom in the height of the pesti-
lence a coffin-pedlar tried to sell a coffin. It was while
arguing about this book that he said to me, "I don't care
a damn for my reputation."

Curiously enough it was just when success came to
him that he began to take a much smaller interest in it.
I speak now of the time when the very fact that he had
been given a Civil List Pension of £150 a year seemed
to bring more money in its wake. He began to sell his

books in America: agents offered him their services. When Methuens published *A Shepherd's Life,* this was arranged by a well-known agent on my advice. Once again, in this he reminded me of George Gissing, who seemed to dread agents, though he did much better when at last I got him to deal through them. Hudson for years refused to have anything to do with them, and although his first trial was very successful he never repeated it. He believed, and believed quite wrongly, that he could get as much money for his work as any agent. The reason of his desire to make money was, however, not avarice, or not avarice for himself. As usual he left me to find out the reason, which he never openly acknowledged. He wanted to make some money for the Bird Society, and now began to save for that purpose. If any ever found him hard to deal with and highly conscious of his market-value, his words and actions must be attributed to this, and only this. Elsewhere I shall have occasion to remark that when I obtained for him a price beyond his expectations, he showed not gratitude but a disturbance which surprised me. It took me long to discover the reason. It was that on looking back he felt that after all an agent might have made more money for the birds than he had made without such help. This passion of his for the Bird Society dominated all his later life, as, indeed, it influenced the beginning when he dedicated one book to Mrs. Philips. It was this that led him to resuscitate *Fan,* for none knew better than he that it was not good. But the Bird Society weighed down the balance against his own judgment and mine.

CHAPTER XI

In 1893 Hudson published *Idle Days in Patagonia,* a
book discovering, even better than his earlier work, the
wide range of his speculations, which is memorable to
me in that Hudson and I discussed many of the subjects
there treated. But chiefly do I feel affection for it because
the sixth chapter, "War with Nature," is but an ampli-
fication and development of *The Settler's Recompense,*
published in a dead magazine called *Merry England.*
This paper I have spoken of before as one which opened
to me first the great reach and possibilities of the writer's
mind. If that paper is reprinted as it first appeared I
shall be glad, for then others may read it and understand
how I felt when borne newly upon its strange and urgent
flood. It is true that in distant lands I had learnt something of the everlasting human war with other forms of

life which is the ancient and ever-present lot of man, his
training, his destiny, and his joy, until he passes with
his great natural antagonist and moulders into the final
shadow, and therefore could understand it. The lesson
Hudson taught, that the fight and not the victory remains
man's reward, is ancient and yet new. He had seen it
in action and approved the struggle. Yet even those
who have been forced to live at second hand with Nature
in cities of dim smoke and pallid sunshine, and among
a world of dusty books, will find something that appeals
to the half-subdued instincts which grew so mightily in
their forefathers. I cannot imagine anyone reading what
Hudson wrote who will not feel the better for it, and
the stronger, though his battles must be those set in the
arena of cities, where he is deprived of the great stimula-
tions of sun and air and the subtle and ceaseless struggle
against the pampa and the forest.

And again, in the chapter named "Snow and the
Quality of Whiteness," there comes the first great proof
of Hudson's "animism."   As he says, this was not the
"animism" of the anthropologists, of Tyler, Robertson
Smith, and Frazer. Hudson's "animism" was in truth
an emotion which in different types and orders of mind
may flower in pantheism or in mysticism.   But both
pantheist and mystic lose sight of nature.   They sink
it in a philosophic scheme or subjective vision: they do
not become part of it, nor do they include it and grow
the greater thereby.   But for Hudson "animism" means
here not a doctrine of souls that survive the bodies and
objects they inhabit, but the mind's projection of itself
into nature.   And in those great hours that come to but
a few, he did not "project his mind" only, but lost his

sense of separation and floated, as it were, into the great flood of universal life and energy. In another place, when noting some of Hudson's favourite haunts, "some woods of Westermain" or an ancient city, I shall have to speak of his powers of historic vision which were allied to this mystic animism, and therefore shall not dilate upon it here. But I cannot leave this favourite book of mine without noting that it was to Hudson that I owed my first knowledge of Herman Melville and his magnificent achievement, *Moby Dick*. Often Hudson and I wondered how it was that the Americans still looked forward to some great American book when all they had to do was to cast their eyes backward and find it. Some day they will turn upon their path and see that in the cloud and mist which covered their passage they have missed one of their two great monuments of literature. It is obvious, of course, that *Moby Dick* is not flawless. There are pages of it in that fatal style which is not prose and yet has not the majesty of poetry, but when we contemplate it as a whole it has a strange unequalled power, an insight into character hardly to be surpassed by its grasp of great natural phenomena, and with all its terror there is also laughter. It is said to be a book of the whale. It is also a book of the ship and of the sea and of man, and Hudson knew it and learnt from it and spread its name.

If all these pages were but a criticism of Hudson's work, it would be natural and here convenient to dilate more upon *Idle Days in Patagonia*. Especially it would please me, and just a few who have been subdued to the magic of great flat open spaces to speak of Hudson's chapter on the "Plains of Patagonia." If I might add

one word to his explanation of the magic which plains
possess when we are accustomed to them, and he put
this down to our reversion to very ancient and primitive
states of mind, I would say that the possibility of seeing
great distances is, and always has been, a great safeguard
to man in a state of nature. It was Hudson's ill-fortune
that he never had the opportunity of observing his own
feelings among great mountains or even among the
greater hill-ranges of England. It suggests to me very
forcibly that man was originally a plain-dweller, or
wanderer that, after two years in the Australian plains,
a visit to the mountains and hills of the Upper Murray
seemed to stifle and choke me: and the fact that I could
not say whether some stranger was near or not appeared
to raise in me a primitive sense of caution and alertness.
I never succeeded in my endeavour to make Hudson
spend a summer among the hills of the Lake District,
and I believe that at least one of the reasons why I
failed was that Salisbury Plain and the open uplands of
Cornwall dominated him to the last. In them there was
something, however faint, of the green pampa and the
grey plains of far-off Patagonia. In *Nature in Downland*
Hudson wrote that "when we once get above the world
and have an unobstructed view all round, whether the
height above the surrounding country be 500 or 5000
feet, then we at once experience all that sense of freedom,
triumph, and elation which the mind is capable of." This
is a natural enough delusion. How great a delusion it is
only those can know who have climbed great peaks, and,
with a sense of power over difficulties that their race
never struggled to overcome, have looked down in peril-
ous triumph upon a strange new world.

Birds in London, published in 1895, is not one of the big books, and is perhaps chiefly remarkable as being the earliest work of Hudson's which showed his mind as regards the preservation of such birds as still exist in a great city. Here he first speaks of bird sanctuaries being made in London, and shows, when he writes of the trees lopped and polled in Greenwich Park, how deeply he detested the tree-murdering public authorities of London. Even as I write I can look out and see acacias, that were once a glory, reduced to Borough Council monstrosities; and planes, that formerly gave a gracious shadow, polled to mere pillars which Nature can now decorate with but a few green leaves.

The book which came next was the one I referred to just now, *Nature in Downland,* Hudson's earliest master-piece of simple and characteristic observation in England. In it he disclosed new powers and surpassed all his predecessors. There is little need to indulge in com-parative criticism at any time, since a writer should be judged as if he stood alone, but no one has ever equalled Hudson in his power of beautiful consecutiveness of thought and pure observation done in simple and pellucid English. It is true that the simplicity of White of Sel-borne is exquisite, but the fact that his book was written as letters takes away something from its solitary purity of contemplation, while too often in Richard Jefferies there is an over-eager and haggard anxiety to put down everything, which makes his writing an uneven mosaic, or a mere string of beads. I shall not endeavour to criticise Hudson's book of the Downs, but one may note that in it he first disclosed his peculiar passion for for-gotten worthies, for minor poets upon whose work, as on their tombs, a century's moss had grown, and for shepherds. Now, too, his sense of colour increased, the colour of distances and of flowers, such as the viper's bugloss. In later years, as I shall show when I come to definite talks with him, this flower in masses or sheets had a great and peculiar effect upon him which apparently it failed to produce when he first wrote of it. How strange it is to think that with his great and ever-increasing colour-sense he yet lived when in town among sombre and subfusc surroundings!

In *Nature in Downland* Hudson also discovered his curious passion for snakes and adders. Snakes of all kinds interested him throughout his life. He intended to write a long book about them and accumulated a mass of notes sufficient for some great general ophiology. But the year before he died I found him destroying them, and he refused to let me look at the mass still unburnt. They could, he said, be of no use to any but himself, and now he could not hope to live to do the book. But in some ways the most notable thing in *Nature in Downland* is not Hudson's observations of the world of animals and adders, but his bitter attack upon the city of Chichester, of which in after years he often spoke to me. His temper was so equal, his tolerance so immense— (how else could he sit and talk calmly with Whitechapel bird-catchers at their nets?)—that any such sudden ferocity seems surprising. But the things he hated most after cruelty were inability and pretence. In spite of his want of orthodoxy, and here I give myself the liberty of using a meiosis, he had many friends among the clergy. They were a class, almost a curious species, of man, and, therefore, to be observed without prejudice.

But when he came to a cathedral town in which they were either so indifferent or ineffectual that drinking-shops abounded which sold—"wrecked lives of innumerable men, broken hearts and homes made desolate: famine and every foul disease: feverish dreams and appetites, frantic passions, crimes, ravings of delirium, epilepsy, insanity, and, strewn over all, the ashes of death," then his reserve perished and his just anger grew. The words I have quoted are his own. They represent a very noble indignation that more churches than one might bow the head to hear. That in this drink-haunted cathedral precinct he fought, and fought in vain, for the liberty of a wretched white owl imprisoned in a fiery kitchen, doubtless accentuated his bitterness. For owls, those mysterious, semi-sacred birds, he had a peculiar regard, and when he failed to free this prisoner he was ashamed to go near him. "For I had promised him his liberty and could not keep my word." The day must surely come when words like this will not be needed. If that be so, and it be not a vain hope to trust that the frail plant of human mercy shall grow at last into a tree under which all can shelter, Hudson will be looked on as a prophet, who lived in a dim time of dawn.

Nature in Downland was published in 1900. In 1901 it was followed by *Birds and Man,* which has a special interest to me, as the chapter upon "The Secret of Flowers" was the continual subject of discussion between us for years. His attribution of this charm to human associations, and especially that of blue to the suggestion of blue eyes, seemed wrong to me, and something which resulted from our talks may be found on pp. 155–57, though his attribution to him, who spoke as a seaman, of the phrase "a kind of bloom on the intrinsic beauty of things," is, perhaps, not correct. The Dr. Sutton of whom I spoke will not be recognised by many. He was Dr. Henry Gawen Sutton, once the colleague of Sir Andrew Clarke at the London Hospital, and a notable man, who had a great influence on many through his rugged, downright phrasing and a philosophy which made him, in the true and best sense of the word, an anarchist. For he, like Hudson, held that man was noblest and happiest when under the rule and domination of the great natural stimuli of the earth and free from fetters that he and his ancestors had forged and could not break. It will be seen that Hudson approved my notion that the blue of the sky influenced our feelings with regard to blue flowers, though he still clung to the view, in his own case rightly no doubt, that human associations and memories were the dominant factor. Deeply do I now regret that I never asked him whose blue eyes it was that he chiefly remembered.

More, and much more, might be said of this book, but since it and all the others are so well known I shall in speaking of any confine myself chiefly to points about which I have some special knowledge, however small. For I cannot but believe that they will interest even those who do not agree with me and would rather have pure criticism, of which I profess myself incapable, than any personal comments.

In 1902 those critics who had never seen *The Purple Land,* or in the rush and hurry of the 'nineties had forgotten it, and had learnt to regard Hudson as a "mere" naturalist, might have seen reason for revising their opinion. For in that year he published *El Ombú.* In

more ways than one Hudson was the strangest of mortals.
He learnt to shrug his shoulders at his own big stories.
I have even seen a passage in a letter of his in which he
says, "I am no judge of fiction, as it is not my line."
But all writers with various powers and faculties have
hours in which one region of their work seems most
worthy of cultivation, and what he said towards the
end of his life has little bearing on the value of his
tales. However highly Hudson's other work may rank,
these stories must in the end stand by his best books.
They grew naturally, as naturally as the ombú tree itself.
On the title-page of the book stand the lines—

"Cada camarca en la tierra
Tiene su rasgo prominente,
Brazil tiene su sol ardente,
Minas de plata el Peru:
Buenos Aires—patria hermosa—
Tiene su Pampa grandiosa:
La Pampa tiene el Ombú."

And so it might be said that this very little book stands
nobly upon the pampa, so wide and green, of his general
achievement. I shall not devote much space to it, since
many, not without vision and balanced judgment, believe
the first tale in it the greatest short story in English.
Such an opinion is sometimes my own, though when
looking over the range and wide extent of tales which
challenge it I have in certain moods denied it so high
a place. Assuredly it was Hudson's opinion, often declared to me, that the one story he looked on as his
best was not *El Ombú*, though it contained the very
essence of his native country, but the more mournful
and dreadful tale of imagination, *Marta Riquelme*. The

reasons for his preference must be obscure to most readers and even to critics who are not merely casual reviewers. But I think it may be made clear why he preferred it. *El Ombú* was purely a natural growth. Such tales as Nicandro related had been told many times to Hudson by old gauchos and peons as he sat with them under the shadow of the ombú trees about his early home. But writers, like all other men, chiefly delight in the exercise of powers which, perhaps, had not been suspected by themselves. In *Marta Riquelme* Hudson endued the robe and mantle of a priest of Loyola and, without the shadow of belief in a priest's creeds, told a fervent and passionate story of a religious mind among the superstitious of far-off Jujuy. It is possible that many will not perceive in the relation the deep and pitiful irony which is its very marrow. In most places it is not intruded, but in one passage it comes out perhaps too plainly. For when the holy and learned Father Guevara bade the Chiriquanos remember the danger they incurred by refusing baptism, they told him they were glad to learn that the fires of hell were unquenchable, as that would save them infinite labour in preparing fire. "So hard it was for their heathen intellects to comprehend the solemn doctrines of our faith."

Tales of the Pampa, printed in 1916, contains all the stories in *El Ombú* and also *Pelino Viero's Confession,* another story somewhat in the vein of Edgar Allan Poe. I read it in script many years ago, but did not, and do not, think its addition adds to the value of the collection. Whenever in *Fan* or any story there are to be found traces or even suggestions of other writers, Hudson is never at his best. His greater fiction has its pure source

in Spanish America seen through the eyes of one whose
blood and instincts were English, to whom Spanish was
yet a native language. Bathed as he was in later years
in the great flood of English literature, this combination
of influences gave him qualities which are without parallel, though they could not bear dilution. For imaginative literature must mostly spring from early emotional
experiences, and thought and observation are but ancillary
to these.

Of *Hampshire Days* little need be said here. I note
it chiefly because it was after its publication in 1903
that I urged him to go to Cornwall. Yet in every way
the book is the purest Hudson, and his account of the
cuckoo in the first chapter is not only the most valuable
in all natural history, but a great example of his powers
and perseverance in observation. Anything like a real
appreciation of this full book would be itself a book, for
there is not a page which might not lead to comment.
It may, however, here be noted that Hudson was often
too easy to please, or at least, not to anger, by illustrations which adorn and explain nothing. In spite of his
early desire to become a painter and his continued love
of many great pictures, he lacked something as regards
this branch of art, or, perhaps, added so much from
his own imagination that dead and lifeless pictures became living to him. In the copy which he gave me he
went back for a moment to the Spanish, for in it he
wrote "de su amigo, W. H. Hudson." It is inscribed
to Sir Edward and Lady Grey, and is one of the very
few books with dedications, which in late years he came
to dislike greatly. Truly he must have felt that his
books were written not for one or two, however beloved,

but for all those who were in tune with him or for those whom he might at least influence.

Hampshire Days was followed in 1904 by *Green Mansions,* of which I have spoken elsewhere. *A Little Boy Lost* followed it in 1905, and then after three years' silence came *The Land's End.* When considering the ceaseless attempts I made to get him to visit Cornwall, I feel I have some claim on those Hudsonians who know "dark Bolerium, seat of storms." Of Hudson's curious casual obstinacy I have had occasion to speak. No, he would not use a glass for observation! And as for a bicycle, what did I take him for? Had he not legs? And what, in the name of heaven, was this Cornwall I wished him to see? Were not Hampshire and Wiltshire and Sussex sufficient? Why, a man could spend his life on the Downs or near Salisbury or in the New Forest and find occupation till he was a hundred. But just as he took silently to glasses of eight diameters and then to a bicycle without so much as mentioning it, so one day in 1905 he went off to Cornwall without a word. It was just as if he said to himself, "I'll stop this absurd clack about Cornwall by going there. Probably there isn't a bird in the place. R—— doesn't know a chough from a raven!" He might have been right, but so far he knew little but land birds and, at least, knowing a gannet from a herring-gull, I was certain that the seas and cliffs of the Land's End and those of Tol-peden-penwith would enchant him. He got to love it all. Did he ever express gratitude for my accursed insistence? That was never Hudson's way. And how deeply I was to regret that I ever spoke of Cornwall! For in later years I cursed it every winter and cursed myself for

having told him tales of the Cornish coast, where with
a few hard-scraped pounds in my pocket I used to wander
from Polperro to Fowey and Looe and Mevagissey, and
away to Falmouth and the Lizard and the wild end of
England, looking down on the Longships, the red shore-
ward lights of the Wolf, the far-off gleams of the Bishop
Rock and St. Agnes and Round Island, and the lightship
at the Seven Stones. Often he was to see these, and
out of it all came *The Land's End,* but out of my early
insistence came in later years Penzance, the one place
in Cornwall or on the coast that I hated and could not
live in for gloom which fell upon me in it. But the
town suited him and that was so far good. Yet it was
only once that I could get to him there to spend a happy
fortnight, happy so far as being with him was concerned,
but apart from this a wretched one by reason of the
warm, wet damp, the ceaseless rain, and the abundant
dullness of the most westerly quarter of England. They
call it the English Riviera: and there are days in summer
when the Foot of England does seem as if it were about
to stride into summer seas; when the sea is purple wine
and bands of emerald and amethyst lie beyond the shining
surf; but in the winter, when there is fog, or mist and
rain, and a dim rare wet sun, and the chill of winter
with a damp as of the southwest monsoon, and all the
world is wet and running, and mud is underfoot, and
the sheltered sea lacks the stir of the ocean, such as one
is comforted by at St. Ives, why, Penzance beats for
concentrated winter dullness all the places I know.

This is an excursus, and an anticipation, since it was
ten years later that Hudson took to wintering at Penzance. When the book was written he cared little for

it, for Zennor and Gurnard's Head, that mighty rock
buttress thrust out into the Atlantic like an outlying
foot or field-work, and St. Ives, chiefly drew him. Yet
at St. Ives he saw cruelty rampant, since there he found
that people baited hooks for the migrant birds and slew
them cruelly in thousands—golden plover, sanderlings,
and lapwings and smaller song-birds. The passage in
his book and letters about it inspired that fierce Conservative and obstacle to reform, Sir Frederick Banbury,
to a Radical legislative fury for which much may be
forgiven him. He rushed a Bill through both Houses
which forbade the evil practice, and now the folks there
think, no doubt, that they themselves reformed. Yet
Hudson's words excited fury at first. He wrote to me,
"I have received a letter from a gentleman at Camborne,
inviting me on behalf of the Literary Society to go and
discuss Cornish character with the Cambornites, who
will be delighted to meet me face to face and hear what
I have to say to justify my charges against the people
of Cornwall. They want me to know what Cornishmen
really are, etc., etc. The Cambornites have a name for
roughness: they very nearly killed Will Thorne when
he went to meet them face to face, and I shall have to
ask you to come with your gun to back me up."

In reply to this I advised him on no account to make
himself a target for a rough mining population which
considered itself insulted. He did not go.

In 1909 came *Afoot in England,* a book which seems
to me to have as much sap in it as any green shoot in
spring-time. It is full to the brim of his intense passion
for England, England untouched and undefiled in her

green spaces. Many have explained Greater Britain to
England, but who like Hudson has explained England itself? His sense of life in this country and his passionate
desire that what is beautiful should remain beautiful, and
that all that is ugly and of ill repute should pass away, are
what has drawn and will draw English hearts to him.
The book has the qualities which came from a naturalist's
freedom after being long pent in London's prison. It
goes back to the very leanest years of Hudson's and his
wife's poverty, even to the poor days of Ravenscourt
Park, when starvation and a cup of cocoa made a day's
provision for an unrecognised master. There is great
pathos in the simple words with which Hudson began
the fourth chapter:

"The 'walks' already spoken of, at a time when life
had little or no other pleasure for us on account of
poverty and ill-health, were taken at pretty regular intervals two or three times a year. It all depended on
our means; in very lean years there was but one outing.
It was impossible to escape altogether from the immense
unfriendly wilderness of London, simply because, albeit
'unfriendly,' it yet appeared to be the only place in the
wide world where our poor little talents could earn us
a few shillings a week to live on. Music and literature!
But I fancy the nearest crossing-sweeper did better, and
could afford to give himself a more generous dinner
every day. It occasionally happened that an article sent
to some magazine was not returned, and always after
so many rejections to have one accepted and paid for
with a cheque worth several pounds was a cause of
astonishment, and was as truly a miracle as if the angel

of the sun had compassionately thrown us down a handful
of gold.   And out of these little handfuls enough was
sometimes saved for the country rambles at Easter and
Whitsuntide and in the autumn."

Those were rare days of liberty from which he returned to write much in this very book which was rejected
at the time by many editors.   Not a little of it was
written when I was tramping in Western America, for
it covers a long period and was put together long after
the bulk of it was written.   Though in some of the
chapters he speaks of times "on my wheel when flying
along the roads at the reckless rate of nearly nine miles
an hour," he often walked with his wife and once speaks
of "my companion."   This roused Emily Hudson to
remonstrate.

"Why do you speak of me as your 'companion'?" she
asked.

"Because a companion *is* a companion, and very often
a wife is none," said Hudson, and she was satisfied.
She had a very kindly, simple heart.

In Hudson's chronology the following year, 1910, is
memorable for *A Shepherd's Life,* one of his very greatest and most characteristic books, in spite of the fact
that birds and beasts take a subordinate place and a
man, the shepherd Caleb Bawcombe, is the dominant
theme in a fugue of Salisbury Plain.   It is possible that
a musician with a wide mind and imagination, who was
steeped not only in the tides of his own art but in those
of literature, might discover many analogies between
books and forms of music.   Such secret likenesses, hidden
from most of us, could surely be found in much of
Hudson's work.   But never have I found that musician,

and of music I know too little, as little even as Hudson,
who put finally all his passion for it into prose. Yet
some of his work has the construction and true consecutiveness of music and, like it, means so much more
than it says that, according to the various emotions of
the reader, it has notably various effects. No doubt it
will seem absurd to the technical musician to compare
this book with a fugue. Perhaps it is liker to the looser
prelude, and yet the way the theme flies and is treated
and comes up again and again so that expectation is
justified or, if not merely justified, is overpaid by what
none has looked for, gives it to my ignorant mind some
of the qualities of the beautiful set form that Bach has
made a delight for ever. If such be criticism it may
stand for it, though I determined here not to criticise
but just to say what I knew of these books. Truly of
this I can say nothing that is not expressed in it, but
I think he meant once and forever to put down his
feeling for the soil, and for man who sprang from it
and did not leave or disdain it and seek far cities instead
of his native earth. There is in Hudson's dearest villages the beautiful quality of some human sanctuary
where men and women might grow naturally and be at
peace, such peace as he desired for birds and the greater
fauna of the world, a fauna of which man was chief.
So, in spite of his native conservatism, even political
conservatism, he resented bitterly all those who would
cultivate pheasants rather than man, or, in the endeavour
to grow rich out of the ploughed soil, would stamp the
autochthonous to unhappy dust. Let those who doubt
this read again the eighth and ninth chapters with their
bitter indictment of the law and a juridical devil "in a

black cap." When I proposed for Hudson's epitaph, "He loved birds and man and the wind on the heath," it was said by some that he did not love man. To those who ate their fellows he would have denied the name of man.

It is in *A Shepherd's Life* that "Winterbourne Bishop," Hudson's favourite village, is first named. As many know now, there is no such village, and Hudson always refused to tell anyone its real name. He received many letters asking for it and invariably answered that he had vowed not to reveal it. One determined lady set out for Salisbury and searched the country for it, and wrote reproachfully to Hudson saying that she had not found it and had therefore determined to settle for a time in the village she liked best. It was "Winterbourne Bishop."

"Did you tell her that she had found it?" I asked.

"Certainly not," replied Hudson. "I'd vowed I'd tell nobody. I won't tell you."

How he did tell me by implication I shall relate in a conversation and the curious must read the truth there, or at least some indications of the truth.

Adventures Among Birds (1913) was more or less finished at Wells-next-the-Sea, Hudson's favourite lonely place in Norfolk, a spot very far from the world, which I had once visited before he knew it. The ancient, secluded peace of Wells, set on its harbour amongst the saltings facing the rude winds of the North Sea, its simple, poor population of humans, and its grey visitors the wise wild geese, attracted him to his last day. For all Hudson's love of the least among birds, for the grasshopper warbler or the wren, there was a passion in him for the big and powerful masters of the air. The wild geese,

> "Wrapt in the darkness of the night,
> Gathering in silence on the shore,"

it may be reminded him of the greater birds of the pampa, when in a country where most were small. So when watching them he could recall the crested screamer, a bird of mighty powers of flight and a mighty voice, whose gatherings and tremendous music he had seen and listened to when a boy. I think no other bird in England ever gave him such a sense of community of spirit and deep relationship as the wild goose, so brave and strong and wise a bird. More than once he has written, and many times spoken, of imitating with his arms the flight of birds, and so in imagination launching himself in air and flying. The wife in *Pelino Viero's Confession* rubbed herself with some magical ointment and grew wings. When Hudson watched the wild geese at Wells I am pleased to think that he, too, grew them for a while and gained a noble freedom. But now he has gone with them. In some of the more fantastic flights of his imagination he dreamed of magical possible things, and therefore those who now stand lonely on the wide saltings he loved may for a moment believe in the transmigration of "souls" and imagine him rejoicing with his great brethren in some splendid desolation.

I shall say but little of *Far Away and Long Ago,* the best and greatest story of a man's boyhood in all English literature. The only part which I saw when he was writing it was the seventeenth chapter, "A Boy's Animism." This subject was discussed by us in many talks and in letters, for everything connected with animism, however interpreted, was of intense interest to him. The book was published in 1918, but took long to write. He has spoken of the illness which seemed to have brought back all his memories, but does not say that he was cared for in a Catholic conventual hospital, which he often remembered gratefully. I do but mention it, however, because of a characteristic incident that happened there, to which I referred briefly in a previous chapter. One of his nurses was a novice, who presently proposed to take the veil and submit her whole life to the authority of the Church. There are women, doubtless, for whom such a fate may be beautiful and seemly: they can mother the poor and helpless and satisfy their souls. Yet there are some for whom one must hate the cloistered life, even though it be not spent wholly in vain worship but turned to actual human service. To Hudson this nurse seemed one who belonged not to a cell but to the natural and sacred service of the world. And so he set himself, as he lay there, to move her towards the wider freedom he desired, and presently prevailed so that she renounced the convent and went back into the world. To him it seemed as if he had freed some bird from a snare before it became for ever the creature of a cage. I have related this incident because it reveals much of his attitude to life. None can rightly renounce life or submit themselves to any narrower authority than that of human instinct. How bitter the trivial rule of theology-ridden men may be I myself know, for once I met a nun of a closely confined order who had been bred by the sea, and during an illness felt a wild longing to look on it once more before she died. Her superior and the

priests considered this rebellion; for with a common
human life she had renounced the sea and all that therein
is. With them was also the bishop, a rigid old man,
and it therefore seemed as if her desire could never be
satisfied. I know it pleased Hudson to learn that Nature
worked a miracle, for her illness became so severe that
she had to be sent for treatment to a place which could
only be reached by a sea passage. I have heard only
lately that this nun is back in her convent and happy.
And Hudson's liberated novice is, I believe, married and
a mother of children.

Hudson's early struggles to get free from the shackles
of an outworn faith are related in this book of which I
write. They resemble and recall the conflicts of many
men who have attained freedom at the price of wounds
that healed but slowly. Yet he did attain freedom and
desired it for others, and was moved when I told him
of a man bred in the savagest form of Presbyterianism,
who after sixty years reached a late and bitter freedom
and said to me, "I have destroyed the greatest and best
part of my life." Hudson owned that at hours even
bare existence, however barren, was better than blank
nothingness, but in truth when he concluded *Far Away
and Long Ago* with the words, "I could always feel it
was better to be than not to be," he meant deep in his
heart that "to be" was being free to follow the native
and natural laws of mankind.

Something may be said here of his occasional papers,
many of which he used in his work. A number of
them will doubtless be reprinted, and most of them, even
the slightest, would declare themselves as his even were
they unsigned. One of these, published in some maga-

zine, brought him nearer to unpopularity than he ever
came to general acceptance. It was written to denounce
the practice of keeping dogs confined in a town, and
was especially bitter against making parasites of poor
pet dogs. For once he spoke almost with venom, for
he looked on dogs as agreeable companions for the
country, while his healthy dislike of the poor diseased
animals known as "toys," which are bred perhaps as a
special variety from some of the less vigorous of a normal
kennel, amounted almost to disgust. His paper, which
suffered from no want of strength, raised a chorus of
remonstrance from those whose taste he questioned. His
senses were acute, and amongst them his sense of smell
was almost dominant. That dogs were kept close in
houses showed how grossly this sense had decayed in
modern man and woman. And the substitution of a
passion of this order for the normal passions and affections of women truly distressed him. To his eyes
they became almost the peers and equals of their caged
and pathological specimens: they were themselves degenerate and morbid. Yet many of Hudson's books
speak of his love for the nobler dog who retained his
strength and faculties in the open air as the helper,
comrade, and guard of his master, or even for a vagabond
"on his own" with never a master but one whose voice
and aspect recommended him as the head of the pack,
though it were but for one day's ramble. If Hudson
suppressed this paper he did so out of an enlarging sense
of pity for the feebler of his own race. Man, he knew,
was the creature of fate, and, though it was a grievous
thing to see the worship of a diseased and useless creature,

even that was a matter of ungenerous destiny. It was better than selfish aloofness.

Of some other books I shall say nothing, but in what follows shall speak of *A Hind in Richmond Park,* which in many ways, especially in indicating the richness and fullness of his mind and the way it worked, is perhaps the most characteristic of them all.

CHAPTER XII

Style—Peasant or artist—Hudson's fullness—His memory—*A Hind in Richmond Park*—A summary of his mind—The place of art—Art and life—"Amateurs" in art—His writing not without flaws—Pater and Stevenson—His method and plan in *A Hind*—The end of the book—Art and energy—Life as art—Hudson not a philanthropist—Pseudo-philosophers and Hudson—Critics and his friends—His own critical powers and weakness—Living writers and self-advertisers.

So far I have said very little about Hudson's style, his manner of writing. There are, it seems, already two views held about his style: one that he wrote "like a peasant," and the other that he always wrote divinely as by plenary inspiration, just as birds sing, though none knew better than he that even birds go, as it were, to school for song and labour ceaselessly for perfection. In studying *A Hind in Richmond Park* we see Hudson's writing at a high level of excellence, though it may possibly lack some of his greater moments. As for the note of the "peasant," one may let it go with contempt, having heard the same of others who do not endeavour to force a style "of their own" after the manner of those who cannot speak in plain English, but go about believing that originality may be manufactured. Hudson wrote so far "like a peasant" that he was always clear, and did not seek "alembicated Gongorisms," or out-of-the-way phrases, or strange turns so that the youthful might exalt him as a master. He became a master by much writing and much reading, and so attained speech fine enough to express all his deliberate thoughts, and also his instinctive feelings, an infinitely more important thing to him, without weakness or taint of sentimentalism or affectation. That he never had, and yet none can read him in places without seeing how one less a master might have failed lamentably or have gone down into mere words as Richard Jefferies too often went. At the back of Hudson's prose there is steady power, the stream is controlled, but has "head" and weight to it. Often we wonder why he stopped: he always had more to say and avoided saying it. He wrote and re-wrote, and if he did not play with "beautiful words" as Meredith did to his detriment, he looked for the best and mostly found them. There are times he chooses the wrong one, but this may have been due to his knowledge of Spanish. In one tale an old gaucho uses "interval," a word in English not suitable for a son of the pampa, but the Spanish word is "intervalo," and Hudson, listening to the tale, perhaps translated wrongly. But flaws like that are rare: his chief fault in later books being an occasional lack of clarity, due not to want of thought but to the carelessness in revision not unnatural in one growing old.

Much of the beauty of his work depends upon its fullness: he never lacked material or tried to fill space, since his effort was to condense or suggest rather than to dilate and expand. However he might run memory down and cry out for notes and notebooks, he had the fullest memory of any man I ever met as well as the most fertile mind. He grew crops and thrashed and winnowed his own grain, but, just as a great vineyard, Château Margaux or La Rose or what not, may crush its own grapes and then take in others from neighbouring vineyards, and, by using its own sacred secret and peculiar ferment, turn out an equal true quality, so Hudson borrowed from other lands and other peoples and stamped what he sent out with his own incommunicable mark and charm. He made a thin thing full-bodied, gave it aroma and colour and bouquet so that one could drink and say, "This is a Hudson, 1916," and be satisfied. Above all things it was fullness which was his mark—fullness not only of memory but of thought. As he speaks one sees another unwritten chapter, and he, too, sees it and remarks on it lightly and puts it aside with just a word. In many ways it seems to me that he did no such full book as *A Hind in Richmond Park,* for every page is a store of suggestions, and out of each he could have made yet another volume, and a curious commentator could make one if he had eyes as well as curiosity. The book sums up Hudson's mind. He wrote of a thousand, of ten thousand things, and with every stroke drew himself. He was strong as a Nasmyth's hammer and as delicate as an epeïra spinning cobwebs in the sun. He is even like the gossamer spider: he shoots out a filament and departs on the wind, going one knows not where. Or, singing, he is a grasshopper warbler in a secret place, or again a peregrine swiftly dividing the day, or a condor over Aconcagua.

It is no purpose of mine to comment on *A Hind in Richmond Park:* it would take a lifetime, but since it fell to me to put together as best I could the last illegible words he left, making them as coherent and logical as I could, and knowing, as I did know, that there should have been yet another book to come, or even more than one, as it seemed we had the right to hope, I must say some words on the end, and perhaps thereby clear up some doubts, or, if not that, suggest what was in his mind that he did not express and left for a later time that never came to him. The whole of the book expresses clearly his constant underlying theme, that for him man was one of the animals, the best, the most terrible, the greatest, but yet of the mighty brood of the fertile earth, fertile of herself and fate, unfertilised by "spirit" or any of the gods. He shows plainly enough in a hundred ways, but never puts down in so many words, as he did with me in talk, that all the arts in which man glories as a special heritage or privilege of humanity were to him just what singing, dancing, colour, and plumage were to animals and birds. With Wallace he attributed the glories of birds not to any thought-out Darwinian scheme of sexual selection, but to the over-plus of energy, the free energy of Ostwald and the great physicists, working itself out and developing colour and plumage and dancing and singing, and he believed that all the arts of man were parallel with these, the result of his free energy, and, alas, of energy diverted too often from real living which was man's greatest art of all. So when folks talk, as some have talked and will talk, of Hudson as if he were some wind-bag of a philosopher who spouts at large of something like spirit that is not spirit and more than spirit and a creator, he was finally, and in the end, a great physicist half without knowing it, one who saw clearly that out of the furious energy of things working in the fine and delicate conduits of flesh and bone and fur and feather came alike the glories of ornament and the arts of man. Had he known it he would have approved of Spinoza's dictum, "We do not know yet what body can or cannot do." And what of those who ask, "What is that which shall replace art, art that has failed?" and then proceed metaphysically into bogs that Hudson would never have trodden? What he meant should be obvious. In this his last book he came back by his own secret way to some of the philosophy of *A Crystal Age,* but a saner, sounder, more possible philosophy than the theory of that beautiful and inhuman imagination. The art that should replace the arts was the greatest art of living. Art for art's sake was folly and disease. Nor again was life for art's sake. Life was for life's sake, and art would never fulfil its highest function till it became instinctive and glorified man's every action. So when I said to him that there should be no professional artists, that they were morbid growths in a sad dull world, but that all should be "amateurs," true natural lovers of art who used up their spare time and strength in art that sought no recompense and recognition, he agreed warmly. Life could not be made beautiful by taking artistic means to make it so: it had, in the end, to grow beautiful, and when he trod the heather of a wild moorland, or the springy turf of a high down, and looked out across the blue of viper's bugloss and became one with Nature, he saw the dim possibility of a world that put art under and behind it and lived, lived, just lived and breathed and worked and joyed and lived again. A vision, a vision! But he saw such visions, and after many æons of pain they may come true at last. It is such a philosophy which gives Hudson his rank, not the due order or high quality of his verbal symbols. But he did not waste himself among mere verbal symbols, nor did he

belong to the vain order of metaphysicians, a class of
thinkers not so rapidly diminishing as Froude fondly believed.

It would have been an easier task to write of Hudson's
work if nothing had been written of him. Many years
ago I came to certain conclusions as to his rank and have
seen no reason to modify them. But since his death, and
even before it, a chorus was raised that made out of him
more a great writer than a man. Adulation without dis-
creet limits produces reaction. Were it not for that, who
would have any mercy for the few who deprecated his
being placed amongst the greatest English writers? There
are some who judge an author by his mistakes. A split
infinitive destroys the value of a prophecy: a *nominativus
pendens* neutralises the value and visions of a seer.
Technically speaking Hudson's writing was not without
flaws. No writing is without them. One prefers the
wilder worshippers of Hudson who lift him upon a mountain above the greatest and flood the vales beneath his
feet with clouds of incense. A writer is not merely a
writer. It is possible to write beautifully about nothing
or a broomstick. There are who kneel before the oily
shrine of Pater, whose work was often harsh and tune-
less: a charmless, artificial product of labour and polish.
Others worship Stevenson at his worst, when patient work
on a natural style has taken life away and given the world
the mere corpse of fantasy. What Stevenson could
achieve is seen in the fragmentary *Weir of Hermiston:*
what he could destroy in that which many call his best
work. These, however, are writers of no high order,
though they are held to write prose which might make
Landor sigh to think he failed to reach such perfection.

But there is no great writing without great thinking.
So many make us think just of them and of their little
methods and we leave them, as we might leave the Royal
Academy, without a new thought, or any purification of
the heart, or any of the stimulation that such a man as
Hudson gives by the infinite suggestive variety of his
mind. They work in studies and cellars: they breathe at
the best the air brought by an electric fan. Hudson
dipped his pen in red blood. Now and again he was careless: his heart was tired: he rested at the expense of the
perfection he sought. But he never esteemed the vehicle
above the matter. He wrought no regal carriage for a
beggarly conception: he would rather have wheeled a
king in a barrow. More than once I said to him, "Your
critics, in books and out of them, seem to think you write
by the light of nature: that you throw things off in the
authentic manner of the traditional genius." And then he
laughed. For he worked with slowness, with care, with
much labour and with many pauses, and often wrote
pages and passages, and even chapters, over and over
again. To get the writing adequate, to see that no one
was likely to rate the manner above the meaning, was,
when he wrote, his conscious and unconscious aim. In
speaking of it he would say as much, but truly what ruled
his methods and his writing was the fullness of which I
have spoken. Too many of our best prose writers, or,
if not our best, those whom fanatics esteem exemplars,
have little enough to say. Even such a writer as Froude,
whose style is usually one which compels attention, many
times filled three pages with the matter of a paragraph.
Hudson had no need to use any such "padding," as he
never had space to say what he could say. In this last

book, eminently one which shows the careless richness of
his mind and the miraculous intellectual curiosity which
found food wherever it turned, he throws aside thoughts
full of suggestion and flows onward like a full river.
There is, indeed, in many of his books, and most of all in
A Hind, the suggestion of a great river system.   The
book rises in Richmond as it were in a spring by which
the hind lay, and as it flows, affluent after affluent runs
in until at last the varied sparkling stream runs out into
the very sea of philosophy itself and ends in a space of
great horizons.   I would use the same metaphor for all
his work, and those who have once launched themselves
upon its flood will surely follow it to the ocean.

This wandering and discursive method of Hudson may
appear to some critics the negation of art.   They look
for a plan and easy pattern, for continued argument, and
fail to follow him as he moves, or, as it were, dances
in the most intricate pattern and plan he ever wove.   I
do not say he set it down aforethought with a "con-
spectus" or some drawing of his purpose, but he wrote to
me and said in talk that in *A Hind* his "plan was to appear
to have none."   And so he sat down to weave a beautiful
fabric with embroidery and colour and infinite suggestion,
making of "brute wool" bright clothing for his thoughts,
whether they were deep or fanciful.   To be thus a conscious artist before work and yet fervid and unconscious
of design is to rank very high in any art.   Let us remember, too, that had he been what the barren and over-
polished call a "peasant" writer, that through peasants
there still flows in many parts of Europe a beautiful
stream of colour and ornament, while not a few who rank

high in academies might envy in despair the free noble
designs in the Magdalenian caves of Altamira.

As I have said, it happened that I had something to do
with the end of *A Hind in Richmond Park.* I refer to
that fact because the conclusion of the book has been mis-
conceived and its tendency misinterpreted. But if there
is any part of Hudson's work more wholly characteristic
of his outlook on life I do not know it. He seems to
speak aloud in the paragraph which appeared to me, as I
went over the difficult and almost indecipherable script,
the most natural end of the book. He was satisfied with
suggestion and wished to write of other things. He
would not begin another volume (and here again one
sees his inexhaustible fertility) by speculating as to what
should replace art, which seemed to him, and seems to
many, more or less a failure. Such a failure, he might
have told us, is what was to be looked for. Artistic im-
pulse in whatever form was a biological variation endeavouring to establish itself as a permanent and general
human characteristic. But each art fights against every
other art. Even like tissues in healing may fight for a
blood supply only sufficient for one. And yet how feeble
is art in man, in how few can it display itself, how few
can appreciate it! They have not even the surplus energy
to develop a possibility of seeing, however vaguely, what
the artist tries to express. It is impossible to blame them,
for in most cases the poor, one might even say the
wretched, artist has not himself sufficient power to work
out his dreams, to accomplish even part of his vision.
He is not powerful, not full of energy: he remains almost
a parasite in an overworked, unhappy social organism
which understands neither life nor art, nor how the two

should be one as speed and colour are one in the humming-bird and the tanager. Was not this the reason that Hudson agreed with me a score of times that it was professionalism which destroyed and nullified art while it seemed to perfect it? Some happy casual votary of beauty, not wedded indissolubly to his art and dragging it about with him as an organ-grinder drags his monkey and organ, but a free lover of the joy of life, was what Hudson asked for. The artist should not be a beggar or a parasite, not one forced to conform to Academicism, which is after all nothing but a glorification of the taste of those with sufficient money to hire architects and painters to debauch their gifts and their art in popular buildings and popular paintings; he should be free to live and paint and sing and mould clay or bronze or carve marble as he would. If, at any time, such changes took place in the forms of society as enabled the gifted to use, not to torture, their gifts, then others, not artists yet, though their children might be, since every happy child sings and dances and is an artist, would turn to life rather than to the means of it; and to turn to life and hold it and live it and make it a brave thing, an art in itself that made the arts a mere means to the greater glory of happy living, was what was in Hudson's mind, as old and worn and still brave and wise and full of desire to live and work, he drew towards the end of the unfinished but glorious book, *A Hind in Richmond Park*. If I am mistaken, then I know nothing of the man and someone who knew him not must set me right.

In later years he and I came back once more to such discussions and arguments as characterised the days and nights at Shoreham or our busy afternoons at Tower

House. I have many letters from him about the charm of flowers and migration in which he never hesitated to belabour me for taking what he thought an academical scientific view. But this book cannot be weighed in the scales of the Royal Society. If it were estimated by its pure scientific value it could not rank among masterpieces. The field-naturalist outweighed the man of science in Hudson. He was what he was because he lived so with Nature, while those who work in science must take into steady and calm account the work of their co-labourers. Anything or anybody who "threw rocks" at pure science appealed to Hudson. He objected fiercely and humorously to my opinions of Samuel Butler. Hudson was a Lamarckian rather than a pure Darwinian, and Butler had supported Lamarck. As I believe, he had been an advocate who did more harm than good. His "inherited memory" was an importation of psychology into realism in which memory, however defined, had no relevance, and, though none is now a pure Darwinian, Butler's "inherited memory" and the Hering-Semon "mnemes" are false and circular explanation. They suggest that organisms grow because they know how to do it, and that they know how to do it because they remember how to do it, a statement which is not logical and, explaining nothing, takes explanation for granted. Hudson's views as regards smelling also lack a scientific basis. He had no knowledge of physiology, though he was interested in any clear exposition of its problems. He believed firmly in telepathy and in certain "occult" phenomena, which, however, he denied were occult except in the sense that they were obscure and not yet explained on principles which asked for no spiritual or "spiritualistic" basis. In nothing did he allow any ancient theological or religious prejudice to influence his judgment. In one of his letters to me he refers to himself humorously as "an atheist (religious)," which implied that all the religion he needed was human kindness and his own interpretation of animism by which he became at moments, or even for great hours, a part of the visible sonorous, tangible and odorous world.

I should like to say one word more about the end of the book and its very last sentence. That last sentence was the sole one I rescued from an indecipherable fragment. It, therefore, had no set place. But it was too characteristic of the writer to lay aside. I had to consider where he might have put it, if he too, as he sometimes did, failed to decipher what he had written. As soon as I asked myself the question I saw it as his last word and put it there. For ever he wished to go forward, to live in and yet to leave the past, to pierce into the future as far as his strength and joy in work permitted. A thing done was done. He knew its value, but why with ten thousand things to say and do should he linger by past achievements? Those who turn back to their books, to their paintings, to their carvings, have done their work. Hudson had not done his: he would not have done it if he had lived to be a hundred, and thus endowed with the energy of a magical giant for all his bodily troubles, the next piece of work was what he wished to set his hand to. "When I have done a book I begin, rover-like, to hate it." How far he could rove those who know his work may say, and as to hating it, why, no, that was a figure of speech. He hated to linger, for to stay was death: and life was the flowering of the energy he kept almost to his last hour.

A friend of Hudson's wrote that Hudson was a poet surgeon, who gave the myopic, even the blind, their sight. It may be that he performed operations on a few. But it was by accident. He cared nothing for people's sight, since he never in his wildest moments thought they could see as he did. He knew they could not. He wrote as Turner painted his water-colours, not for others' delight but for his own, to satisfy an instinct, to fulfil a function. He worked as some birds sing, and yet listen to others in order to learn. He has noted that some birds thus improve their song. So did he, but Hudson was not like a bird singing to a mate, rather was he like at times to the grasshopper he speaks of in his last book, that ignores the female in his artistic fury. I do not like the endeavour to paint Hudson as a philanthropist. He had great interest in, but little respect for, humanity. He hoped to make men ashamed of cruelty, and, if that was impossible, to restrain them by force, by ridicule and shame.

Here I may also note a letter that he wrote about Benjamin Kidd's view that the "sex fury" must die out for man to develop "as destined," whatever that may mean. Hudson's opinion of such a view may be guessed, though perhaps he never quite recognised the essential futility of this writer or of Bergson, both of whom are more or less wind-bags of flatulent philosophy. How could any know to what man was destined? To one who studied the rise and fall of species, or genera and families, of all living organisms, was it so sure that man *must* rise? Hudson would have hated the notion of loss or even great diminution of passion. He wanted kindness and liberty, not castration. The great neurologist Hughlings Jackson said to a friend of mine, in frank language which I refrain from putting down, something that meant "the end of the human race will arrive by the development of culture at the expense of the animal passions." He regretted the prospect. If *A Crystal Age* shows nothing else, it shows that Hudson would have shaken hands on that. He would scarcely have listened to sermons on life from Origen.

Soon after his death I wrote this note—"In arranging the end of *A Hind* I put an isolated sentence last. It summed up so much of Hudson. A book was yesterday's work. Yesterday was dead: he waited to hail the morning sun. When he had written a book the artist in him made him loathe, yet work upon, proofs. The truth is he wrote his books for himself: he laid hold of far horizons and made them part of his environment. He hated dedications and in later years dedicated no book. To whom could they belong? He rarely hoped to teach, but he might shame some of the cruel." I think this is true. It is certainly not false idealism and may possibly be of use to minor critics.

I never knew Hudson indignant with critics on his own account. But when they were unjust to those he loved he got furious: there was no name too bad for them. So when I was mauled by some, or neglected, or put off with a few cheap clichés, he rose up in his might and asked the earth and the heavens what they meant by it, on such occasions using his head voice, as he always did when angry or surprised. To hear so big a man (had not his very bigness deluded a dozen into believing that he had a "booming" or a "deep rich voice"?) using a high, bird-like falsetto was remarkable, for in such a mood he

was pretty sure to be more unjust to the critics than they
had been to me.   To his amazement, voiced in still more
surprising head notes, I often defended them, saying that
they could scarcely be expected to understand always or to
show it if they did, and then he swept me and them away
in a flood of indignation.   In some odd kind of way he
then reminded me of my own father, whose view of
some critics was murderous.   Hudson on such occasions
seemed to look on me as if I were a promising son, likely
to be crushed by injustice, and he could hardly understand
that I felt able to stand without great impatience anything
some reviewers might choose to say.   It was their business to say something and to be paid for it, and if they
were clever so much the better, while if they were fools,
why not let them fill their space and as much of their
pockets as possible?   No one with the faintest sense of
letters was likely to mistake every reviewer for a critic,
and if one happened to be a critic it was something to
thank heaven for even though the discovery was painful.
Hudson accepted this view for himself, but for others—
no, a thousand times no!   I have seen him raving at the
injustice some ineffective third-class poet received when
a few verses or a line or two had pleased him, and for
one passage or thought he would forgive and even rejoice
in some poor story.   This may show he was no great
critic.   Some may think him the greatest critic after all.

And yet he could be very severe, often unjustly so.   It
would be possible, but painful and perhaps libellous, to
give some of his *obiter dicta* on contemporary novelists
and other writers.   His knowledge of current literature,
good and bad, was almost unequalled.   Few critics have
gone through such bundles of chaff for a grain of wheat,

or even some poorer cereal. The very last day I was
with him he made a ten-minutes' autopsy of the latest big
success. He was so amusing that it might even have done
the author good. He knew a thousand negligible writers
of the eighteenth century and picked up their stray
grains with avidity. But of professional writers he had
on the whole a poor opinion, and it is, therefore, not
surprising that he admired those most who had to write,
not for money, but most obviously because they had
something to say. He would have agreed that any com-
mercialism in art debauched it. To have to sell work
was loathsome, and to have to consider opinion worse.
He even argued that he, an "unsuccessful" man till far
over seventy, was overpaid. Had it not been for the
Bird Society, to which he long meant to leave money if
he ever had any, he would to the day of his death have
taken any price rather than chaffer, or even have others
chaffer for him. Had not many of our greatest writers
been unprofessional? So men who wrote because they
were out to make a living were not to be esteemed for that
unless they also had something to say that was sane and
far-seeing. Those with axes to grind or fanatics, even
when on his own side of the fence, or touchy megalomani-
acs were anathema or, better still, subjects for laughter.
Of one such he said, "Well, the man is a cad. But he's
going out." He held a reasonable view of his own work,
and never in forty-two years did I see one sign that want
of fame or its late swift coming tended in him to such exal-
tation as marked poor John Davidson in poverty or some
that could be mentioned in abundant success. Rarely did
he resent criticism. "They just don't understand."

Of such living writers as he loved it may be necessary

to speak. But the very fact that he loved them implies that they would hardly be gratified by a plain statement of his affections in public. He loved them not primarily for their writings, but because they were men who could write as they did. They had to be men, not mere creatures of a full ink-pot, bawling self-advertisement, protesting that their most disagreeable traits were prophetic of future high humanity, or reactionary fanatics on their knees to outworn conceptions which they esteemed theology.

So far I have said little of Hudson's letters. If all of them had been preserved they would probably have outnumbered those of any writer with whom the world is acquainted. And he was insatiable in his demand for many and long replies. If Lamb denounced *biblia abiblia,* Hudson scorned letters which were not letters, and though he wrote innumerable postcards himself, objected almost furiously to getting them from others. Combined with this readiness to write letters he had in many cases an eager desire to get them back and destroy them. "Have just got back 3000 letters and have burnt them," he wrote triumphantly to me. I believe I have already related how he distinguished himself in one house by burning a boxful which he found by accident. He was totally unconscious that this was, to say the least, a somewhat queer thing to do. He had written them and had a right to make this holocaust. But those he chiefly wanted to destroy were written to women friends, who treasured every scrap. He made no attempt to get mine, though he suggested more than once that I might put them on the fire, as he did those I wrote to him. This I refused to do and he never asked for them. That we were very much together prevents my collection from being prodigious, but even so they run into hundreds, and may some day be printed all together with the exception of some which he would probably have wished to be destroyed. Almost all letters that he received went into the fire at once. The very few he kept were scrupulously labelled for destruction and were duly burnt by his executors.

His script was sometimes intolerable, but the matter almost always clear, direct, and often not a little humorous. There is a naturalness about the style which is very charming, and at times he would run on and on and only cease, it seemed, from mere finger fatigue. Never did his mind dry up: he was a perennial spring. Of late there has been in England some resurgence of interest in letter-writing, and I cannot but think that Hudson's letters, when some final collection is made of them, will occupy a place not far removed from the highest. For one thing they were never meant for print, and though we forgive Chesterfield his evident intention to publish what he wrote, yet that very intention is against them. They have a kind of intellect akin to Macchiavelli's, perhaps, but no real charm beyond that of mere beautiful execution. We cannot love Chesterfield as we love Lamb, and as many yet unborn may love Hudson even apart from his books. I may over-rate what was written to me directly, yet I think that in this respect, as in respect to the great bulk of his work, I have kept a level head, since over-praise was of all things the most disagreeable to him. In the end, however, they must speak for themselves. As regards the matter of them, it may be found that some are difficult or obscure, since they are often arguments against views I held on subjects which were of interest to him, and often of interest to me chiefly because they were his pet subjects. I took very great trouble to get information for him which he could not, or would not, look for, and sometimes had to do my best to prevent him showing that he had not considered other views. But many of them prove that he was always eager to learn, if any fresh knowledge could be brought to him.

CHAPTER XIII

SINCE I have discriminated a portrait in words from a biography, a discrimination not so unjust as it might appear if we put aside the few masterpieces in English, it is obvious that this book can stand only if it determines something of the living aspect of the man, his inner nature, ambitions, failures, faults, passions, and virtues. Criticism of the simplest historic nature is no more than an accessory. But I have not chosen to depict Hudson against a red curtain with a book in his hand. In my apology for the method, I determined to speak of him just as I knew him, leaving others to write of their knowledge as addenda, or even as a substitute. If, then, my own state of mind as regards him seems now a background to the true subject, I may be excused for declaring it. I wrote the first draft of this book in fragments at different times just as if I were recording separately those things for which "memory is no good." Obviously it was the proper method (I speak according to the rubric) to recast these documents and make them "literature." By this is meant a book written to please the critics and done in the accepted method with polish, urbanity, and as much, or as little, truth as may be convenient. I rejected this method with regret, since it is an agreeable thing to please everybody, and have left these fragments, written for my own melancholy pleasure, practically as they were when I put them into a portfolio. It is possible for a cunningly, or even simply, arranged bundle of sketches to acquire in the mass a quality denied to each particular essay. I am the more inclined to insist that this method is here the best, if it is not the best in every case, because to keep a timid eye on the subject and the other on the critic and the public is the prevalent vice of the modern artist and writer. When to this is added a painful proleptic sense of what friends and relations may think when the book appears, it seems certain that any portrait is damned before birth.

Though I believed these separate attempts were adequate, because they were truly felt, they yet lacked something for that very reason. They were the result of many long years of intimate contact and correspondence: they represented profound impressions slowly made and again and again reinforced. They were written as it were by instinct rather than by taking thought and in them, I knew, there might be, not merely errors of fact, but conclusions due in some way to the mind of him who wrote them. It was not until two or three years before Hudson's death that the remotest notion came to me that I should ever write of him. Indeed, it was only on the 10th of November, 1920, that it occurred to me that a direct record might be made of him as he lived and spoke. It seemed difficult to do, and almost disloyal to imagine the death he so abhorred. But I felt that he could hardly last long, and who else was there who knew him so well? There is something in a big man of any order which belongs to humanity. He is a teacher and more than a teacher. That day I saw in my great old friend lying on his couch one whom it was good that the world should know. If St. Francis still remains as an influence of mercy by the little most men have heard of him, it seemed possible that something of Hudson's exact speech, noted in secret and with simplicity, might help a little to further the aims to which he dedicated his life. My only regret is now the fact that these records were begun so late. And yet if they had been commenced earlier they must have spoiled the naturalness of our converse, its erratic charm and varied flow. I should have been led into directing the talk, into asking questions instead of taking what the gods gave. What is preserved may, perhaps, suffice. I have tried to be accurate, and in some of the following sections have been greatly aided by another friend of his, my stepdaughter, whose memory has often corrected and enlarged my own. The more I read them the less satisfactory they appear, but they may serve where better are wanting. I can put down as much as may be remembered of his talk, but how can anyone hope to suggest the ways of his mind and speech and the infinite variety of his mobile and expressive face? I have known none with gifts for showing the inner man, which is beyond all words, that were equal to his gifts. While writing I seem to see him in Tower House or Penzance as he talked of all things in heaven and earth, running easily and rapidly from philosophy to anecdote, from satire to approval, from character to biology, or to music, or painting, or the song of birds, or dancing in man or the animals, and while the warm human flow of his speech went on I can recall how here he laughed with all his face, and there squeaked suddenly in indignation, or again fell into some passing gloom over the flight of time or the death of some species that would never return to his England, and once more showed by a shy glance or accent some acknowledged affection, so that memory reproduces him as a perpetual spirit of knowledge, kindness, criticism, or queer remote speculation. For those who knew him such an empty sketch may mean just a little. It may serve to bring back to them hours that might have perished or moments that truly did perish. But for such as have learnt to love him only from his books, so many of which "talk" even to strangers, my few ineffective words can be of small advantage when they strive to build him up for themselves merely from what he says and from the dim adumbration of him in some poor sun-picture. Yet that is all we have of so many noble and great men of the past, and when I think how much we prize even some passing note of these, and how infinitely we should value even a word, though of some careless passer-by, about Euripides or some of his peers, then I am consoled even for the inevitable failure to which time and time alone can give some quality.

One knows when writing that many will think him diminished in these pages. These are his true lovers doubtless and may be justified in their faith, since they have remembrances that surpass the power of words, even those which accomplish much. It may be that Landor, had he been a friend and a survivor of Hudson, might have put into prose something which would satisfy such remembrances. But for those without Landor's gift of massive carving or that of passionate sorrow which, joined together, make him in great instances the peer of those who wrote or carved in classic Greek, simpler methods must suffice. Others there are, I know, who will say he has been magnified. Let that be as it may, for, indeed, such words of his as I can recall without the man himself seem curiously feeble and unjust to him. Yet I believe that such critics will be those who never knew him and have but read books enough of his to give an opinion, apparently based, which is worthless, since they have no real share in him. I have protested against the mythopœic faculty being set to work on Hudson, and have endeavoured to stay the process by delineating him as I knew him. But the very "faults" which make a man human may well accentuate his high qualities. They are the shadows of the picture. So even a poor representation of his casual talk which, at its best, only depicts him as an interesting and curious character, may throw into relief the work which he did in solitude. This is at once an apology and an explanation. Little as I have been able to put down, and none can be so conscious as myself how little it is and how inadequate, it shows something of Hudson in company when he was no longer struggling with pen and paper

and the very fullness of his own mind. In no book but
A Crystal Age, and only in part of that, is Hudson, as
it were, in full dress. Elsewhere he is natural and simple
and yet is an artist. To be an artist means conscious
and unconscious selection, to say nothing of second
thoughts and revisions. But when Hudson talked he
talked as a pure instinctive: he followed himself, let
himself go. His flood spread in a thousand channels,
irrigated many fields: no longer did it turn the mill of
books. I want to show him with his coat off, in his
shirt-sleeves; and these talks of his do, at the very least,
suggest him at his ease and in an easy-chair or on a
couch. I have no other method than this and, therefore,
let these notes go.

Have I not said that during all the forty-two years
of our friendship it rarely seemed possible to me that
any could make a portrait or even a poor sketch of
Hudson, for the more I saw of him the more elusive he
appeared to grow? And he was always so young that
he appeared a contemporary: one on whose death none
could or would reckon: perhaps an inhabitant of another
world, to whom death would come very late or not at
all. In any man's life there are memories not to be
imparted: to yield them to others would seem a kind of
treachery, and, even worse, a rending of the veil which
hides us from ourselves. Yet there is a man still living
who has written a book of his mother which has added
beauty, melancholy, and knowledge to the world. My
own relations with Hudson were not of this sacred order,
nor can I assume that anything I ever write can rank
with the book of which I speak, but still there have been
hours when it was impossible to write of him: when it

seemed best to take all memories of him into the rising shadows. Yet why should even a little of such a man be lost if it could be saved for the very few, now or hereafter, who would wholly understand and love him? And when this came to me I began, as it were suddenly, to see Hudson clearly for the first time. The clouds rolled away or rose a little, and he no longer resembled a landscape "of hamlets brown and dim-discovered spires," or some woodland god as elusive as the daughter of the Didi in *Green Mansions,* but a big and simple man, whose very simplicity mocked sophisticated eyes. There is an ancient game for children in which a place is chosen on a map and others are bidden to find it. Some choose a village in the smallest print for its inconspicuousness among a crowd of like places, but those who know the game best choose, as one might in a map of the Argentine, some big-lettered, far-spread title of a province, such as Jujuy or Catamarca, and its very size will defeat the search of the curious. It seems to me now that this was my experience with Hudson as his days drew to an end. In all those forty years I had lived with him as a *Traveller in Little Things,* taking him just as he came, and never seeking to look, as it were, beyond his Quilmes, the village of his birth, to the big letters that revealed his whole great country.

It was not that in his later years he withdrew himself, or that I stood farther apart from him. Rather did his friendship increase and sometimes prove itself by queer sidelong acknowledgments of affection, by an increasing desire for companionship, by opener speech, by self-revelation, as though a man conscious of the inevitable end should take apart some intimate and say,

"These are things you will see to some day and look after for me." And then he was once more almost elfish, purely and simply human, satiric, gloomy, joyous, all in turn. So he might be seen clearly, and then again it was as though night drew down "her gradual dusky veil."

If this was so to me who seemed to know him, with what difficulty can the task be essayed of rendering him clear to others, not by way of idealisation and suppression, or vain guesses and unfounded inferences, but by straightforward representation, plane by plane? It seems as if there was but one way: to put down just what was seen and heard and to trust to the intuitions of those who look at these pages to fill in what they will by sympathy and knowledge of his books. Nothing I can write will show Hudson as a great conversationalist. He was no phrasemonger, no polisher of impromptu epigrams, but lucid and lambent rather than sparkling. After such a prelude these notes of his talk must answer for themselves. That they should contain certain repetitions of what has been said already is a fault which cannot be avoided, since when writing them I regarded them only as material on which I might some day work. I have in set purpose left them almost untouched, save by the elision of some names and of a few passages which might annoy or distress certain people.

November 10, 1920.—I went to St. Luke's Road to-day and found Hudson in bed with a big bed-jacket on. He looked very big and fine and picturesque in it, although he was lying down on account of his heart. He spoke about Arthur Keith and then went on to talk with humorous contempt of Belloc and Chesterton shouting, as

he called it, that religion, religion, had come back! He
put it as if somebody was yelling across fields that Lord
So-and-so had come home. His contempt of orthodox
religion is really extreme: I have hardly so much myself,
since dogmatic religion is an interesting human phenom-
enon. Somehow young Massingham's remarks about
him in the *Mercury* came up, and I said that Massingham's view was that Hudson's one real lack was religion.
He likes Massingham.

H. "Perhaps I've got as much as Massingham, or more,
but it's hard to say what religion is."

R. "I'm afraid Massingham is here not so wise as
he might be, for your very *raison d'être* is a remarkable
human inhumanity! Why, you're a bird-man without
morals!"

H. "Well, well, but folks like Massingham prattle that
mysticism springs out of religion. On the contrary, religion, in a great many, springs out of our natural mystical
feeling, that oneness we may have with Nature. I was
never so sure of this, that's to say I never had such a
sense of oneness, as when I was once on the Downs near
Burlington Gap. It was a beautiful day, the sky was a
deep wonderful blue, and before me there was a great
spread of thinly growing viper's bugloss, such as I had
seen on the pampa. It was so wonderful a sight that I
became the blue of the sky and the bugloss and the air!
Why, I didn't seem to walk, I just floated, floated! Have
you ever felt like that?"

I spoke of what I had felt in the Columbia Valley,
in the Campo Santa at Pisa, and of a kind of ascetic
ecstasy, through starvation in San Francisco, and also
of the feeling which I described in one passage of *The*

Wingless Psyche. All this seemed to please him, as it supported his view.

H. "I remember a wicked old gambling and most unholy gaucho who was with me one day on the Pampa, and I found him looking as if he was filled with content, and smiling. Suddenly he said, 'It would be good for me now if I died.' 'Why?' I asked, and the old gaucho replied, 'I feel at peace with everybody and everything, and I know this comes sometimes to us all, and it is well known that if people die when they feel like that they go straight to heaven without any purgatory.'"

R. "There's a certain amount of mysticism hidden in all of us. It may come out any time. What Massingham wants is that you should be a theist, or, at the least, believe in immortality. Some will sigh and let you off with that."

H. "I have no belief in it, none. What I want is just life: I want to live, to live!"

I do not know how it was that we came to talk of someone I knew well, but to my amazement Hudson said he had a foul mind and told horrible stories. Curiously enough, although I had known the man well for very many years, he never told me anything indecent, although he once showed me a book with pornographic illustrations which he said somebody had brought for him to see and he didn't want to see it. If anybody else but Hudson had said he had such a mind I could not have believed it. Many people might think that Hudson with his very free morality would not mind this kind of thing, but after that he never saw him again and did not even know that he was dead. Curiously enough on this day Hudson spoke of the possibilities of passion still existing in him. I note this because in forty years of friendship we have spoken of such things no more than three times, and I cannot remember that he has ever told an unseemly story for its own sake and very rarely as an illustration. To him all natural instincts, if they are natural, are not good or bad or beautiful or ugly, they are just part of the air he breathes. I might say he is a kind of Whitman without any desire to thrust nature down the throats of others, but he fears all emotion now lest it should kill him. He is frightfully nervous about living and dying, and kept on repeating that the cold he had must bring on bronchitis. He said it would finish him. I told him he was doing too much, even in destroying papers, and argued against his fatiguing himself in any way, and explained to him how cerebral fatigue might itself damage cardiac action in a case like his. He is always intensely interested in a plainly put scientific or physiological view, and he is alternately vexed that he can't understand all my last book, and proud in an odd, elder-brotherly way that I have written it. When he spoke of it I reminded him that it was his talk that had first led me towards biology and physiology.

H. "I never was scientific and I think very little of academic scientific people. However, I had no education, you see."

That, of course, was satiric: he knows he had a very great education. I said that I wanted to write a little about animals as I remembered them.

"No, I wouldn't if I were you," said he. "You've probably forgotten all about them and now you've only mere impressions. Memory is no good."

He often says that. And yet he wrote *Far Away and Long Ago*.

I asked him if he had appointed any particular literary executor, for I saw he had been destroying papers.

H. "No, I haven't. That's why I'm destroying now."

R. "I thought you might have made Garnett your executor."

H. "He wanted to be, but I refused."

R. "Why did you do that?"

H. "Because he would have raked up every fragment and scrap that I'd ever written, and printed it. That's his way."

R. "If you really want one and I survive you, I'll do just what you tell me, absolutely."

H. (*impatiently*). "If you survive me! Don't talk rot. No, I won't! You'd say, 'He was my friend and everything he wrote is of value.'"

R. "Don't you make any mistake. You know I shouldn't. Have I ever cracked up everything? I'll give you my word of honour I'll destroy all I don't really think of literary value."

He made no reply to this, but smiled, and then began to tell me a long story he had written and thought of destroying, in which someone said, "Well, wasn't Satan in his way a man of honour?" Then he added, laughing, "That's for you." I am not quite sure what he meant, though I think I know. He went through the whole of this story, a pretty long one, and I asked if I could see it, and even offered to revise it for him.

H. "No, but you can look at it. It's partly typed. I'll get it all done, then you can have it."

I doubt very much if I ever shall see, now that he has this fit of paper destruction.

He then described part of another book, *Ralph Herne,* in which he had drawn the great yellow-fever epidemic in Buenos Aires. He forgot that I had read it over thirty years before. It seems that he was in Patagonia at the time, but his brothers and sisters told him all about it. The one incident that struck him greatly was when a man with a cartload of coffins tried to sell one to his sister as he was taking his merchandise through grass-grown deserted streets. I spoke about the epidemic of influenza two years ago in Rio Janeiro, when 18,000 people were said to have died, and for some reason he absolutely refused to believe it. I said Koebel had told me. He had corresponded with him, but somehow he would not believe his report. This talk about Rio led to Cunninghame Graham, and of course to his hand-writing. He abused mine, and admitted his own was sometimes awful. I remarked that neither I nor N. could read one particular word in his last letter to me.

H. "You should have deduced it, just as you and I read Cunninghame Graham's letters."

R. "To read Cunninghame Graham's script is a logical and scientific training. We have to make hypotheses and discard them one after another. It's all trial and error. But he is a confirmed criminal and you are only casually as bad."

He went back again to his own books and manuscripts, and he said he had destroyed two whole books not long ago, one of them a full-length novel, and regretted having done away with it.

R. "You destroyed the whole or a great part of the book from which.*The Purple Land* came."

H. "It wasn't any good and most of *The Purple Land* is no good now."

R. "What nonsense! Don't tell me 'Lock and Key and Sinners Three' and 'Manuelo, also called the Fox' are not great things."

H. "Oh well, I daresay!"

As a matter of fact he quite loves those particular chapters himself.

Somehow or other we got to the migration of birds and, as we used to do in the old days, he found the facts, I made hypotheses, and he shot them to pieces with more facts. But I noticed that he was rather more rigid in his mind than he used to be. He couldn't hear out a piece of reasoning in his old patient way. He had a queer lapse of humour when I told him N.'s little jest about migration, when she attributed the hens' delay to move to their desire to grow a few more feathers or get themselves up in some way. He replied: "Oh no! In so many species the males and females don't travel together at all."

I didn't attempt to explain the little joke to him. Our migration talk lasted over an hour. He was frightfully keen on the birds, all birds, having a sense of the magnetic north, an idea he thought all his own, although it certainly was not. At the end we came more or less to some kind of agreement and by that time it was dark.

H. "We must have a light."

R. "Don't move, I'll light it."

H. "Oh, you can't light that lamp."

R. "Why, of course I can."

H. "No, you can't. It's a very particular lamp."

And he tried to get out of bed to show that this very particular lamp would only attend to him. Before he got to the lamp I had it lighted, rather to his surprise and perhaps his disappointment. So I shoved him back into bed again. Then it was a question of the fire.

R. "I'll make it up."

H. "Oh no, you can't."

R. "What's the good of talking? You know perfectly well you can't do anything with your hands, and I'm far more dexterous than most people with them."

I told him of Ruskin, who, when his mind was failing and he lay in bed, made the servant bring him the coal-scuttle so that he could choose the pieces of coal which she was to put on. He laughed, and though he had partly got up to go to the fire I made him lie down again. Soon after that I came away.

During this talk he was very amusing about a book written by a man I knew. The indecipherable word I had mentioned turned out to be "cartload." He had written that this man had indited a cartload of worthless books about the country. He added that a cartload of books was what Lord Jeffreys had accused Baxter of writing.

November 12.—Before going to see Hudson to-day I wrote a very long note on the migration of birds with a few suggestions of my own in it, but the body of the note dwelt chiefly on the question of the sensibility of birds to the magnetic north. I put in something about the two magnetic poles in the Northern Hemisphere, and the theories of Russian writers upon the subject. When

I got to Tower House I found he was up and destroying papers vigorously. As it was about tea-time, he made coffee for me and tea for himself and we talked for two hours. I read him part of the magnetic part of my note and he received it, very much to my surprise, with something quite like gratitude. He seemed really pleased, whereas he usually accepted such services as a natural right, never thanking one for them. Indeed I believe he would render them himself and never look for thanks. One part of his character comes out very curiously about the *Telegraph* leader on Arthur's Keith's dinner at the Authors' Club, at which I took the chair.

H. (with indignation). "But why don't they mention your name?"

R. "Why should they?"

H. "You were there, you were in the chair!"

R. "But really I don't count, not from the newspaper's point of view."

H. "That's rot! Of course you should have been spoken of in the same way."

R. "I don't care a damn personally and don't want to be spoken of."

H. "Well, I think that's *most* absurd!"

It was quite difficult to console him and I could not convince him that my name ought not to be mentioned. I passed it off as it didn't interest me, and asked him more about the story he was to show me.

H. "I've destroyed it."

R. "Why, you said I was to look at it!"

H. "It was bad, too bad. Now I'm destroying everything about my old serpent book."

This was a book I had heard of for over twenty-five

years, or may be thirty-five. He had been making notes
about snakes at intervals all his life, and I used to ask
him periodically how it was going on. I was disturbed
to hear he was destroying it and begged him to let me
have a bundle of the papers still unburnt.

H. "No, I won't. There's nothing good in it, it's
only notes, and I myself can hardly make anything of
some of them."

R. "It's a great pity to destroy it."

H. (*pettishly*). "Well, you must destroy *something!*"

I do not know how it was, but he began to speak
afterwards of immortality and he said about someone
whose name I've forgotten, "I don't suppose he believes
in it any more than I do. I had an intimate woman
friend once, not so long ago either, who is a very religious
woman, and she used to say to me, 'You are already
dead. I think anyone is dead who doesn't believe in
another life.' She was frightfully keen on it, but she
never thought her irregularities were a sin."

R. "Your friends the Spaniards are right. *Pecado
de carne no es pecado.*"

H. "I was thinking this morning of my earlier days,
when I struggled so with new views while I held on
desperately to the old religion."

R. "It seems very cold without it at first. It's like
landing in a new country where you have no friends."

We talked more of migration, but I had to hurry away.
Just as I was going I said, "To-day, Hudson, you somehow look more like a big bird than ever."

H. "Yes, I suppose I do. A friend of mine used to
say that I crossed the street like an eagle, walking with

a prodigious flopping, waving my arms and plunging across the road."

R. "All right, we'll call you *carancho.*"

H. (*indignantly*). "A carancho's a vulture."

R. "I know it is! Very well, any eagle you like. Or a Magellanic owl."

He cackled in his queer, high-pitched voice. It always seems strange that so big a man should speak so often in such a high tone. When Hueffer wrote about him he spoke of Hudson's "deep, bell-like voice." I mentioned this to Hudson, who is quite aware that his voice is not deep or bell-like, and he was very scornful, just as he is of over-praise. It was this day that we talked a lot about a lady whose work he used to admire and still thought very clever. He cut her to pieces "on the table."

November 14.—I found Hudson lying down. He had gone through the whole of my migration note, part of which I had discreetly left unread.

H. "Why do you say 'and others' about the magnetic north? It's my idea."

R. "Is it?"

H. "Yes."

R. "I think others have had the same notion if you look it up."

This, of course, is a fact, but here again one sees the lacunæ in Hudson's reading. He will very seldom look at any text-book or compendium which gives general clues to all that has been written, although his special and general reading among books is amazing even to me, for I fancy sometimes that I have read nearly everything myself. I suppose this is the reason he jumps so at conclusions. So he jabbed me two or three times for not believing that he, and he alone, had created the idea of a magnetic north sense in birds. Curiously enough he often says cutting things, and at times I have wondered whether he meant to do so or not. One great friend of his said to me that he liked to hurt his friends. I do not think that he does, but he is often careless in his speech and regrets it. I never heard him say a really disagreeable thing about any who could truly claim friendship with him, or even of those who could have done so once. Yet again this day Hudson showed himself peculiarly jealous for my reputation, as if, indeed, I had any in particular, and the very next minute he snorted at me and called me "Academic." This was because I owned to reading all round every subject of which at the time I was thinking. Curiously enough I could not get into his head the notion that, even if a bird *had* a sense of magnetic direction, that was not an actual motive for movements of migration north and south.

He was rather gloomy at one time during this afternoon and I asked him what was the matter. He spoke reluctantly about his wife, saying that she might die any day. For the first time he told me something about her age. She was always curiously ageless in appearance and I never had any idea how old she was. He said, "I believe she's ninety-five, perhaps even a hundred. I only knew a few years ago how much older she was than I." I was sorry to hear about her serious illness. She had been very kind to me in the old days. He broke off the talk about her very soon. I had brought with me a set of proofs of a book of verse and I showed him some verses called "An Epitaph." He pushed the slip away impatiently and said, "That's not my way of thinking. Death is too horrible to think about." This was said quite pettishly, but he afterwards asked me to leave the proofs. He went on to give me a talking to about one book of mine, which was mainly about women, his ground of disapproval being that the book was a special case. I did not argue the matter, for he was very hard to please at times. I do not know why a writer should not deal with special cases. However, soon after that little lecture I said—

"We've known each other forty years and never had a shadow between us."

H. (*looking down on me doubtfully*). "Haven't we?"

R. "No, never."

H. "Well, there's been time enough to forget."

R. "I tell you there's never been a cloud between us and you know it."

H. (*with a curious smile*). "Well, *that's* a very good thing!"

R. "Do you remember that I 'parted brass-rags' with Gissing once for a whole year?"

H. "Yes, I remember."

It is really remarkable that we never had a really jarring word between us in all those years, although at times I think he really tried to make me fire up. But I never would or could quarrel with him.

He said something about women which reminds me that a girl who knows him once said to me, "What does he think of women?" I replied truly enough that I did not quite know. If he numbered them among the animals, he numbered himself among them too. I believe he thinks that women are all right when he wants them about him. I told her that probably he looked upon them as agreeable or disagreeable birds, or as dear or detestable animals of his own species. But he loves to be loved by them, even to be liked, and when I go to lunch with him at Whiteley's and happen to turn up without N., he seems surprised and even cross and wants to know every possible reason why she hasn't come. I remember George Meredith said that in a man's old age beautiful women were like a sunset glow to him. But at eighty Hudson grew almost afraid of them. Many of them call him "Huddy." I think I never did until I heard the Galsworthys do it, and then only in jest. I have never called him anything but Hudson, and he has never used my Christian name except once in a letter. His wife always calls him William. It's a name that seems an outrage on him. He should have been called Hawk Hudson or something like that, for he is more like a splendid raptorial every day. The pampa women were right about Dominic.

Once more he spoke of the time before he got rid of all dogmatic religion. He reminds me at times of an amiable American tough, who used to prelude some stories with "When I was in the Penitentiary."

November 21.—After a spell of illness I went round to Tower House again this afternoon and found him reading in bed. He kept on talking about his heart, and presently I felt his pulse and found the same old fairly regular irregularity. I could detect no murmur, though Pardoe said he thought Hudson had aortic regurgitation. Any murmur of mitral disease had ceased long ago. I cheered him a little, and presently he rose and made

tea and coffee.   He spoke very bitterly about the fate
of the Plumage Bill, and presently spoke of Lord Grey,
for whom he has a great admiration.   He said, however,
that Chalmers Mitchell seemed to have gone over to
the enemy.   He was very bitter about it: I don't know
how justly.   It seems that Hudson urged Grey to speak
on the subject of the Bill and he promised that he would.
He spoke of Lord Grey's sight.   To Hudson the loss or
failure of sight was something terrible.   He then went
on to poetry.   He has a great admiration for Hardy's
best lyrics, though curiously enough he has never read
The Dynasts.   He said, quite wrongly, that Hardy had
no technique and scarcely belonged to time at all, but
that he hammered out his verse carelessly.

R. "He carves verse on the rocks of a wild moorland
and is eolithic."

H. "Ah, an eolithic poet!   That just suits him."

R. "What do you think of Blake?"

H. "I can't read his long mystical stuff, but of course
I like *Songs of Innocence*.   W. H. Davies now and again
gets a note from Blake.   I met Mackail at dinner the
other day and luckily remembered he'd written about
Morris, so we had something to talk about.   But I do
not care much for Morris, except in 'The Defence of
Guinevere.'"

R. "That's right.   The poems in that book are all he
wrote that are really worth anything.   What a sense
of colour and decoration in words!"

H. "Morris will belong to literature—and won't be
read."

Presently he spoke of Ezra Pound, with whom he
sometimes corresponded.

H. "I don't like his work."

R. "What sort of a man is he?"

H. "Oh, well, he talks!"

He showed me a letter of Ezra Pound's, which read: "Your discontent with your books is probably a matter of health. They are really quite good."

R. "And that's not a joke? What damned cheek!"

Presently I happened to ask him where I could find his sketch, a most amazing one, of Humming-Bird Gould.

H. (*with sudden petulant sulkiness*). "I don't know. I want to forget it. I want to forget a lot of things. I'm destroying all the time."

That afternoon when I reached No. 40 the housekeeper, Mrs. MacDougal, handed me a letter he had just written to me. When I told Hudson of this he betrayed a curious anxiety that I should not take away the unused stamp, so I tore it out of the envelope, and, somehow, I think by way of "The Purloined Letter," we got on to Edgar Allan Poe. Then he recited most of "Annabel Lee," and did it very badly. I know an even worse reader than Hudson: one has some dreadful experiences among men of letters.

H. "I don't like the last verse."

R. "What about the last verse of Keats's 'Ode to a Nightingale'?"

H. "Oh, that's *all* wrong: Did you turn out that last verse of your own that I spoke about?"

R. "Yes. You were quite right."

That pleased him. This afternoon he cross-examined me for a whole hour about anthropological points. He was very keen to know all about Neanderthal man and so forth, but of course he has his own theories and is stubbornly set on holding that Negroes are descended from a different sub-human stock than that from which the white races derive.   He will not read up a subject, but if he has no different pre-conceived views, always likes to be told things provided they can be put in a clear light.   He spoke again about his beautiful collection of South American agate arrow-heads, mentioned in his Patagonian book, all of which were lost in crossing a river, although he had taken such particular care of them as to carry them about with him, while the ruder weapons, which were sent roughly packed in a mere wagon, came through safely.   Some of these arrow-heads were barely half an inch long, but were most beautifully worked.   His description gave me the impression that they must have surpassed the very best neolithic work I have ever seen or seen described.   He gave a particularly vivid description of the prehistoric village in which he had found them.   This, it seems, had been buried by time and then had been swept clear once more by strong winds, pamperos, so that he came across its remains in a far-off wilderness, looking as if they had been but lately destroyed, with signs of fires about them, hearths and the like, and here and there these precious arrow-heads.   He also told me about a big snake-stone, as they are called by the gauchos.   These are rare stones which fracture conchoidally.   They are very smooth and about an inch and a half in diameter, with a hole bored through them.   They have been rubbed to make them round.   Two of these were found in the home cultivation paddocks or ploughed fields of his father's ranch.   Nobody knew who had made them or what they were for, though I believe the natives connected them in some way with snakes, perhaps as a cure for snake-bites. They must have been valuable, but both were lost.

When I was with him last he spoke of a paper written by Carpenter, the author of *Towards Democracy,* about mysticism or the kind of mystic feeling which Carpenter himself experienced.

H. "Carpenter seems to think nobody knows what he's talking about, so he has to explain it very carefully."

He went through the essay and its intentions and asked my opinion.

R. "Well, I want to see the paper."

H. "If I can find it I'll send it on to you."

When it came in a day or two I read it and agreed that the author seemed to think he was specially favoured by fate. Hudson now asked me what I thought of it, and I said I was of his opinion.

H. "Yes, it's all damned nonsense. Why, we've all got some mysticism in us: it's nothing to brag about. It might be something to complain about if he hadn't any of it."

R. "It's the ascetic ecstasy again that I spoke of the other day, and your 'oneness.' "

To this Hudson agreed and went on to talk in such a way that I began to see he regards almost all mystical insight and feeling as inferior examples of his own occasional uplift and communion with nature. He made one inclined to agree with him. I wish I could put down the impossible.

November 24.—His heart was troubling him a good deal. He talked at large about it, and as far as I can remember this is what he said:

"I don't believe the physicians understand anything! At any rate no better than I do. All of them always talk the same way. Price wants me to take digitalis until my pulse is down to seventy. But I don't feel so well when it's low as I do when it's up. Now my idea is that I've got used to having it eighty and over, and that if it goes at a different pace everything goes wrong. What do you think of that?"

Of course I was in a difficulty, such a difficulty as I frequently found myself in with him. I should not have sent him to Mackenzie and afterwards to Price if I had not thought them as regards cardiac conditions the best men in London, whose opinion was worth paying for and whose advice was worth following. But at the same time if I defended their views regardless of his feelings I was tolerably well convinced that out of sheer obstinacy he would take the exactly opposite path. So I hedged a little.

R. "I can't pretend to know a hundredth part as much about the heart as Price, Hudson, but when a degenerate heart is running too big licks it usually wants to be slowed. But perhaps there may be something in what you say. I daresay Price would be satisfied if your heart went down to seventy-five."

So a doctor says "you may take a little whisky," though he knows the patient would be better without alcohol, because a man forbidden to take any usually ends in taking too much. But I felt this was about as far as I dared go, and, indeed, there is, maybe, just a modicum of truth in what he said, as it is sometimes to feel moderately well with a fast-working heart than to feel tolerably seedy with one a trifle slower, so I went on to say:

"After all, I daresay you'd prefer to live five or ten years comfortably than ten or twenty years much less comfortably."

After a protest and a snort or two at my generous suggestion of twenty years he agreed more or less with what I said, and the net result of it was that he agreed to go on with the digitalis, as he had been told to do. A little experience of this kind shows what a difficult task a physician may have, for a wrong word of any kind with Hudson would make him dismiss his doctor. He got me to listen to his heart again. Of course, as Pardoe says, it's awful rubbish of a heart. I had no stethoscope, and he asked me why I didn't have one, for curiously enough he seems to have more faith in me than in the head of the cardiologists. He told me about his heart in youth after he had had rheumatic fever. He used to get the most awful palpitations, his heart "went mad." He used to fall down almost insensible and lie motionless, or barely able to move, out on the pampa in the rain.

H. "Once I was out shooting ducks and got much excited. I shot one duck, and when it fell down I fell myself about forty yards from the river and I lay there for hours, it seemed, until I wanted water, and I crawled inch by inch towards it and drank some out of my hand. After another hour I was able to get up and crawl home. Of course, that is why the doctors said I'd die, that my life was worth nothing."

Soon after this he began to talk again about Mrs.

Hudson. It seems she expects him to stay the winter at Worthing.

H. "I can't do it, I just can't! It would kill me. My being down there gave me this bronchitis."

He spoke again of her age, and said she was sometimes almost childish and then wakes up, as it were, and becomes extraordinarily intelligent and alert, and, although she is now bed-ridden, she is always proposing to get up. Hudson says he is going direct to Penzance and will write to Mrs. Hudson's companion and doctor to tell her that he will come when he is better of his cold.

Somehow we got on to his *Shepherd's Life* and spoke of "Winterbourne Bishop."

R. "I can't find any such village on the map."

H. "There isn't any such village. I called it that."

R. Well, what's its name?"

H. "I swore I would never tell anybody. A lady wrote to me asking about it. She said she'd been looking for it for several summers, but had at last given it up and settled down for her summer holiday in the most beautiful village she found. It was Winterbourne Bishop, though she didn't know it."

R. "Didn't you tell her?"

H. "Certainly not. Why should I? There's a Bustard Down close to it and in the village there's a Bustard House."

I never mentioned that this would inevitably enable me to find out where it was, but I naturally supposed that this was his way of getting round his absurd oath not to tell anybody the name of the village. What it was that led up to it I do not know, but he afterwards told me that the first time he fell in love was with a

little girl about seven when he himself was eight. It
was a very desperate affair. On the table there was a
pile of manuscript, and I asked him if the things were
for me to look at. He said they were and gave me a
long ballad. I began it at once and had not read a page
or two before I said:

"Why, Hudson, this is very good. What are you
going to do with it."

H. "I don't know. Give it away, I suppose, or destroy it."

R. "What nonsense! Give it to me, I'll sell it for you."

H. "You can't."

R. "Well, let me try, anyhow."

H. "Oh, very well, but you'll do nothing with it. They
might print it in some poetry book or another, the kind
of thing they put anything into nowadays. I've destroyed
much better things, two whole volumes of poetry. I
wish I'd kept it all now."

Among these manuscripts was a mad story, about a
ride on an omnibus from Kensington to the City, which
he thought very amusing. I took it home and read it
there. It was mad enough but fell between two stools.
It was too realistic and too fantastic at once. On the
whole I thought nothing of it. There was also the *Ralph
Herne* book with the Buenos Aïres yellow fever epidemic
in it. All these things I took away with me. He talked
a good deal about *Dead Man's Plack,* and told me that
he had sent a copy to Lord Stanmore's sister. He wondered with a smile whether Lord Stanmore might not
show a certain passage of it to the Prince of Wales.
He evidently rather wished that the Prince could hear
what he had said of him. He spoke contemptuously of

somebody's idea that they would make "movies" of *Dead Man's Plack*. He again threw out dark hints, so to speak, that he was somewhat disturbed at my not thinking it so very good when I read it first. As a matter of fact I was rather inclined to under-rate it, or under-rate all but the very beautiful and curiously characteristic introduction. When speaking of that I said:

"What a peculiar thing it is, this almost general belief, or the belief at any rate I have found fairly general, that you are such a highly gifted individual that you rush and write down instinctively all you have to say and leave it at that."

H. "Oh yes, I daresay."

R. "Why, look at the beginning of the *Plack*. There's a lot of low cunning about that, Hudson. You know some of them will be for saying that you believe in spirits and are a religious mystic or something of that kind, but you got the right effect by working for it and you know it."

H. "Why, of course I worked."

He spoke with great affection of his story "An Old Thorn," as he seems to think it's perhaps the only surviving bit of tree-worship left in England. He was very angry that in the picture of the thorn tree they put the name of the place. He talked about going to Penzance.

R. "Well, I shall come too and bring N. if I can afford it."

H. "If I pull off something in the United States I'll send you your fare."

He was curiously affectionate and much less casual than usual. He has the most extraordinary power of instant detachment, and frequently after being really

affectionate when I say good-bye and shake hands, he'll
say "good-bye" without turning towards me as I go, a
thing I couldn't do unless I was actually angry with
anybody. Speaking of "An Old Thorn," I mentioned
N.'s denunciation of the unforgiving old tree, and he
was much tickled and laughed in his curious high-pitched
voice. He spoke of May Sinclair's liking the story and
went on to jeer at her raw Freudism, but indeed he does
not in the least understand it. I said he understood as
little of it as most of the novelists. Presently they will
be writing "glandular" novels. He will call Freud Frood,
and when I said Freud rightly he kept on repeating the
name wrongly in the most obstinate manner. But finally
he actually asked me to explain the basal theory of it,
and listened patiently enough and agreed to much that
I said, especially when I pointed out that "repressed
complexes" might not only be the foundation of disease
or hysterical manifestations, but also quite naturally the
normal basis of good character. As I went away he
actually came to the head of the stairs with me, and
when there I said casually, as I had the manuscript under
my arm, "I suppose if I can get you" (and I named a
price) "for this poem you will let me sell it."

H. "Why, of course I would, but you can't do it!"

R. "We'll see. I shall come to the station to see you
off and bring N. if possible."

We shook hands, and as I went downstairs he looked
after me all the way down, a thing I don't remember
his ever doing before. I don't mind saying there were
tears in my own eyes. It wouldn't surprise me very
much if he himself were a little moved, for he knows
quite well that when we part we may never meet again.

CHAPTER XIV

Soon after the last notes were written Hudson came
to tea with us in order to meet my friend Sir Arthur
Keith, who was much interested in him and his work.
I cannot dilate on Hudson's views as to the one big
man of science he ever took to with real heartiness, since
it was Keith's kindly help with regard to work of mine
which first made Hudson desire to know more of him.
His strict avoidance of most purely scientific books kept
him ignorant of the contributions to anthropology made
by the Conservator of the Royal College of Surgeons,
and it was only when I gave him second-hand information about the mixed races which compose the population

of England that Hudson began to think that Keith could clear up some of his own particular problems. Hudson's interest in race, and his rare keenness in this discrimination of types, can be seen in many of his books, though his conclusions are often vitiated by want of special knowledge.

It is a pity that I can give no detailed account of the conversation between two of the most interesting men I have ever known. But the first thing that Keith said to me was, "He's a real true Beaker man." It was most interesting to note the difference of character and skull-form between the two as I sat and listened and said as little as might be. Hudson subjected Keith to an eager interrogatory as to the Mediterranean man, the small dark fellow who came up from the south and still can be seen in Wales and elsewhere. Notes of their talk would have extended to a small volume, for their interest was mutual and so obvious that it did not need the corroboration I got from both of them afterwards. I think it may be said that, for Keith, Hudson was a very rare type, for though he belonged to the dominating Beaker man, who is still apt to be a conqueror and a master of others, his visible intellectual curiosity combined with native charm, and his very bigness which accentuated in some ways his native courtesy, put him in a class all by himself. And Hudson went away so full and satisfied with more to think about that I cannot here report his opinion, and must merely say that his objection to pure men of science was greatly modified by finding one at least with a wide mind which refused the narrow limits of a single branch of learning.

When I reflect upon that afternoon and compare the

conversation with my own old talks with Hudson, my feeling grows that to "write a life," which so many undertake with rash cheerfulness, is a wholly impossible thing. What are events and what do they matter compared with a man's mind? One true and long report of six hours' argument and fight with Hudson would give more of him than any exact chronology and laboured comment.

Hudson's talk never wearied anyone. We weary easily of the very brilliant talkers. It is like living under an arc-light: we end in wishing them of less candle-power. There are some who talk pure literature. I spent some days in the company of a young American woman who told stories of the poor whites and Negroes which might have been taken down and printed. They were good stories without a doubt, but the narrator presently appeared to me as an incarnation of *Harpers'* and *Scribner's,* a terrible magazine, impossible to put down or throw away. But Hudson, simple, curious, and discursive, with short interludes of deep seriousness or rollicking absurdities, fell in no such pits of monologue. He was always eager to have others talk and silence in his company was impossible.

Soon after he met Keith, my step-daughter and I went to Paddington to see him off to Penzance. He was waiting for us and was wearing a threadbare old overcoat, which must have been in his possession the past thirty years, for he never paid attention to appearance. After greeting us he said he was much disturbed because he had left his flask of brandy behind. This he always carried when he was travelling and he seemed to rely on it greatly. I found I could not get him any, so **he**

had to go away without it, and as he was only going
to Exeter he was not in the corridor part of the train.
We had not much time to talk, but he spoke about the
ballad and said, "Whatever you sell it for, take half
and come down with N. to Penzance." I declined this
commission but promised to come if we possibly could.

"For how long?" asked Hudson.

"Perhaps a fortnight," said I.

"What's the good of a fortnight? Can't you stay a
month?"

However, I thought we should be lucky if we got away
even for a couple of weeks. He seemed rather less
depressed. He always liked travelling.

After he had gone I took his poem and managed to
dispose of it for a good price, certainly more than he
would have obtained for it, since he judged it only from
a literary point of view and forgot that it was a "Hudson" and unique in its solitude. He wrote much verse
and destroyed whole volumes of it. To say that he was
a poet would be to say too much, and yet, if he had
always devoted himself to poetry, if he had been able
so to devote himself, I believe he might in the end have
ranked high. My success with this sale received peculiar
rewards. For the first time in his life he wrote a peevish
letter to me. I should not have sold the poem where I
did: the price was far too large: I should get him into
some kind of trouble: what the deuce did I mean by it?
And at the same time he proposed a commission which
I thought more absurd than his complaints. I even began
to look forward to our meeting in Penzance with some
apprehension. I came to the conclusion much later that
Hudson really regretted the price at which he had sold

some of his later books, especially in America. Though he was cross with me, he was savage with himself, being then dominated by the desire to leave as much as possible to the cause of the birds.

We went down to Penzance on the 22nd of December. It was a most wonderful day till we reached Exeter and then it rained. This was the Riviera as seen on the advertisements of the Great Western Railway! They ought to be indicted by the whole south of France. At Penzance it was pouring, and I could not help remembering that before Hudson took to Penzance he wrote to me, "To stay in this squalid place is impossible," and once more, "When I feel able to move out of this unpleasant place." But I never dared to remind him of his early impressions. I put on my waterproof and in the dark discovered 23 North Parade in the centre of the town. Since he had been away he had fallen off one of the high Penzance pavements, a drop in the dark of four feet into the roadway, and had bruised his knee and cut his hand by driving a stone into it. It was a marvel to think that a man of his age, near to eighty, had not smashed his femur and been laid up for the rest of his life. I now return to my notes and, therefore, sometimes use the present tense. His hand was in a bandage and he complained rather quaintly that he had been stiff, and then added, almost like a child, "I suppose it's because I had that fall." He went on to speak about his heart, which had been very bad, I suppose from the shock. He said he had had insomnia and was obliged to sit up with a candle for a great part of the night.

H. "And the way my heart went on was something quite amazing. It seemed to be tumbling all over the

place. I didn't know what to do and I said to myself,
'They'll find me dead in the morning, that I'm sure of.' "

I remarked that he seemed to have nice people looking
after him. The girl, a niece of his landlady, seemed
very much attached to him. When I came in I asked,
"I believe you have been looking after my friend Mr.
Hudson?" and she said warmly, "I do all I can." Hudson
told me a story about her which was very characteristic
of him. He reconciled her and her aunt. *À propos* of
something, he spoke of Wilfrid Blunt having no real
politics and added that Blunt remarked, "I'm just against
the Government, that's it." And we talked a little about
Auberon Herbert and that wonderful old man's flints
with markings on them that he believed to be very ancient
writing.

I found Hudson quite a little savage with me about
the ballad. Why the devil had I gone to that particular
publisher? He had promised to give him the refusal
of everything, and now he would presently be writing
reminiscences and saying that Hudson had acted dis-
honourably!

R. "Nonsense! I've found out your market value,
that's what it is."

H. (*peevishly*). "I know my market value. If I'd
wanted money I could have taken it to him and he'd
have given me something for it."

This more or less confirmed what I had said, but I
refrained from saying so, though I felt inclined to come
out with "Here's your poem and the letter about it.
Take it and do what you like." However, I held my
tongue. To have any kind of a quarrel over such a thing
after more than forty years wasn't to be borne. I turned

the conversation and would not go back to the poem, though he kept dragging it in.

I pretended to admire Hudson's room and said what a nice clean room it was without any infernal pictures or ornaments, such as one finds in country lodgings, and it seems he has had it decorated himself. It had been dingy with dark, dirty paper and crowded with what he described as beastly pictures. These he had replaced by proofs of H. Gronvold's drawings for the *Birds of La Plata,* framed in a rather dreadful red.

H. "I couldn't stand it and at last went on my knees to my landlady, and finally she said crossly, 'Oh, Mr. Hudson, do what you like!' So I had the whole place stripped and nearly all the pictures taken out of it."

The walls are white now and the furniture is clad in blue chintz. He keeps fruit on the sideboard for some child friends.

Although I knew Hudson was glad we had come to Penzance, I left the house depressed and irritable and came back in soaking rain to discover that my waterproof wasn't waterproof at all, at any rate not waterproof in Penzance. I have also discovered what the mental side of cardiac irritability may mean.

December 23.—N. and I went to Hudson's this morning. We found him in a much more amiable frame of mind because he had slept well. But he objected to my wearing a big overcoat, and soon I realised that he would object to anything. I had taken back with me the *Herne* manuscript and suggested that I should do some work on it for him. He showed obstinacy at once.

H. "No, I shall send it as it is to Knopf in New York. If anyone else touched it, it wouldn't be mine."

R. "Come, let me do a first chapter for you to see how it looks. I asked H.D. about it and he said that collaboration in your case wouldn't matter. They just want you, and that means anything with your name on it."

H. "No, I'll send it to Knopf just as it is. I never pay any attention to what anyone says about my work. There is one man now going about in New York saying he made me in the United States, when it was another who wrote to me first from there and asked me to let him try what he could do to get me an American sale. I don't care what *Ralph Herne* is like, whether it's good or bad."

We then had a struggle over *Fan,* which I wanted to keep in obscurity. He owned it was not good, but meant to sell it for the Birds. That settled it and I let it go. There was obviously no moving him. With other script I had sent him back his rather absurd 'bus story.

R. "I think it falls between the two stools of fantasy and realism."

H. "And I think it's real enough. I sat in a 'bus once with a man who talked all the way from Bayswater to the City about his stocks and shares. Besides (*with a gurgle*), it's your lack of humour! I have destroyed it but I rather liked it."

He showed me Galsworthy's letter from California.

H. "He sent me *The Awakening.* I liked it, but I gave it away, as I do most books that are sent me."

I felt rather inclined to ask what he does with mine, but I think he keeps them. He showed me a letter from his friend **Curll** and spoke of *Shadows out of the Crowd* with very great approval, but was much disappointed with Curll's later work. He talked of *South Wind*. He said Douglas is better than his book, but there were great things in parts of *South Wind*. *À propos* of someone else he said suddenly, "I can't read Maeterlinck's *Bees*."

R. "I can, and I make it out a bitter criticism of the awful hive of men."

H. "That's you, not Maeterlinck. For me he makes his bees human and all false. I prefer Fabre. Let's go out now. I want to go to the library. N., what are some good children's books?"

N. "Well, Mr. Hudson, what about Mrs. Ewing?"

Hudson objected to Mrs. Ewing apparently on the general principle of objecting to everything, just as he objected to my coat when I came in. Perhaps it's all cardiac.

R. "What about Mrs. Nesbit?"

H. "Children want incident and so on," just as if E. Nesbit had no incident.

So out we went to Bridger's shop and he bought two modern children's books, I don't know what. He saw with great pleasure his *Argentine Birds* in the shop and also *Birds and Man*. It is obvious that his irritable statement that he doesn't care a damn about the books he's written, but only about the ones he's going to write, is not wholly well-founded. He left us at the top of Market Jew Street to see the children to whom the books were going. I said to N. when we left him, "He's better to-day, and, thank heaven, not a word about the ballad."

We all have our strength and our weaknesses and both come out some way or another, perhaps quite plainly without any strangeness, but in Hudson there is certainly a strangeness that runs through everything he says or thinks. So I have often heard him speak as others do of the sudden strangeness that may lie in beauty, but there's maybe a strangeness in some ugly qualities, or what would be ugly qualities by themselves or in others, and one finds that in him. When we got back to our lodgings down by the sea, N. said, "I hope nothing wrong will happen about the ballad, but didn't G. say that Hudson, perhaps, had never quite forgiven him for making him better known in America. He said he seemed sore about it ever afterwards." Certainly Hudson "got his knife into me" about this ballad, though he forced me to take a commission on the transaction rather than quarrel with him, a thing not to be thought of calmly.

To get out Hudson a solid and real and live thing of three dimensions can't be done by thought or taking care. He must be developed like a plate in one's own brain and it's long odds on under or over-exposure. I feel he's on my mental plate for certain, but with what fear and trembling does one try to get him out, reasonable, captious, bright and irritable, man and bird, the ancient shepherd, the mystic poet, the ruthless mountain, sky-haunting eagle, who damns all idealists who live in cloudland, those who are devoid of real instincts, and devoid of his particular kind of pitiless pantheism! It is a hard, an impossible task. At this moment it occurs to me that during all our long friendship I have never written anything about him, as I did of Gissing when he was alive. The reason of this was, I believe, not only the difficulties he presented in analysis, but to my feeling that he objected to being understood. A wrong word, or a hint of real insight, might have caused trouble.

It was rather strange to hear him talk of Garnett and Garnett's views on Ireland. So far as I am concerned Hudson's clean adherence to England's cause, whether right or wrong, is more than attractive, although, as he told me, he comes from an Irish grandmother, his father's mother. One thinks of his beautiful care and thought for children and the young of all things, and his bitter, almost brutal, rage against the aigretted women. Directly after he has spoken beautifully of beautiful things there comes out some strange, wild irritation. All are fools, thrice fools! He's as moody as a wild April, everything by turns and nothing long. One sees him bitter, and then a winged angel whose wings shed balm and blessing. I said to N., "He's a dear old chap, with a damned old heart, like a clock out of gear. That's it, he's just like an old clock, our ancient clock that strikes or doesn't strike, goes or doesn't go, is affected by frost and fine weather and rain, and perhaps even by a gloomy day, and, playing the devil itself with time, wants help and yet, as it seems, resents it." Many years ago these failings of Hudson were visible faintly, now they come up at times in the bath of ill-health in bold black and white, and then again he looks at me or at N. with quite visible love. It's strange, I think sometimes, to note how she has quietly taken him as a real friend.

Again we went in together at five o'clock and found Hudson yawning, but he brightened wonderfully, as if we'd blown his clouds away. He then talked about Trollope, for whom he has a very considerable admiration, but, just like George Gissing, was ferociously angry with him for saying, 'Now, if this were true,' or at any rate he was angry till I agreed, when he averred it didn't

matter. Then we talked about Gissing, and he said with
a kind of snap that he would probably repent of the
moment after, that Gissing was "rather mouldy now."
He keeps himself strangely up to modern standards, as
one sees in poetry. He talked about the value of books.

H. "I've sold all my Gissings but the best one, *Born
in Exile.*"

R. "I'm glad you think that the best, for it is the
best."

I rather expected him to deny it then, but he didn't.

R. "If you say 'rather mouldy,' perhaps you've seen
Swinnerton's estimate of him as the connecting link with
our age or the last of the Early Victorians."

H. "I didn't know Swinnerton had written of him."

We then talked about the Cornish sense of humour.

H. "I know a man here who came to me and said with
a kind of shamefaced triumph, 'I've written a novel and
I've got a great title for it.' So I asked what it was and
he said, 'Well, you see, I first called it *Will Tregarthen.*
Now that's good enough, but it wasn't just what I wanted,
and I kept on thinking for days, and at last I spoke to a
friend of mine, and he said he'd think it over, and next
morning he came down and he said, "I've got it!" And so
he had! So I've called the book by a great title, a splendid title, *Will Tregarthen, Cornishman!*' "

Hudson's face as he told this story of two powerful
brains elaborating such a new and magnificent title was a
picture of humorous joy. From the twelfth chapter of
The Land's End we know what he thought of Cornish
humour. We went on to talk of Trollope's *Orley Farm.*
The forging of some document by the heroine was, N.
said, perfectly justifiable. Hudson displayed peculiar

amazement at her endorsement of this breach of law. He showed with extraordinary plainness his old conservative side. His affection for law and order is very strange in a man of his past life, and yet one sees the Conservative in him at every turn. He even made stern objections to homeless, houseless men seizing upon empty houses, and when I backed them up mildly, not ferociously as I felt like doing, he was amazed, although he knows me so well. I told him he was a Conservative and yet wouldn't he burn a woman with birds in her hat to save birds? Hudson simply wouldn't answer this question, although N. and I both pressed him. He went on to expatiate, with concentrated quiet bitterness, on bird-collectors. This quietness of his on such a subject was very remarkable, but, as I said before, he knows he must be calm. He has to be. He wants to live. He seems to be able to stop at mere irritability. He told us of his plan to put a stop to rare bird-killing, which he maintains is entirely due to the high prices given by that accursed body of men, mostly rich, who are bird-collectors. This plan was to forbid private bird-collecting by law. He might have all kinds of ideas concerning liberty, but, when it came to the liberty of slaughtering rare and beautiful creatures in his heart he'd send liberty to hell at any moment. He spoke with quiet savagery of a certain important person in the Bird Society.

When Hudson told him about his motion, this fellow, a very rich man and a Member of Parliament, said angrily, "I'll oppose it in the House in every possible and conceivable way." Hudson, when he told us of this, spoke without rage. That's what is so surprising in him. He is irritable and almost angry at the least little thing, but when it comes to a big, serious matter like this, in which his whole heart and life have been concentrated for so many years, he manages to preserve a remarkable quietness. As I said before, I suppose it's protective. He dare not let himself go, and yet nothing that I could say, and I said a good deal, was too much for this man whose rage was because—"I'm a collector myself!"

That's where the trouble is, and so, as Hudson told me, the Bird Society hires watchers to see that certain rare birds are not molested, at least in the mating season, and these men are approached and bribed to betray their charge, because even members of this community for protecting birds want at all costs yet another specimen for their cabinet. As Hudson said, it's the bird-collecting squires and scoundrels of this order whose money fires guns at every rare visitant that comes to the shores of Great Britain. Sometimes I think Hudson modifies even his hatreds, because the follies and brutalities he laments are the result of men's deep destructive instincts. For a thing to have a basis in ancient instinct is with him to have some kind of justification. One feels that in all he says, except when he talks of bird-collectors and feathered women. Even of them I have heard him speak without visible anger, though never without contempt. To attribute mercy, and kindness and goodness to all women, was ludicrous when one saw how their damnable decorative instinct developed and reinforced callousness in so many of them.

When Hudson spoke of photographs, for he wished N. to be photographed, he went on talking of portraits generally, and the book of Rothenstein's in which his own portrait appears. He has, I think, a certain harmless and perhaps even beautiful vanity about himself, as he does everything within reason to avoid looking very old, and he spoke of this particular portrait with great dislike.

H. "Why, all the lines in my face were accentuated and made deep black and white! I hid the book away!"

I doubt if he understands Rothenstein's method, or indeed whether he appreciates any of the more modern forms of art except modern poetry or even pseudo-poetry. He spoke presently of people one meets who desire to be pleasant to authors, and told us of one lady in particular, whom he called a pleasing hypocrite, who has read absolutely nothing but makes beautiful speeches to wretched writers. For if she has to meet one she hastens to any who know him with the words, "Quick, dears, tell me what he has written!" Then, said Hudson, she goes flowering in speech to the unsuspecting writer: "Oh, I do so love your books!" And Hudson said he turned upon her and said, "Look here, I like you just because I know you never read anything, so don't talk to me of my books, please."

To speak once more about his keeping his temper in the matter of bird-slaughter, I have noticed these last years in his talk a notable and steadily increasing tendency to great and even striking sobriety of statement about such things as seem to him most detestable, though he gets angry about trifles. This may be due to his deep conviction that argument isn't necessary, and that the briefest, coldest statement of fact should put others into the rage he himself avoids. Physiologically this tendency has been most interesting to me, as I am sure it springs from his natural and increasing fear of rage. As he himself might say, it is a nascent self-protecting instinct, but many of us have a deep dread of great anger.

December 24.—It's been raining hard all day, half a gale from the south'ard, with driving scud overhead. This day we were going to St. Ives and couldn't possibly go in such weather, so we went up to Hudson instead. He seemed surprised.

"Well," he began in his high-pitched voice, "so you've not gone to St. Ives!"

There was a kind of curious indignant remonstrance in his tone. He appeared unutterably amazed that we hadn't gone, rain or shine, wind or calm.

R. "Why, no, of course we wouldn't go on a day like this."

H. (*in reedy tones of wild surprise*). "What? A day like this! Why, what kind of a day do you want? It's a splendid day!"

And he looked out of window with an air which seemed to say that Penzance in a black squall reminded him of the Tropics.

R. "Well, as a matter of fact, I don't mind telling you that we wanted a day not like this present fine day of yours, but one more like yesterday, which for Penzance wasn't so bad."

H. "Nonsense! This is a fine and a very good day."

After that, as I saw he was in the mood to declare that a hurricane, volcanic eruptions, and red-hot lava made up real holiday weather, I dropped the subject and asked him what he was writing. There were papers on the table.

H. "I'm writing letters, tons of answers to letters! They come from everywhere, many from the United

States. Why, I've got the title-pages here of three of my own books. I'm supposed to write on them and send them back."

He told us that a man once sent him a bale of his books to autograph and return and left him to pay the postage. He did so, but it wouldn't have surprised me if he'd given the entire set to the nearest library.

H. "Here's a letter you might like to see. It's from a distant cousin of mine whom I've never met, a Mrs. Merriam Garick who lives in Portsmouth, New Hampshire."

After I'd read it he entered on a long history of the Merriams, his mother's family. It seems they all sprang from two brothers who migrated to America long ago. It appears there's a history of the Merriams somewhere. Then he spoke of his father, who had been a tolerably good athlete until he met with a severe accident caused by running at top speed along a big row of barrels in a brewery. In doing this he hurt himself and ruptured a vein in his leg and was laid up for a long time. After he recovered he was sent away and went south with a man called Rockwood, who was a pretty bad case of tuberculosis. They went to Rio and after that to Buenos Aires.

H. "Of course Rockwood was in very bad health and he lived upon—oh, worse food than you do and even less of it—and one day, after he had been dieting for years, he went to a doctor out there who said to him, 'That's all you eat, is it? But don't you want to eat?' 'Why, yes, of course I do,' said Rockwood. 'Well, what do you want? What would you like to eat?' Rockwood declared that of everything on earth he wanted salt pork. 'Then eat it,' said the doctor. He did and got quite well!"

Hudson thought this was a triumphant tale against most doctors, but the medical profession are quite aware of cases, in which they are supposed to have been wrong, when they have really cured a man by strict dieting who, on his recovery, declares that the first good meal he took was the cause of his getting better. I do not know how we got to it from food, but I said something about *Green Mansions* and its success in America. I had no idea it was the success it is.

H. "Why, I've made two hundred a year out of the book for some time, but they will keep sending me drafts for the money payable only in the United States. These I give to the bank, which sends them back to America, and then the U. S. Government takes 8 per cent. out of it and the English publisher takes 10 per cent."

R. "Yes, but the exchange as it stands at present more than makes it up to you."

Hudson growled at this but said nothing. I mentioned casually that X. had sent me a Christmas card.

H. (*snorting*). "And to me too. I suppose he sends them wholesale."

In spite of my efforts he began to talk about the poem again and wanted to know whether I'd sent it to Knopf.

"You did? I can't think why you sent that stuff to him. He's not a rich publisher."

I couldn't see why a poor publisher shouldn't print Hudson's work, but let it pass and refused to speak of the ballad any more and turned the conversation in spite of Hudson's spadework to keep the current of talk as he would have it. I remember thinking at the time that some might say he didn't really want me to come in at all, considering the way he talks and sometimes pinpricks me, but they would be wrong. The very moment I wanted to go he would urge me to stay almost excitedly, and if I really had to leave him it was always, "When are you and N. coming in again?" As we stood arguing about this, N. did come in with a marketing basket in order to see if I was there, as she had a question to ask me. He was quite delighted to see her and begged us to come in at tea-time. Would we want tea when we came? We said, however, that we shouldn't want tea, but would have it before, and then he sat down to the table and, with his usual strange power of detachment, he had begun writing almost before we were out of the room and hardly looked up. After all, there's not a touch of real old age about him, for all his irritability may be seen any day in a young cardiac or gouty subject, but now he's wonderfully of the *genus irritabile vatum*. As I went away I said to N., "I'm in a great stew, for I want to know if he's made his will and who his executors are, and I'm hanged if I know how to find out."

We went in again at about a quarter to five.

H. "And why are you so late?"

So really he is very eager for society, and though he can look like a green persimmon there's no one on earth with a more charming smile when he's all right. As soon as he had forgiven us for not coming in before tea he was all anyone could wish him to be. He talked about the earthquake in South America, the great one at Mendoza in the old days, when the earth had opened, and went on to tell his strange story of a gaucho scout who had at times been employed by the Government against the Indians. His name was Soza, and having happened to kill somebody he skipped out for Patagonia and was liv-

ing with a band of brother ruffians, desperaaoes, and out-
casts, on the Rio Colorado, just at the time that this great
Mendoza earthquake occurred. It seems that they were
camped in a dead calm and were having a meal, when
Soza rose up suddenly and without a word held out his
hand. The others asked why he did so and he replied:
"To feel the wind; and there's no wind, and yet I see
the leaves of all the trees, the red willows, trembling."
No one else could see them move, but allowing the time
for the tremor to travel across the pampa, that was the
very hour and moment of the great Mendoza earthquake,
when thousands lost their lives. This is in *Idle Days in
Patagonia,* but his narrative was better than what he
wrote there. So then we got upon hearing and ears.
Those who know all his work will remember a passage
in which he speaks of making, or wishing to make, large
wax ears and putting them on to see if he could hear
better. Then he mentioned Smollett's *History of an
Atom* because of a certain man who held his hand to his
ear. Hudson went on to remark that it was the beastliest
classic in the English language, and that this one thing
was the only good observation in it. He proceeded to
dogmatise in his usual way about hearing, for he knows
nothing of the theory and might never have heard of
Helmholtz or anyone else. However, he was quite certain
that the brain did it all and was curiously positive that the
brain received nothing but what we thought we heard. I
couldn't get his notion clear and tried to show him some
of the traps and difficulties of his own and other theories,
and he grew reasonable, as he almost always is when anyone tries to expose scientific difficulties and theories to
him. But the way he rushes in on instinct and intuition

where physiologists fear to tread is quite wonderful, and sometimes I think he's more right than anyone after all.

Having disposed of hearing and having settled it and me, he talked on about titles, especially of a journalist whom he seemed to like.

H. (*scornfully*). "Of course his knighthood was not given him by the King, he was given it by Northcliffe."

R. "Well, he's a very good chap anyhow. I know him quite well."

H. "Why, where did you meet him?"

R. "At the place I sometimes play chess in, in St. Martin's Lane."

H. "To be sure. I used to dine there occasionally with a very peculiar society of Humanitarians. I wrote *Roff and a Linnet* for them. It was a vegetable place: I always had indigestion after dinner. Once I went in early and sat down, and presently a very queer-looking young enthusiastic-eyed fellow danced up to me. When I looked at him he said, 'May I ask if you are a Humanitarian?' So I replied, 'Well, I subscribe to them,' and he began to tell me how much excited he was because this was his first visit, and he so terribly wished to see Edward Carpenter and other famous people whom he named. Now in the room where this little dinner was to take place there were many other tables, for it wasn't kept entirely for the Humanitarians. After a while a big man with a large moustache," perhaps an Admiral," said Hudson (for he didn't know that an admiral wouldn't wear one unless he had a beard), "who had his wife with him, came in. He looked a real fighting man. They sat at our table. Then the young enthusiastic person rose up and danced round the head of it to them and bowed low and said, 'Pray pardon

me, but may I inquire if you are Humanitarians?' The man
who was asked this absurd question looked fairly dazed,
but at last got out, 'Why do you ask such a question?'
'Because this table, sir, is reserved for Humanitarians,'
said the young stranger from the country. 'Oh, is it?'
asked the big man, 'and are they dangerous?' This fairly
stumped his questioner and he then turned to his wife and
said, 'Perhaps we'd better go to another table, my dear,
they might do us some damage here.' "

I remember his story of the "antediluvian," but reminded him of it. I must put it down somewhere and
here is as good as anywhere else.

When Hudson was one day walking from Tower
House to Notting Hill Gate by way of Portobello Road,
over twenty years ago, he saw a crowd gathered outside
a rather poor house in front of which there was a little
garden. On stopping to find out what was the matter he
saw a long, thin man with something like a wrapped-up
picture under his arm endeavouring to get away from his
wife. So far as Hudson could gather the husband proposed to pawn what he had in his parcel and his wife objected strongly to this being done. Their argument was
long and impassioned and was accompanied by cheers and
laughter from the gathering crowd. The husband at last
turned towards all those who were assembled in the road
and, addressing them, shouted at the top of his voice,
"Now what I want to know is this: Is a man a king in
his own castle or is he an antediluvian?" To Hudson this
was a most exquisite joke, though perhaps to others it
may seem no more entertaining than the lighter amuse-
ments of some other illustrious men, such as Spinoza
and Robert Burton, but seeing the numbers of times

Hudson and I, as well as others, have set our wits in vain
to find out what this man really wanted to say when he
used the word "antediluvian," it has had a longer life
than most casual jests. To this day Hudson is ready to
repeat it with infinite gusto, always turning round to
those in the room to ask what the man actually did mean.

After talking about many other things he came back
this afternoon once more to hearing. It seems he had
read in a book of someone's experience in a belfry, and he
had made up his mind to get inside one at all costs.
While he was at Wells, a favourite haunt of his, although
he admires too much the front of the Cathedral, which
has no revelance to the rest of the architecture, he found
the bellringers entering St. Nicholas. He spoke to one of
them and asked if it were possible for him to go into
the belfry while they rang the peal. This man said they
could not allow it, for no one could stand the noise.

H. "When he had said it couldn't possibly be done I
gave him something for himself and went up while they
stayed below in the rope chamber. But they sent a boy
into the belfry to look after me, though the young fellow
really stayed outside. The truth is that the bell-ringers
below were quite right: the sound was truly awful and
horrible. I do not mean the musical waves of sound,
but one awful steely note that pierced my brain like a
hot arrow. I stayed in the belfry perhaps twenty seconds
and got out upon the leads. Again and again I went in,
and this most awful sound absolutely hurt me and drove
me out. There was something unutterably unmusical
about it. It was as if I was in a place with a gigantic saw
cutting steel, and yet it was a fine peal of bells. I could
not understand why that appalling sound came to me in

such a way when I was close to, seeing I heard nothing of it from the street."

Perhaps a campanologist or any musician might say what was the cause of this, but I suggested that as no bell in existence is or can be quite true, he heard some discord or some peculiarly horrible beat in the note. I was not aware at the time that what he heard is known as the "tap-tone." This is the actual sound produced by the blow of the hammer or clapper, which has nothing to do with the true bell tones. I tried to make him see how the bell's compound note is made up, and he waved me aside and proceeded to assert that nowadays any bell could be made true. I soon found out he knew nothing of the triple note of a bell with all the complex overtones. When I rather stumped him by mentioning such things as "tones" when talking of hearing, he replied in a lordly fashion but not without humour, "Such things make the subject unnecessarily complicated." And once more, when I urged that no note was a simple thing, he accused me of taking a simple subject and inventing complications for it.

He continued talking of music, one of his passions, of which, however, he knows nothing technically, not even the rough physics of a vibrating string. I did my best to explain it out of my own abundant ignorance. When I told him that I could make a wonderful bell for him with his big poker and a bit of string, he got me the string at once.

R. "You see, I hitch the middle of the string to the top of the poker. Now take the ends of the strings over your thumbs and, bending a little, press your thumbs into your ears."

H. "And what will you do?"

R. "I'll strike the poker gently. I don't want to deafen you."

He did what I asked and I struck.

H. "Now, that's wonderful! I couldn't have believed it. Do it again."

I did it again. He was just like a child with a new toy and make me keep on striking the poker. The pleasure he got out of his senses was extreme. He put his new bell down with reluctance. His senses were keen to the last. He could read and write without glasses when over eighty.

It was odd, however, that hideous and prolonged discords did not always annoy him. At midnight on New Year's Eve the uproar in Penzance, especially the noise which came from steamers in the harbour, was, it might have seemed, enough to drive mad anyone with a touch of musical feeling in him. But not even some drunken engineer who blew his accursed discordant whistle for over an hour worried him. He was surprised that it worried others.

It might have been considered that he presently desired to give us an example of uncomplicated musical tones, for picking up a volume he began to read a poem by a dead soldier, and he read it so badly that I could barely understand a word of it. He admired it a great deal more than I, and did so for reasons which I was totally unable to follow. I took the book away from him and said, "May I read it?" Oddly enough he allowed me to do so and I made it at least intelligible to N. I only know one worse reader than Hudson, and this man is always eager to read aloud. It is certainly wonderful, the way he keeps up his appreciation of new poetry of all sorts. I remember how much he liked Doughty's poems, which some people regard as a kind of touchstone of feeling for poetry. Those who admire Doughty are allowed inside the circle, and those who don't admire Doughty are wretched outsiders. For my own part, I would rather put down as a test admiration for Thomas Hardy's poems. After poetry we went on to modern politics, and it seems that Hueffer had written to him, as he had done to me, about the Irish question, asking him to write something about it. Now seeing that Hudson is typically English all over, and in nothing so English as in his Irish views, this was a little too much. He said, "I wrote to Hueffer that I wouldn't write about what I didn't understand and knew nothing about. I never read newspapers." Nevertheless he is in his way, as I think I said before, more anti-Irish by a long way than I ever was in my most savage and unreasoning moments.

December 25.—This is Christmas Day and at eleven o'clock I found Hudson, who was very cheerful. We said nothing about Christmas, although he smiled at the so-called carol-singing of some croaking boys close by. The chatter of choughs would have been musical to them. They certainly didn't make me smile. He had read a story of mine.

H. "I laughed all through it, but there, it falls between two stools, the stools of fantasy and realism."

As this was what I had said of his 'bus story, he added, smiling, "but it's not like my 'bus story." He went round the room looking at his bird pictures, the full sheets out of the *Argentine Ornithology,* which he has had mounted and framed in stained wood of a dreadful colour which he seems to admire. He pointed out the best drawn birds with great complacency and described most vivaciously the song of the oven bird. His letters came in while I was there. One was from the head of the Ornithological Museum in Philadelphia, praising the Argentine bird-book. Hudson was obviously pleased, but outwardly he maintains an attitude of more or less rigid ingratitude. He opened some of the other letters.

H. "This one's a Christmas card. I never send any now."

One lady sent him a Japanese drawing of crows which pleased us both. He remarked that 2*s*. 6*d*. was written on the back of it. "She forgot to rub that out."

This somehow led to a very long tragic story of a doctor he knew, and indeed lived with in the same house at Hammersmith, who married a very dreadful woman who drank and had all the vices. After years he cut adrift, went to America, was divorced in the United States and again married. He went to another country and was very successful but was discovered, pursued, and ruined by the first wife.

H. "The poor fellow drank himself to death by drinking port. ●We all tried to do something, but no matter what we said his answer always was, 'Well, I've nothing to live for!'"

One of this man's daughters was a very beautiful and clever child who died of meningitis, much to Hudson's grief. He had great love for beautiful little girls, but this particular child was a tragedy of sorrowful passion to him. He said she was so strangely brilliant and even, as he put it, "wildly promising." I suppose the

poor little thing was a kind of Marjorie Fleming, the
most wonderful child we know anything about. Hudson
told the story very simply, but even as he spoke it was a
tragic novel he unfolded, for he sees his people so well
and remembers with utter clearness their salient points.
He spoke of one of the doctor's relatives, and as he spoke
I seemed to see a bright, beautiful woman die down into
a coarsened, gross, unmoral creature. Another in the
long story was a young girl who became, as it were,
atrophied, "sublimated" into nothing but an enthusiastic,
sexless creature, and under one's eyes the poor drinking
doctor, once so brilliant, so successful and happy, changed
gradually into a shiftless, hopeless, loveless, alcoholic
wreck.

On this particular afternoon I kept on thinking, while I
was out of the conversation and he was talking more
particularly to N., that the last old man of eighty and over
that I had sat with was dear old William Rossetti. How
strange a difference was this! Here was Hudson, save
for the crack in the pitcher, his heart trouble, as sound a
piece of humanity as one could wish to see, keen on enjoyment of all that remains to him, brimming over with
life, proclaiming that a million years would not be too
much, eager, ardent, full of knowledge and readiness to
discuss all things on earth, and there was poor old
Rossetti, stretched out in a long chair, with a skull-cap
over his white locks, and his delicate, beautiful face worn
out by life, saying to me, "Ah, Roberts, it's time I went.
A man can live too long." Never could I imagine Hudson saying that. Why, the only sign of illness that he
has, beyond his occasional irritability, is at times a little
morbid pink flush on his cheeks. And he is always as

busy as a bird or a bee in a flower-garden, talking steadily and so easily, moving from life to art, from birds to men, from wild young dancing dervishes of children to quaint and quiet old women, interested in everything that earth can show except politics and what he terms with such resolute confidence and contempt, "academic science." Such a robust contempt in him is not really a sign of old age, but a common characteristic of many observing naturalists when they contemplate those dull biological birds upon their perches in museums who call themselves professors. After all it is the same kind of thing one sees in the clinician, who is impatient of physiologist and pathologist. Naturalist and physician know alike that they must go to work at once with some instinctive certainty or fail. So they are apt to resent the tendency of those who by new knowledge or new doubts make them hesitate. Hudson likes to work with certainty.

One sign of his oncoming failure is a new slight incapacity to see as he did, and that's why he seems so glad of company. To be his companion once more as I've been these last few months brought back to me much of the old days and nights we used to have in London at Tower House or away in the country, by the sea or on the moorlands, or some wild country such as that at the back of Cookham-on-Thames, where I myself at last found him a grasshopper warbler. When I think of those times I remember, "They told me, Heraclitus, they told me you were dead." Yes, in those days we not only tired the sun with talking, but wore out half a moon as well till midnight came. I remember how often he proposed a problem and I set up an hypothesis which he "knocked endways" with a fact, and more than once we've worked for hours until between us we got a theory which no longer seemed like a glass house at the mercy of any stray stone. Nowadays I notice I'm not allowed to hypothesise so much. When I remarked this very morning that for some children their day was, as it were, life to them, and that night when it came was a kind of death, he denied it utterly for all children and immediately began to say that I must not substitute a difficult explanation for an easy one. That was good enough, it's a sound rule, but I might have retorted that not he nor I nor anyone should in haste adopt an easy explanation which was no explanation at all. I said, "Right, old chap, don't worry, but that doesn't get rid of direct observation nor of my own childish memories." Hudson settled me with a broadside. "I just don't remember anything of the sort myself," said he. When that kind of thing happens nowadays one has to let it go, and soon he's away on another tack and all's well.

I know well how slight and trivial some of these talks sound, and yet "sands make the mountain" and out of many little things life is mostly built, and in them character shows and sometimes shines as brightly as in its few great moments. Rarely, very rarely, did I leave Hudson without feeling that his most trifling word was pleasing to remember. Out of them all, though much be forgotten, there comes his "landscape," of meadows as well as of "antres vast and deserts idle," when he sat sole upon the shores of old romance.

CHAPTER XV

December (? 27).—I didn't go to see Hudson this morning, but I went in later and found that he had been rather unwell. He began on the dislike often shown by people who are well for those who are not.

H. "I think it's a natural feeling, it's an instinct. It has something to do with the feeling that cattle have towards those who are sick, they're a danger to the herd, a weakness. But of course all this dislike of the ill tends to be overcome when you're in a city."

He seemed to regret this, very curiously, and went on to talk at large and rather contemptuously of what he called super-humanitarians.

H. "Why, I know a lot of people who would feel just as if a knife went through them if they saw a boy pulling a fly's legs off."

R. "Isn't that natural?"

H. "No, it's absurd."

R. "Why, I'd like to have the boy whipped, and whipped hard, if I saw him doing it."

H. "Such a feeling is ridiculous and morbid. But as to hating the ill, I had a friend in the Argentine, a strong man of thirty who was a Captain in the National Guard to which I belonged as a boy of eighteen, who once said to me suddenly, 'I wish you were dead.' I was very much upset and asked why he said such a dreadful thing, and he answered, 'You're being ill worries me.' He liked me very well and was always coming to me for information about birds. He wasn't a super-humanitarian and I could see that in some ways he was quite right."

When we went away that afternoon N. said to me, "It's curious the way he spoke of flies and such things, but I knew he was like that or he could never have lived to his age." We went in again in the evening and found Hudson garrulous, very garrulous indeed. He turned his mind towards so-called psychic things and talked about hypnotism, clairvoyance, telepathy, and the "physical phenomena" of séances. He believes that many queer things really happen but, after saying so, added, "Only fools would put down such things to spirits. As to hypnotism, I can't be hypnotised even when I try to be, nor can I hypnotise myself. I knew a little girl who could hypnotise anybody. I saw her hypnotise other people, but for some reason nothing would induce her to try it on me. As to telepathy, why, of course I believe in it."

He told us a long story of two telepathic brothers whom he saw practising a game of so-called telepathy on the beach at Bridlington. I suggested that it was only the Zancig business over again, but he was quite certain that it was not after having a long talk with them. N. interrogated him as to his attitude about bird-catchers, for in one of his books, I forget which at the moment, he spoke about sitting down with some of them and talking about their business.

N. "How *could* you do it?"

H. "Well, wasn't I accustomed all my young life to be with scoundrels and murderers? Why should I show any agitation with bird-catchers?"

He said this quite simply. He went on to talk of the persistence of type in human beings. His wife's folks were Wingraves, and there was another branch of Wingraves who were pickle merchants at Shaftesbury. Hudson saw some of them and found them exactly the same type as his wife's nephews, although no relationship could be traced between the two groups. *À propos* of something or nothing he spoke of those people who tell lies and end in believing them. This was, I remember now, about people who go to séances and gradually convince themselves that they have seen more than they dreamed of at first. He believed in the phantasms of the dead and living and in ghosts, and has a kind of vague notion that ghosts have a life, a short one, and then disappear. I suggested this years ago, just as a fantastic base to stories. I told him about a medical friend of mine and the séances held in Harley Street with a clairvoyant where queer, "impossible" things were said to have happened. Somehow humanitarianism came up again and he chuckled at the

absurdity of people who don't like picking flowers. Now
this is a thing I often feel queerly and I thought he would
have felt it. No, such an idea was quite morbid! He
spoke this evening of Ralph Hodgson, whom he knows
and likes. He showed us a book on fishing by Zane Grey.
Z. G. is a great admirer of his. He said he ought to send
him a book. It seems that more title-pages have been
torn out and sent to him to sign. He groaned over them
sadly. Still his growing popularity pleases him, though
he won't admit that it does. What worries him is having
to send these things back to the enthusiastic inconsiderate
people who pester him.

December 28.—Hudson talked a good deal about his
family this morning, especially of one of his brothers who
had a ranch on the southern frontiers of the Argentine.
This was in a part of the country still liable to incursions
from the wild Indians. One day, when his brother was
luckily absent from home, a party of Indians rode up,
and breaking into the house wrecked it more or less. The
curious thing was that the damage done seemed the result
of some particular objection to paper. Every particle of
it in the place and a tremendous number of letters that the
Indians had got hold of were torn up and scattered to
the winds, so that when the owner of the place came back
it actually looked as if there had been a small snow-storm.
H. "I only once went to stay with him and I rode
there with no more than two horses, and they got pretty
tired too, and one night, a good time after sunset, I heard
galloping and two Indians charged down on me. At least
I thought they meant to knock me over and take the
horses, but I pulled up and got my revolver out, and they,

finding me wide awake, swerved and passed me galloping. One of them as he rode past squealed in the curious, high-pitched voice the Indians always use in talking Spanish, 'Friend, your horses are tired!' They passed me like a whirlwind and very late I got to my brother's. I didn't stay there long, it was far too much exposed to incursions from the south. As a matter of fact I didn't sleep there. My brother and I used to go together to another house not far off and stay the night. There were more men there. A lot of us galloped together. We used to tell stories, sitting and smoking, but there was no one in any way pre-eminent, until one evening a very poorly clad guacho came in. He had only one horse, and as usual begged permission to stay there that night and make his bed. So when his horse was turned loose he brought in his saddle and presently, after answering all the usual questions and asking such as occurred to him, he began to talk and attracted everybody's attention. The man was a strange and really wonderful genius. He talked about everything: the country and its conditions, politics and statesmen, the condition of the poor man, the follies and wickedness of the rich, but all in such a high strain of true, natural eloquence that he kept us on the stretch to hear every word he said. After he poured forth what seemed like untold riches hour after hour he stopped talking and rolled a cigarette, and then one or the other of us asked him some question and set him going again, so that it was almost dawn before we were satisfied and went to sleep. So far as words were concerned he was the greatest genius I ever saw."

December 29.—Hudson showed me and N. his queer,

fantastically queer, hard side to-day. He brought out a manuscript page of contents for one of his new books. In this one paper was called "The Vanishing Curtsey." N. asked if that meant the going out of the custom of curt-seying. He didn't hear what she said and she repeated it. Curiously enough he answered her almost rudely. Perhaps he was annoyed to be reminded that he was now at times a little deaf.

H. "Why, whatever else could it be about?"

As a matter of fact she and I had both fancied it might have some reference to some mystical story, as he had been talking of spooks. However, that was not his hard side. Among his papers was an inconsiderable one he proposed to destroy.

H. "I've cut it out and shan't print it."

R. "Why not? Isn't it good?"

H. "Not particularly. I did a sketch of a man, and to make it interesting I exaggerated his good points and published it in a magazine. And this fellow actually wrote to the editor saying he was the man described and asking who I was!"

N. "Did you tell him?"

H. "No! Certainly not. Why should I? He had no right to do it."

R. "He oughtn't to have done it, of course."

H. "It annoyed me very much."

R. "After all, Hudson, it was only harmless vanity on the fellow's part. I don't see why you shouldn't reprint it."

H. (*pettishly*). "Well, I won't! I'm not going to gratify his vanity. He shouldn't have written."

N. "But, Mr. Hudson, perhaps he only just wanted to get into touch with you again."

H. (*indignantly*). "Yes, that's just it, and I didn't want him to get into touch with me. I've had all I want out of him and he doesn't interest me any more. As I said to you, it's like that with little girls. When they're very small they're interesting, and when they're a little older they are not interesting, and I don't want to know them any more, and they and their mothers won't understand that."

He was much more charming when he came back to migration and the manners and customs of birds in migration. He drew a very pretty picture of the curious evolutions of shearwaters, when coming to England, which he saw on the extreme verge of Cape Cornwall.

R. "Tell me, what about the sparrows hawking for flies? Hartley said he saw the sparrows hawking for flies and had never seen it before."

H. (*shouting*). "Never seen it before! Why, anybody can see them do it! They hawk for crane-flies constantly. Once when I was in London I saw all the sparrows leave the streets and go up to the roofs. They sat on the chimney-pots and on the extreme edge of the parapets, and were constantly flying up and catching daddylonglegs. They had a regular feast of them."

He then talked at large about starlings and the way they know by the withered grass where the wireworms are.

If Hudson's directness of speech, independent of his occasional irritability, is sometimes a little trying, he let us know quite plainly that he did not preserve his kind of directness only for his friends. He told us about his going to a shop in Penzance to buy paper, and on his rejecting it and asking for a rather better quality without flaws in it, the woman attendant banged it down on the counter before him and said with asperity, "See for yourself."

H. "So I looked at her and said, 'No, I won't take it at all now. I will go to your other shop and see if I can find someone who is not in a temper.'"

He talked after this about some physiological points and especially about deep breathing and its true value, since a shallow breather in good air has fouler air in his lungs than if he breathed properly in bad air. Then I told him of my conversation with Martin Flack the physiologist, and presently asked him if he knew anything about the mechanism of breathing. I found he was like most other people who think that breathing in and breathing out is a simple matter requiring no explanation. So I told him briefly something about the muscular mechanism of breathing.

H. "Now that's *very* curious! I never thought of it. Oh, by the way, I wrote to Hueffer about that Irish paper he wanted you and me to sign, and I said to him, 'I like your poetry, but I don't know anything of politics.'"

We talked afterwards of several women authors. He had lent me a book by one of them. I said, "You left a letter of hers in the book. You'll find it there."

H. (*as if discussing the contents of the letter*). "Oh, yes, she said——"

R. "Well, of course, I didn't read it, old chap."

H. "There was no reason why you shouldn't."

R. "I shouldn't dream of reading a letter left in a book like that. Nor would N."

N. "Why should I? It might have been left in by accident and I like to be on the safe side."

H. (*much surprised*). "Goodness gracious, there's no reason why anyone shouldn't read a letter in a book. If it were private it wouldn't be there."

R. "It might have been left by accident. Of course if it's pasted in that's another matter. But I wouldn't read one left in loose."

H. "I think that's very absurd. I put letters from the authors in all books given to me which I keep."

But that's surely quite another matter.

December 30.—I took him Arthur Keith's letter, wishing Hudson all the New Years he wished to see.

H. (*gloomily*). "That would be a million."

He proceeded to tell me how he and Stanhope Forbes had talked about noises which are apt to wake one just as one is going off to sleep, for, sounding like pistol shots, they make one jump.

H. "Forbes had a strange idea, which was that this was caused by the snapping, the breaking, of small veins in the brain.

R. "That's a strained and superfluous hypothesis. He seems to know very little of his subject and devilish little of physiology or pathology. He wouldn't be painting long if it were correct."

H. "So I explained it to him and he was much relieved."

R. "And how the deuce did *you* explain it? Did you tell him that they were really the faint noises in the room, such as cracks in the furniture, which to one's somnolent brain sound as loud as pistol-shots?"

H. "Of course not. That's not the explanation."

R. "I think it is. But what's yours?"

H. "Oh, it's not mine, but it's perfectly correct. It was told me by a doctor. He said that the nerves of digestion and the nerves of hearing were very close together, and that digestive disturbances affected the nerves of hearing and caused these noises."

R. "Then like most doctors he was a rotten physiologist and didn't know what he was talking about. In any case what the devil are what he called 'the nerves of digestion'?"

He couldn't say, and being totally ignorant of the mechanism of digestion it was no good trying to explain to him that there were no "nerves of digestion," whatever they might be, anywhere near the auditory centre or auditory mechanism, but he was as obstinate as a pig going to a fair, and proceeded to argue as if pitch and volume were the same, and he couldn't see that a slight external stimulation might have as big an effect as an internal dream stimulation. He seemed rather ill to-night and I didn't contradict him any more than I could help. After arguing about pitch he again tried to prove that Frederick Price was wrong and that a certain pulse-rate suited him better than a lower one.

December 31.—I have a note that we talked about Meredith, about Fred Chapman, Oswald Crawfurd, James Montgomery, who wrote *The Pelican,* for which he has some admiration, and poor Robert Montgomery whom Macaulay slaughtered. He went on to speak of Masefield, for whom he has a certain but not overwhelming admiration.

H. "He's not as good as Chaucer."

R. "Well, that's pretty high praise."

Then he talked again about Edward Thomas, who was killed in the war. He liked him very much. I find that my note says that we talked about Z. and his children, and I repeated what another writer had told me about his house manners. As seamen talk of "a land-saint and sea-devil," and as the Germans say a man is a "haus-teufel und strass-engel," it seems that the same could be said without much exaggeration of Z. After this he came round at last to a publisher who had told him that Meredith got swelled head after he was successful and was henceforth no good as a companion. This was false, for Meredith was brilliant till he died.

R. "I don't suppose you ever heard the story, but it is said that when Meredith asked for an account a publisher said to him, 'Look here, after such a long time the accounts will be awfully complicated and take a lot of trouble to make up. What do you say if I give you a cheque for a couple of hundred and call it square?' Meredith replied, 'No, I'd rather have an account and chance it.' The cheque that was paid after that was, I was told, over £1000."

H. "The publisher was a business man and of course he cheated. All business men cheat! Why, X. charged me four times the real price of the paper for the book which he published on half profits. I proved it to him, but he had no shame. I was very angry and told the manager that they were a firm of swindlers. He and I were not friends after that."

R. "I put the Society of Authors' accountant in about a book of mine and he didn't forgive me for that."

H. "Well, what does it matter? Don't I say all business men are cheats? You expect it of them. But X. was a very nice fellow and I liked him, and what did it matter if he cheated? He was a lover of nature and a good sportsman."

R. "I don't understand your point of view. When I find a man a thief I've done with him."

H. "That's absurd! As I said before, they all cheat. Would you never speak to a business man?"

R. "Oh, very well, have it your own way. I've found most business men honest. From my point of view if a man keeps his agreement with me I don't care a damn how hard it is, but when he starts robbing the poor I've done with him."

H. (*in his highest key*). "Well, I think that's *most* unreasonable!"

I believe his notion was that business men were just an interesting species of animal with queer characteristics. He might have added, "We don't abuse spiders for catching flies."

It was later in the day, I think, that he talked a great deal about James and Robert Montgomery.

R. "What did James Montgomery write?"

H. "You don't mean to say you don't know?"

R. "I know he wrote something, that's all."

H. "Well, you *are* ignorant! Just imagine not knowing that he wrote *The Pelican*."

So he proceeded to tell me all about *The Pelican*. It appears that he had thrust it down Masefield's and Edward Thomas's throats, who agreed, perhaps on *force majeure*, that it was good poetry. For once Hudson developed the theme of it to a rather devastating extent, and I told him that he had wasted time on that barren literary period between Byron and Tennyson. I was rather glad when he got round to Cornish cliffs instead of flat-footed poetry. He spoke about his going to sleep in the sun on the far outer slope of Gurnard's Head. He seemed to think he had a very narrow escape of rolling off. I told him that I had once almost gone to sleep with my head on the rail of a railroad in Western America and had been roused by the vibration of an on-coming train, and Hudson capped that by saying that he had been out on the pampa with a party of gauchos and that they all went to sleep at the edge of an old road with deep ruts in it. For some reason best known to himself Hudson went and slept on the road, and in the middle of the night was nearly run over by a huge bullock cart. Luckily for him the driver had pulled out of the ruts a yard or two before and the wheels missed Hudson by an inch or two as he woke. Of course, as he himself said, it was "a damned silly trick to do," and he never told the gauchos what had happened or they would have said he was an idiot.

H. "Sometimes I lost my whip and they were always wildly contemptuous of me and looked upon me as a perfect greenhorn. I don't think I ever heard of a gaucho losing his whip or knife."

He spoke again of Smollett's *Roderick Random* and *History of an Atom,* and remarked on Smollett's love and knowledge of dirt and smells.

H. "I suppose his doctoring taught him a lot of both."

Those doctors and young students who practise midwifery in some of our London slums could perhaps corroborate that, as I told Hudson. He complained of the slowness with which he worked. He was producing so little.

R. "Well, Meredith once said to me, 'Ah, you're producing. I'm not producing. So long as one can produce one is alive.' "

H. That's true. If one ceases producing one might as well be dead. Look at all this stuff of mine. I can't get on with any of the three or four things I want to do. Yet my brain is active enough."

R. "Among all the men of your age that I've ever known yours is far the most active except, perhaps, Meredith's."

H. (*gloomily*). "What he said is quite true: one might just as well be dead as not producing."

This is the first time I've ever heard him say "one might as well be dead." I remembered Keith's good wishes and the million years answer of Hudson. All this, I remember now, was *à propos* of his proposed preface to *Ralph Herne*. He gave it me to read.

R. "I think it is very good. If you do it properly it will be the most valuable part of the book. But why won't you let me work a little on the script? I'd look over it for you?"

H. "No, I won't have anyone touch anything of mine. It's a kind of falseness."

R. "Why shouldn't we collaborate for once?"

H. "I wouldn't collaborate with anyone. The spirit goes out of a thing. I suppose you'll speak of the Goncourts."

R. "Well, they did some jolly good work. And there were Erckmann and Chatrian, and Besant and Rice."

H. "But Rice did all the inventing and Besant the

labourer's work. I'm sure of that. Besant was an old bourgeois. I left the Authors' Society which he founded because they wouldn't investigate an account for me. They said they'd just done another author's account at the same firm."

R. "I wonder whether that was mine."

Hudson complained about his sleeping and said he was always waking up all night through. However, he looked better and was really much better in spirit than he was last night. I forgot to mention I'd then been trying to explain something to him and he said suddenly, "No, I can't understand or even hear anything you say." He was really very ill. Some time this day he told me that his father's mother was Irish and that her name was Malony.

N. and I went in to see him in the afternoon. Hudson was much better and at times quite cheerfully garrulous. He searched among some prescriptions for one with bromide of potassium in it, and I told him the story of an actress taking ninety grains to soothe herself and as a consequence she sat up all night in floods of tears. As he said he couldn't sleep I gave him ten grains of Pot. brom. to use if he needed it. He then told us of his first arrival in England. He came to Southampton and said to those on board with whom he had got friendly, "I'm not coming with you to London, I shall stay in Southampton."

H. "You see, I wanted to go at once into the country to hear English birds. But there was an American who had attached himself to me all the passage home, and this man said, 'Well, I'll stay with you.' I didn't want him. What I wanted was someone who knew about birds to go into the country with me and tell me what bird sang such a note and so on. However, my American stuck to me like wax. I said, 'I shall hire a carriage and drive out into the country,' and he promptly said, 'All right, I'll come with you.' I wished to goodness he'd leave me alone, but I couldn't say so. So we hired a carriage and had a very stolid English youth as driver. It was a funny drive! I don't know what the poor devil of a boy made of it. On one side I kept digging him in the back and saying, 'What bird is that? I say, what bird sang that note?' and on the other side the American, who was wildly interested in agriculture, kept the stolid one busy with, 'I say, what crop is that?' and so on. Then we came to a very good bit of pasture. 'Now what's that?' asked the American. 'Grass,' said the boy. 'Yes, to be sure, but what grass?' 'Why, the grass what horses eat,' and the American cried out, 'What a pity they didn't eat your head off!' "

At the end of this narration Hudson gave a terrific cackle of laughter. It was what Gissing would have called "Hudsonian gigglement." The next day after the drive with the American he did get out by himself to Netley Wood, but was much troubled because he had no one with any knowledge to tell him the name of any of the birds, not even a fool of a driver.

After speaking of a very inferior article on prehistoric instincts, Hudson went on talking about fear of the dark. It seemed that in the Argentine the gauchos much feared a very big monster with great green teeth, called the *curapita*.

H. "This was a kind of gaucho fear-figment. I think we make up a kind of bugbear for ourselves. At least

I did as a boy. So if I was afraid in the dark I was afraid of a kind of short black half-monkey, half-man. I wonder whether it was what you might call an evolutionary bugbear."

I told him about the Australian "bunyip," and then we went on to have a long discussion about subjective visual hallucinations. I spoke of some of mine, those that come as one goes to sleep, among other hypnopompic phenomena.

H. "I always see tapestry patterns in bright colours." Nothing could make him see that they were purely brain figments. He considered that they were somehow upon the retina. He quoted from Coleridge, "A frightful fiend," and said that the poet had learnt all about fear when a scholar at Christ's Hospital. In the old days they punished boys by putting them in a dark room. It seems to have had in some cases a very serious after effect. I don't know what led us to talk of Campbell's poetry. Hudson ran down the patriotic poems, "Ye Mariners of England" and "The Battle of the Baltic," and praised up a great deal of other stuff of Campbell's.

H. "Snobs nowadays are afraid to say it's good."

I thought and said this was bosh, but with our present great poets and writers of *vers libre* (which by the way Hudson calls *verse librer*) we might praise anything nowadays. He was very fond of "Hohenlinden" and tried for a long time to remember it all. He has a very queer idea of what are good stories, and sometimes praises extraordinarily bad ones, as we found out from what he said about some stories in *Pan*. Then he began to run *The Purple Land* down as not being good, and yet when I instanced the great chapters, "Lock and Key and Sinners Three," "Manuel, also called the Fox," and "The Story of a Piebald Horse," he agreed in his usual queer, offhand way, "Oh yes, they're good, of course, for that kind of thing." Again I found one had to be frightfully careful with him. N. remarked to-day that she never saw me so careful with anyone yet. Of course I didn't want to excite him. I said before we went away, "Shall we come in to-morrow? Are you sure we don't bore you?" He turned upon me as if the very notion that I might not come in was a gross grievance.

"Why, of course, come in. I don't know what I shall do when you're gone. There won't be anyone to speak to."

This was very pleasant to hear and I was glad to think we did fill up his time, for talking seems now more than ever a great and natural freeing function for him. It makes one sad to think he may have and must have long melancholy, silent hours.

January 1.—When I went in this morning Hudson told me that he had taken the ten grains of bromide of potassium which I gave him and had slept well. He began talking once more of migration and a sense of direction in birds. I called the expression "sense" in question, because he calls almost every complex faculty a sense, and he seems to resent any analysis of it into reflexes or tropisms. However, I pointed out to him that I felt sure we under-rate the practice of observation in animals and insects and over-rate our own because we thought only about our own.

H. "I don't quite know what you mean."

R. "Why, surely it's no less observation if an insect

sees and acts than if a long set of cerebral reflexes in our brain intervene between seeing and acting. But the fact is we always think of our own damned cleverness."

H. "Analyse it if you will, but a young bee or a young bird just does so-and-so."

R. "How do you know that anyhow?"

H. "Well, when you see dragon-flies first preening themselves for flight they do it straight off without any doubt whatever."

R. "But they probably couldn't do it without seeing. But perhaps both of us are right, Hudson. If you interpret what you call 'sense' in the sense of enforced behaviour or, as you would say, 'just knowledge,' why, I've no objection to your views."

H. "That's it, it's just knowledge."

It's obvious that he greatly objects to having any old idea analysed into factors he has not thought of.

I went in alone in the early afternoon and found him very gloomy. He had received bad news of his wife, and gave me a telegram saying she was very seriously ill indeed. He was very much afraid that he would have to go to Worthing. He knows he ought to go if she wants him, and yet in one sense he really does not want to go even then. He is simply awfully afraid he might have to stay in Worthing, a place which never suits him and which he thinks would kill him in winter. After turning it over in my own mind and trying to think what I ought to say, I came to the conclusion, although I am greatly attached to Mrs. Hudson, who was always very kind to me, that in no case ought he to go. His life is immensely valuable to us all and I honestly fear that the trouble and worry whether she lived or died

would absolutely kill him. I was greatly moved towards
taking this point of view by the fact that Mrs. Hudson
was now at last more than senile and often very de-
lirious. If he went up it might mean killing himself
for nothing. I therefore said, and said it as casually
as I could, "I don't think you should go, at any rate
not without Dr. Miller's permission." He sat and looked
wretched but did not reply. I wanted to ask whether I
might see Miller myself, but felt I had to think this
over. At any rate N. came in then and the conversation
went on other lines. As he has always given her tickets
for the Zoo during many years, he handed over his
packet of tickets for the year which had just arrived,
and told her to take as many as she liked. She took
seven, which he signed. I said to him: "I hate more
and more to go to the Zoological Gardens. I can't help
feeling it's a prison."

H. "I hate to go myself. I don't go often, and if
I do I won't look at any more animals than those I have
particularly come to see."

R. "I daresay you remember Galsworthy got into
trouble for saying the place was a ghastly jail. Certainly
it seems a dreadful prison when I look at some of the
birds and animals, at the eagles and the wolves and
those accustomed to wide horizons."

Hudson agreed with me very quietly.

January 2.—I had a very curious and gloomy morning
with Hudson, who was very much upset by the telegram
of yesterday. It seemed to me that I really ought to
see Dr. Miller, but I had great difficulty in making up
my mind as to whether I dare ask his permission. How-

ever, as I was determined to see Miller in any case, it seemed to me very dangerous to go without Hudson's knowledge. If he found it out later he might never forgive me, so finally I said, "What do you think? Can't I see Miller and have a talk with him about you?" He was, I think, quite glad, probably taking it that some of the weight would be lifted from him. He doesn't want to decide anything. After this I put the whole thing aside and he became more cheerful, and told me a remarkable story that came out when he was staying with the Bosworth Smiths in Dorchester. It seems that Bosworth Smith had corresponded with Hudson a good deal and heard by accident that he was in Dorchester. As they didn't know his address, Mrs. B. S. went down to the post-office to inquire if they knew where Mr. W. H. Hudson was staying. "Oh yes," said one of the post-office people, "why, he was in here only a moment ago. He might be about just now. I'll go and see." Mrs. B. S. followed him and he pointed out a person looking in a window. Mrs. B. S. went up to him and said, "Are you Mr. W. H. Hudson?" "Yes," replied the man, so she instantly invited him to come and stay for a day or two. He said he would be very pleased to do so. He went to the house, stayed two days, and they all got in a state of the wildest confusion. Poor Bosworth Smith said, "Well, he's not in the least Hudson as I remember him. I only saw him once. And he doesn't seem to be really interested in the things he works in. If I talk of birds and so on he puts them all aside." Of course it turned out in the end that he wasn't *the* Hudson at all. Why the man went and what he made of it no one seemed to know.

Hudson talked a great deal about the series *Highways and Byways,* noting that the different writers who write these books ran their own specialty for all it was worth. Thus Lucas when he went over a county thought of cricket, while another took no interest in cricket but was all for churches and brasses. He expressed a considerable admiration for Algernon Gissing's work. He went back again presently to the subject of other Hudsons, whom he apparently dislikes exceedingly. He would never have anything to do with one if he could help it. He was once asked to dine with William Henry Hudson. He refused because he just wouldn't meet him. I told him the story of Oscar Wilde in the British Museum, which led to his telling me that when he was at the Museum Library he took back nine books in order to get the tickets, and the attendant produced eighteen tickets and asked, "Where are the other nine books?" "I never had another nine books," said Hudson. "Oh yes, you've got eighteen tickets. Aren't these your signatures?" "Yes, they're my signatures." But presently he looked at the subjects and discovered that there was another W. H. Hudson with a signature remarkably like his own, so the imbroglio was cleared up. What led him to talk of pain next I can't quite remember.

H. "Pain? Well, I rather like it."

R. "Oh, do you? And what for?"

H. "It's sensation. I used to get bees and wasps to sting me for the experience."

R. "I've never had toothache myself, but I understand from those who have that one experience is enough."

H. "Yes, I own that I don't want to have toothache

twice. My teeth have always been a miserable trouble to me and I was glad to get rid of them."

If he likes pain he certainly doesn't like discomfort, because when I found him with cystitis and took him to see John Pardoe he wasn't patient. In fact I think his notion of liking pain, if not humbug, is just a little pose of his, and I suggested mildly that in spite of having shot himself in the knee when in Patagonia, he had never known what real pain was since he had rheumatic fever.

I went this afternoon to Dr. Miller and we talked about Hudson's cardiac condition and about Mackenzie and Fred Price. I told Miller that I thought it would be dangerous for him to go to Worthing, and Miller agreed. Of course it will be a difficult thing to manage to persuade him to stay in Penzance. As I left Miller said, "I wish you would leave me your address. I don't know anyone to whom I could send in case of accidents, and of course you know something might happen any minute." I gave it to him and told him I believed I was one of Hudson's executors.

CHAPTER XVI

DURING the remainder of our stay in Penzance I made no more notes of Hudson's talk, though I saw him two or three times a day and it remained as free and copious as ever, save when he became gloomy and thought of his wife. His doctor's decision that he must not be allowed to travel helped him, but even more help was the knowledge that she was then almost incapable of recognising anyone. It was a day or two before we left for town that Hudson said to me, "The poor dear must be nearly a hundred! I knew only a very little time ago that she was so much older than I." As a matter of fact Emily Hudson was probably ninety-four when she died, having retained full command of her faculties till she was over ninety. The report of some person (probably a woman), to which the late Maurice Hewlett incautiously, and later to his deep regret, gave currency, that Mrs. Hudson was "weak-minded," is absolutely untrue. Though never in any sense "strong-minded," she was shrewd, courageous, and capable through all the long and trying years in which I knew her best. Her devotion to her husband was without limit: her belief in him, when few or none but she and I believed in him, deep and with an element of pathos because he was so much beyond her. I know that she resented, not always with discretion, the attraction he had for some who found no charm or response in her. But sometimes I thought that if they had known her they would have seen under her dim and faded aspect qualities of faithfulness and devotion which truly ennobled her. More than once I sat with her apart from Hudson and some women who waved censers before him, and she moaned a little about the days when he was all her own. Yet such is almost inevitably the lot of those who marry men of genius. Though she wholly lacked her brilliance, she sometimes made me think of Carlyle's wife.

Had it not been for the ceaseless and pitiless wind and rain I might have stayed longer on the south coast of Cornwall. Though Hudson had many friends in the town he needed then closer contact than most could give him, for intimacy was a plant that grew but slowly in his garden and took years or even many decades to flower. It was with great regret that we went. As he rose late he did not come to see us off, but I went in to him early and said good-bye. I found him in a curious state of mind, half-irritable and half-anxious, and thought that he avoided looking at me, so that at first I wondered what was wrong. But soon I understood that he did not wish us to go away and that in his heart he feared we should meet no more, but hated to say so, or even to look at me because he might show too much. Indeed, when I shook hands with him he sat at his table and did not lift his eyes as I left the room. Again the feeling came to me that I might see him no more, even though I had asked his doctor to telegraph to me if Hudson felt ill. I cannot imagine him sending for anyone: it was impossible for him to make an appeal. He always said, and once wrote to me, that he wished to die alone, even as a sick guanaco leaves the herd and seeks such an ancient Golgotha as he described in *Idle Days in Patagonia*. And yet if any came he was glad and hid his gladness.

I took back to London with me a photograph of him which had been done in Penzance. There is no great satisfactory portrait of him, though Rothenstein's sketch in the National Portrait Gallery at least gives his great intellectual curiosity. A sketch in oil was once done by another artist. Though it was well painted the artist knew it was a failure and Hudson hid it away. So little did it resemble him that Wynnard Hooper and Ernest Bell, his executors, did not recognise it and let it go at the sale of Hudson's things. I was at the time too ill to tell them for whom it stood. I may here say that Hudson did not after all make me an executor, owing to my ill-health. The pencil sketches by McCormick are vivid and life-like. It may interest some to know that they were his first essays towards the big drawings for a little justly forgotten book of mine, *The Earth-Mother*. I now possess these large original sketches in wash and charcoal, and Hudson's head from one of them may be reproduced in this book. I cannot cease to regret that I never photographed him myself, and I know only one snapshot of him, with a raven on his hand, which is truly characteristic. Although I cannot, therefore, put in here anything satisfactory done in paint or pencil or by the camera I am moved to make use of a little sketch in words which seems to me not without value.

In the writing of men's lives, though the author may be the architect, it frequently happens that he himself supplies little or even no material. He is, therefore, a gatherer, and in certain cases achieves more living results than those accomplished by men who were friends of the people they depicted. Such were the lives written by Walton, which still remain models for others to follow. In this sketch, or portrait, of Hudson it was my set purpose to avoid all help, so that the failure, however great, should be my own. It is true that help has been offered me, help for which I should have been grateful if my intent had been other than it was. I deemed it better, however, if the book failed, not to mingle impressions and, it may be, confuse those who looked for the plainest drawing. It was for this reason that I rejected letters and other documents offered to me and even avoided reading much already written about Hudson. Yet such a scheme seems a counsel of perfection, and one sketch of him, which was written by my stepdaughter and is curiously unlike any other, has come so greatly to seem my own, since it corroborates and strengthens many of my impressions and inferences, that

I cannot refrain from giving part of it here. The writer
knew Hudson well during the last nine or ten years of
his life and was with me when we spent that Christmas
holiday in Penzance. I make no claim for her literary
merit, since the sketch was made without any thought
of publication. It was, in fact, written at my request,
since I desired to see how Hudson appeared to friendly
eyes which were not a man's, and which, though friendly,
were acute to observe, and not so prejudiced in his favour
as to deny such flaws as even the greatest may possess.
Whether my request was justified or not I leave to the
decision of those able to judge without saying more than
that Hudson was still alive when the following pages
were written:

"On the surface Hudson and his books are not a bit
like each other. They are sane, spacious, and mellow.
He is unreasonable, petulant, and 'contradictious,' erratic
and often unaccountable. He is himself so independent,
so indifferent to what anyone thinks of him or his work,
that he does not realise that his opinion can hurt anyone.
He has said several times, 'What does it matter what
I think or whether I like it or not? If you please yourself, that's all that matters,' and I believe he meant it.
He would feel deeply for one in any real sorrow, but
has no patience with undue sensitiveness. So he says
things that may hurt people's feelings, but does not know
it, because such things would never hurt his. He's far
too sane and also too arrogant. Anyone could easily
bore or irritate him or make him angry, for he certainly
doesn't suffer fools gladly and would fire quickly at an
insult, but no one can easily wound him. One can't get

at him for one thing. His inmost heart belongs to Nature only, and nothing any human being can say can really hurt it. It's absurd for him ever to have married. Nature is his real and lasting love and any woman a mere incident. It would not be safe to care for him to the extent of being unhappy if he dropped one, for although he has the most amazing faculty for getting something out of everyone, whether prince or peasant, who isn't a born fool, the moment they ceased to please or interest him I believe he would drop them without remorse and be surprised if anyone reproached him. Why should they care what he did? They should be sufficient to themselves as he is. It would be dangerous to let him see he possessed the power to wound, for he has enough of the woman in him to make him want to do it instantly, without the woman's softness which generally prevents her doing it after all. No one knows him really and I believe he is proud of it. It pleases him to think how well he's kept his secret. He is his own 'garden enclosed and fountain sealed up.'

"I am sure he is intensely loyal where his friendship is kept, would rejoice at a friend's good fortune, give help if it were needed as a matter of course, without expecting gratitude or even thinking again of what he had done, and grieve deeply and lastingly if his friend died. Grieve, that is, as far as his instinct of self-protection allows him to agitate himself. But then his friendship must be *kept*, it won't stay just because he has once given it.

"His reading is enormous and his interest in many subjects intense, and he likes to hear about them except when he thinks he knows it all already, when he's as obstinate as can be. When he was younger and stronger he must have been a very delightful companion, and so he often is now, but his impatience makes prolonged intercourse with him sometimes trying to anyone who is nervous.

"Yet these faults, which might loom large in a smaller man, are mere flaws in Hudson and, indeed, since they arise from his intense independence, add savour to and are themselves part of that strange bitter-sweet quality which makes him unique. Behind it all one feels his essential bigness, his genius and humour, and, although he conceals it with feminine perversity, his real deep kindness. And for all his irritability over trifles, he is calmly reasonable over larger things which would anger most men. I have heard him speak of injuries done him with tolerant indifference. Indeed, I believe it is safer to do him an injury than a benefit. I have never known him so ill to get on with, so hard to please, as once when M. R. had done him a service at the cost of much trouble to himself. Hudson raised objections that no one could have foreseen and cavilled and grumbled till I dreaded the subject being mentioned. Yet in the end he showed his gratitude in a way few men would have done, and did it as a matter of course, getting annoyed when any protest was made. It is another peculiarity of his that all his generosities of word and deed are done as a matter of course. When he praises some of M. R.'s work it is without stint, but with no sign of enthusiasm: he states simply that it's 'the best book of its kind in English,' and even shows irritation that it should be necessary to mention such an obvious fact.

"He often shows a boy's pleasure in teasing, and some-

times when he's being very unreasonable and knows it
he has a humorous twinkle that's delightful. Now and
again he looks at one with an expression of affection
that would make amends for many snubs. Not that
there are many to make amends for, so far as I'm concerned: he's always been delightful to me. I've often
wondered why he obviously likes to see me, for he doesn't
talk to me a great deal, nor always seem interested in
what I say, yet he is cross and injured if I don't come.
But whatever the reason for his friendship I treasure it;
for even a small share in Hudson's affection is something
of which to be proud."

Emily Hudson died not so very long after we left
Penzance. Hudson was totally unable to go to the
funeral. She was buried in the Broadwater Cemetery
at Worthing in ground that Hudson chose. He wrote
to an old friend, "I shall meet her in that hollow hole."
It was not the place he really desired for her or for
himself, but the plot he wished for he could not obtain.
He had the grave thickly planted with daisies. He
wished it to be "a continuous white sheet of flowers."
In that cemetery Richard Jefferies lies buried. I think
it pleased Hudson, so far as anything connected with
abhorred death could please him, that a brother naturalist should lie at peace in the same sad place. He had
an affection for Jefferies and yet could not quite understand how it came about that the writer of *The Story
of My Heart* had given himself away with both hands.
For Hudson forever wished to keep his own counsel and
his own secret.

I cannot say to what extent I have elucidated the

mystery, tangle, and pattern of his nature. It may be
that some of the mystery is removed though the tangle
remains. It will help to clear it up if it is remembered
that Hudson knew well he was difficult to understand.
Perhaps the only piece of common vanity in him centred
about this. He was not going to let people comprehend
him. I have seen a letter in which he actually said
that no one could or should. But this was written in
1895 and he changed greatly in the last twenty years
of his life. Yet even to the end he obscured and hid
his motives, his gratitude, his affections, so that some
might look on him as an impersonal creature, and I was
often puzzled to divine the reasons on which he acted.
In some this would have been a pose. In him it was
true nature: his instincts led him into such secretiveness
as leads a bird to build her nest in places where none
shall find it. It was, in fact, impossible for him to show
his heart: he simply could not do it, for his reticence
was so immense that he made false trails to avoid being
known. The actions of birds who pretend injury to
mislead those who might take their eggs, or hurt their
young, had a great and I believe, a special attraction
and delight for him. They, some of his beloved birds,
had here an instinct which was also his own. If he
was a brother to the eagle of the skies he was also akin
to the wild lapwings of the moor.

He did not come back from Penzance till late in the
spring of 1921. In spite of the trouble he had been
through, his physical condition, barring his usual cardiac
worry, was amazing. He could smoke an occasional
cigar, which he thoroughly enjoyed, and for a man of
eighty his appetite was still good, though he chose the

simplest food and rarely took anything with more alcohol in it than a glass of lager beer. He had gloomy fits now and again, but having thrown himself into his book, *A Hind in Richmond Park,* he made that an escape from solitary self-communion. He hated and feared anything like morbid introspection, for his mind was essentially objective: the senses came first and afterwards the intellect might play with the results. It was this which kept him vivid and alive: he drew directly from the earth, and, if that was impossible, from his memories of it. I saw him at Tower House and once more he spoke of migration and the subjects of the book, though he mentioned his wife and told me how he had got on after we left him. I made no notes but was less anxious about him than I had been. During the next month I was on Exmoor, at his "beloved Simonsbath," of which he so regretted having made no notes. On my return our meetings at the Rotunda were resumed: he did not care to ask anyone to his house as he was now living in his big bedroom and had no use for the gloomy drawing-room. So as he loved to talk during lunch, and always insisted on my bringing my stepdaughter with me, we made Whiteley's our regular rendezvous. We met there at least once a week. It was not until the autumn that I wrote down any of his talk. But after his death N. made the following note, which seems to me vivid enough to reproduce:

"I shall miss the lunches with Hudson at Whiteley's dreadfully. It is difficult to believe that we shall never again see that tall figure rising to meet us or towering towards us through the people if we arrived first. I can

see him so plainly, beaming benignantly down at me as
he shook hands, or flapping along like a great eagle in
the old-fashioned tail-coat he always wore, which to my
fancy resembled in shape a bird's closed wings and tail.
He always wanted us both, having apparently no use
for one without the other on these occasions. If M. R.
went without me he would demand indignantly, 'Where's
N.?' or if M. R. was ill, or I ran up first to see if Hudson
was there, it was 'Where's Roberts?' in high-pitched
accusing tones, as if he suspected me of locking him up
somewhere. I never liked to get there first, for if we
didn't take a table he wanted to know why we hadn't,
and if we did it was sure to be the wrong one. When
we settled he would pass round the menu, abuse M. R.
for not eating more, argue with me for choosing the
wrong dishes, 'You can't possibly like that,' and wonder
how I could drink 'brute water' with my food. Then
the talk began: animated discussions and arguments between them about everything under heaven. Sometimes
he was amusing and altogether charming, often 'cussed'
and contrary, when he teased M. R. and contradicted
him till I grew nervous, knowing he would never stand
so much from anyone else. Sometimes he was deliberately absurd and delightful. Once M. R. said that women
thought or did so-and-so, I forget what, and Hudson
maintained that no woman on earth would feel like that.
I happened to feel that way myself, so I said, 'Yes, some
of them do.' He replied very gravely and positively,
'Well, *I* think they don't,' and then twinkled delightfully.
But whether he was amiable or exasperating he was
always stimulating because he was so much alive. So
many people are half dead, either because life has killed

them till they are like Hardy's *Dead Man Walking*, or
they have deliberately slain that part of themselves that
can't be satisfied to save ceaseless pain, or because they
never were alive anyhow. But Hudson was alive all
over. His troubles had no power to crush him. Though
he was so full of vitality he did not obtain it by sucking
the life-blood of others, as some do: nor ever wanted
to impose himself on them. M. R. urged me to repeat
some poem once, and when I would not said to Hudson,
'You tell her to.' He answered promptly, 'No, I won't.
Why should she if she doesn't want to? Let everybody
do just as they like.' He was always eager to do something, and couldn't be idle if he thought there was anything to see. Once all the tables were full, so we went
out on to the leads to wait, and Hudson wandered to
a little tower and began to go up the perpendicular iron
ladder that led to its roof, to find out if there was anything interesting to be seen up there. If he hadn't found
it very dirty he would have urged me to come up to
the top with him, which I wanted to do, but was afraid
it would be bad for him.

"He had his favourite waitresses there who knew him
well, and only laughed when he scolded them because
his favourite suet puddings were not on the menu. But
though he had gusts of impatience or would laugh and
joke like a boy, his manner to me had that beautiful
courtesy which is the gift of age—though I doubt if
the present generation will attain it if they live till a
hundred. Unless he or M. R. had an engagement we
sat there talking till half-past three, when the band began
for tea. At the first sound he would spring up as though
he had been stung, complaining bitterly that he should

be disturbed so soon. The afternoon generally ended by his asking me if I would like some chocolates. As a rule I did like, though when it happened many times in succession I would refuse, and often be overborne."

At one of these meetings about this time N. made a few notes which I shall use. He had been walking with his old and dear friend Mrs. Hubbard either in Leicestershire or Lincolnshire, and they passed a team of plough-horses.

"Isn't it odd that one of those horses is sure to be called Gilbert?" asked his companion.

"Gilbert! Gilbert! Country horses aren't called Gilbert," said Hudson.

"They *are*," she replied: "fancy you of all men not knowing that. If you go into any farm and ask the names of the horses one of them will be Gilbert."

"Nonsense," said Hudson. "I've been in lots and they're called Dobbin and things like that."

He said to us that he could not persuade her she was wrong, and went away chuckling and wondering where she had picked up such an absurd notion. Long afterwards he came across an old book which spoke of a St. Gilbert who had been a great authority on horses and their welfare, and even gave instructions about cutting their tails. It seemed that Mrs. Hubbard might have been right after all, and that horses were even now sometimes called after the saint who cared for them.

From St. Gilbert he came to St. Dominic, and told us the story of the saint's vision, or dream, in which he went to heaven and was shown two men by whom the world would be regenerated. One was himself and the other some unknown monk. When he preached the next day he told his hearers, and in the congregation saw the unknown man who became afterwards St. Francis of Assisi. From this Hudson came to discourse on religious orders and societies generally, of which he had the lowest opinion. He called them gangs of thieves. His opinion was no doubt influenced by early experience. The Catholic priests and orders in some parts of South America have a very low reputation, and have at times given the Holy See something more to think about than Modernism. It was this day that Hudson said his birthday was St. Dominic's Day. He refused to give the date, which, however, is August 4th. I spoke about some pope.

"They don't interest me. Their lives are dull if they weren't unspeakable blackguards like the Borgias."

N. amazed him by defending Cæsar Borgia, I think on the ground that he was in a difficult political situation. But Hudson waved her aside and presently continued on dogma:

"The Catholics explain all the objections to their creed as based on 'invincible ignorance.' I know one lady who goes to confession and says, 'I'm sorry, but I don't believe in the dogmas, I don't believe in heaven or hell or transubstantiation, or anything.' And the priest says, 'Well, that's your invincible ignorance,' and, I suppose, gives her absolution. That's the way they get out of everything."

How just this is I leave others to determine, but I spoke of certain horrible material beliefs as to transubstantiation expressed to me by a fervent Anglo-Catholic. Hudson was at once amazed, amused, and disgusted.

Presently he spoke of tree-worship and his tale "The Old Thorn," and came by that road to forestry and Evelyn's *Sylva*.

H. "I can't stand Evelyn. He's a dull fellow with no æsthetic sense and no style."

R. "There are fine things in his *Diary*. Do you remember his pathetic sketch of his little dead son Richard?"

H. "I haven't read the book. After *Sylva* I didn't want to look at anything else."

R. "I've not read that. Its value is that it's the first English book on Forestry."

H. "Yes, and all utilitarian! He looks at trees and thinks of nothing but the use that can be made of them! Why, he speaks of a field of broom. You know what broom is, its scent and colour, you'd think anyone would feel it in their bones. What does Evelyn do? He looks at it and says the proper thing to do is to cut it and chop it up small and feed donkeys with it!"

We chuckled at his indignation with poor Evelyn, and he joined in with a roar of laughter.

The remaining notes I have of his talk were not written till the late autumn. We went to the Rotunda to have lunch with him on the 31st October. He had been rather "grumpy" the week before, but now he was more cheerful. But even so he preluded the talk with a general sketch of his discontent with the universe because his housekeeper at No. 40 was not well.

He was just then getting ready to go to Penzance. But how could he go if his housekeeper was ill? He had no one else to trust. Last year the man to whom he let his own flat at Tower House for the winter had levanted without paying rent. Perhaps the next one would empty the house! And now his housekeeper was ill!

"She *will* faint," he remarked with sorrowful bitterness, as if fainting were a vice. He looked up with surprise to hear laughter.

He had prescribed aspirin for his housekeeper, on what grounds could not be discovered, and when I suggested that this drug might not be indicated, he showed some wonder. Others, he said quite seriously, had proposed whisky. That was bad: he was sure of it. He now wished to take her to Harley Street and scouted my suggestion of a hospital. Hospitals were scoundrelly institutions which experimented on the poor. I suggested that the medical profession sometimes experimented on the rich at five guineas an experiment, whereas they did it on the poor for nothing, but generally I entered a plea for the wretched doctors. We expected too much of them. He would not hear of it. Now that John Pardoe had retired and James Mackenzie had gone to Scotland, he was inclined to believe that such knowledge of medicine as existed was to be found in Frederick Price, to whom I had sent him. But these women were impossible! They would not go to doctors till it was too late. So after all he relented to the profession. No, he owned men had more sense, but——

"Women are women," said Hudson reflectively. When they ceased to be they ceased to interest him, or rather when they ceased to interest him they were nothing, not even feminine. The whole world existed as a matter of interest and curiosity: little girls, for instance. He spoke of them particularly this day. They had a period of real existence as small wild animals, nurslings of nature, and then they became tamed, domesticated, caged, and repeated what they had been taught. He told us that once there were two in whom he took especial delight. When they were eight their mother asked why he wrote nothing more about them. He explained simply that they did not now interest him, and was surprised to find she seemed angry. They would not interest him again till they developed characters of their own, good or bad. Even a vicious or a bitter woman was interesting. He went on to sketch the life-history of one he knew. He etched it in acid and yet with humour. She was, he said, a perfectly preposterous person capable of satire but incapable of seeing she provoked ridicule.

"But I like to talk to her sometimes. She interests me. Any character does."

He had a perfect gallery, a Hudsonian museum, of human oddities and remarkable specimens. As a naturalist among the sports and varieties of *Homo sapiens* he was at his best purely intellectually. He saw them without the powerful flood of emotion on which he moved when alone with nature, and viewing them in this dry light, dissected them on the table or caged them to observe their habits and customs. He could dislike his own species: of animals or birds or even insects with their many horrible methods of life I never knew him speak other than with understanding, with the single exception of the female in certain species of spiders. He could observe the "spider" woman with curiosity and describe her with humour, though not always without alarm. I met one lady in a house in Kensington who declared her intention to me of going down to Cornwall

in the winter "to take care of him." He fired up wrathfully when I told him of this.

"Is she, indeed? I shall soon let her know she isn't.
I should never get away from her! That's the trouble
in a little place like Penzance. There are half a dozen
of them saying that!"

I said what I thought of poor Penzance, even if it
had a decent library and many jolly people in it, and
asked why he didn't go to the Isle of Wight. He waved
the Wight aside and proceeded to analyse this would-be
visitor till she had no feather to fly with and her very
anatomy was visible. He put the worm on the hook
not "as if he loved it," and finally, so to speak, assembled the poor lady's pieces, and dismissed her with
a caution touched with pity. Of another he said: "She
must hang on someone. But all women must."

And here I may put down a curious example of the
powerful attraction Hudson had for some women. It
seems a certain lady, who farmed her own land, was
for years greatly attached to him. To what extent this
affection was returned I cannot say, but after not having
seen her for a year or two he received a letter asking
his permission to marry. If the passions, affections, and
prejudices of human beings were an open scroll, instead
of being like an ancient palimpsest, or the script of the
Syriac Gospels when first discovered, it would be easy
to determine why Hudson was much disturbed at this
and was at first inclined to request her to remain single.
After profound consideration he came to the conclusion
that the gracious thing to do was to accede to her request. He even went further, and on a later occasion

invited her and her husband to take luncheon with him.
This they did and the incident was closed.

In spite of his satiric mood he looked that day particularly charming and notably more like the last good
photograph taken of him in Penzance, in which he has
a grave and statesmanlike air, than those taken of him
by Marie Léon, where he is the birdman, a kindly, eager
eagle with the wisdom of the bird of Athena. Yet on
the whole they are the best of him in existence.

Continuing the subject of Penzance and the kind but
often troublesome habit some people had of "dropping
in," he observed sadly that one man bored him to death
with politics.

"I don't understand politics."

"And, therefore, are a rabid Conservative," I said
slyly.

He looked up with a twinkle in his eye and then re-
lapsed into seriousness again.

"Well, I want things as they are because they may be
worse. And progress means slaughtering birds and cutting down woods to build beastly rabbit-hutches for
people to breed boys to rob nests. If landlords were only
more decent to poor people and would preserve little birds
rather than big ones! Game-preservers indeed! Why
not man-preservers? And their keepers! Slayers! And
egg-collectors!"

He could have boiled some of these gentry in boiling
oil. He regarded their pretence of scientific aims with
bitter and well-deserved scorn. They bribed the Bird
Society's very watchers. As for politicians—well, there
was Lord Grey, who loved birds, and Sir Frederick Ban-

bury, who, working on Hudson's own initiative, had stopped the Cornish lads from catching birds with baited hooks. It was a strange team, Grey and Banbury, but love of birds made odd bedfellows, said Hudson. As for the opponents of the Plumage Bill——

From birds to bird-pictures and to water-colours and art brought us somehow round to Rothenstein, who was a friend of his. There never was such a conversational bird as Hudson. As he hopped one often had to fly to keep up with him. One man he met at this artist's made him speak of the war and the lives it had brought down into ruin worse than death.

"I don't mean the dead or even the bereaved, but those sent crazy."

He told us a long story of a man who laughed madly and tried to make him laugh too but failed.

"Then for some reason best known to himself he stroked my boots!" said Hudson pensively.

After talk of the wilderness he loved in some of his friends I spoke of Cunninghame Graham, always a favourite of his. I had been to a *matinée* and had seen my old friend Graham there. I first met him with H. H. Champion and Hudson thirty years ago when we breakfasted together at the Café Royal. Hudson was anxious to know all about him. I said he had lost some of his old brilliant colour.

"He's quite white but still for ever the old C. G."

"Good old Graham! How he must hate time! As I do! But hadn't he his old look? You know it."

"He's still the hidalgo," said I. "I wrote of him once that he was 'our only hidalgo'!"

He turned to N.

"It's not only women who hate time. It's so natural to cling to life and feel immortal."

I said I had never done so.

"Nor I," said N. "I don't see why anyone should."

"Then you're both exceptions," he cried hastily. Just as clergymen hate to hear of an intelligent atheist, he disliked hearing of anyone who did not cling madly to life. It was then I told him of a young girl's death. It shocked him, one could see that.

"So young, so young!"

As his hand lay on the table I saw his radial artery with the typical queer pulsation of auricular fibrillation, and spoke about the new treatment of this cardiac state with quinidine sulphate. I suggested he should ask Price whether it would or could do anything for him, although I knew it was mostly of use in young cardiac cases. He made me write down the name of the drug and then went on lamenting about his housekeeper, and about heart-trouble, asking more questions, as he always did about such things. It always encouraged him to hear of faulty diagnosis as regards hearts, and any case where a prognosis of early disaster turned out wrong made him chuckle. He wanted to know about the athletic hypertrophied heart, which Mackenzie disbelieves in, and chortled about a man forbidden to ride a bicycle, who got so miserable about it that he advised him to try it and go easy.

"And he quite recovered," said Hudson triumphantly.

"Well, he might have died," said I.

"He didn't," retorted Hudson: "doctors are often fools."

"Not so often as patients," I returned, but consoled

him by saying that his advice would probably have coincided absolutely with Sir James Mackenzie's in many such cases.

Presently he hopped on to the publishing twig and spoke of Jonathan Cape and Dent.

"Do you know a man called Holmes?" he asked suddenly.

"Yes, if you mean the poet and education man," said I. "We met him and his wife and daughter this summer at Hawnby in Yorkshire."

It appears E. G. Holmes was keen on a book of mine and wanted Dent's to use it in *Everyman*. This book was a particular favourite of Hudson's and his appreciation of it has made up for the many times he damned other books of mine "without mitigation or remorse of voice." But he had a hand in this one, since he urged me to write it on my return from America and therefore regarded it with special favour. As I have made no notes of his bitter criticisms I refrain from putting down his extravagant praise, which overbalanced his unfavourable judgments on other work. Travel and adventure of all kinds always appeal to him if in them he finds anything vivid enough for him to build such pictures for himself as seem to add to his Zoological Garden of the species and varieties of man. So he read eagerly Doughty's *Arabian Deserta,* and *Eothen,* and *Cross and Crescent.*

Hudson continued talking of books and spoke of an old lady named Brown. She had been in post-offices all over Africa from Pondoland to Rhodesia, and wrote to Hudson about his paper on cats in the *Strand* and elsewhere, sending him anecdotes about monkeys. This was when she came to England.

"They were good, but I'd finished with cats and wasn't on monkeys," said Hudson, pettishly. "However I saw her stuff was quite fair and asked what else she'd written. Oh, book after book and none published! What were they? She sent me a mass of stuff about cats and dogs and birds and natives: all very good. So I went to see her and said, 'Why do you want to give this stuff to me? You are throwing away a mass of valuable material. Why don't you keep it and put it in a book?' She replied, 'Well, I've written a lot of books and can't get them published.' 'What kind of book?' I asked. 'I've written an account of my official life.' 'We don't want that. What else?' 'And I've written my impressions of London, my first visit after being all over the world.' 'We don't want that. We've had thousands of first impressions of London, and there's an army of practiced journalists giving us impressions every day. What else?' 'A novel—two or three of them.' 'We don't want your novels,' I said sternly. 'You've obviously done everything but what you can do! Write your personal life in all these outlying parts of Africa and put in all the stories you've sent me about Zulus and every kind of black beggar you know, and serpents and insects and birds and pets, a book like the *Story of an African Farm.*' So she said she was going back home, that is, to Africa, and would write the book if she spent the rest of her life doing it. She has a farm left her by her father, so she can give herself to the work. It will be a good book and I shall tell Dent to ask for it."

His stern, authoritative way with this ambitious lady made us chuckle, though I have little doubt his actual talk was more gentle than the brief impression he gave of it. I asked him if he had heard the rumour that the *Story of an African Farm* was mostly written by O. S.'s father and only finished by her. He was much interested and remarked, "I can believe that. The last third is different and not good. No, the end is good!"

No doubt the phrase "the chickens knew better" got hold of him.

We talked of his last book, *A Traveller in Little Things*, and though I could not say that most of it was up to the level of his best work I remarked:

"I think the one I liked best was that about the two old women in the churchyard. But all the sketches of little girls are good."

N. then spoke of a little girl who had run after her in Hampstead and kissed her hand with a look of ineffable adoration. It had quite touched her, but Hudson was anything but sympathetic. Fond as he was of her he didn't mind doing a little trampling. He never did dislike an odd piece of destruction now and again. At times it seemed almost cruel, but he rarely held in what was in his mind. He grunted:

"That's nothing. Little girls often do it in Kensington Gardens. Women have told me of it, and besides I've seen it myself."

So N. collapsed.

"Yes, I've often known them fall in love with a lady's face and say 'Kiss me,' or 'I want to kiss you.'"

A little later I growled again about his going to Penzance. I knew he wanted us to come down, though he would almost rather have died than say so.

'Why don't you let your flat?"

This to N.

"I don't want to," she said promptly.

"I don't either," said I.

"It would do you good to go away for six months," said Hudson. "Four guineas a week for the flat——"

"Why, that wouldn't pay a hotel bill."

"Oh, there you are with your hotels! I hate the people in hotels."

"And N. hates the no people in rooms."

"Besides, there's our old servant," said N.

"Bah, people chain themselves to a flat or a servant. We're all chained to something. Break the chains!" he almost shouted.

"Bah, too," said I. "You can't! You can only change them. That's freedom, just changing them."

"You're chained to your cigarettes," said Hudson, watching me roll one. "Do you enjoy them?"

"I take them to satisfy and kill a craving."

"But you enjoy them?"

"I don't! They give me a pain if I smoke too many, so there you are!"

"You remind me of a man who said he couldn't drink whisky because it gave him a pain in the head. And he drank it!"

Of course after lunch was over he insisted on buying N. some chocolates. We parted downstairs. I always look after him as if I should never see him again. But now I remember one thing that he said as I helped him on with his coat. He grunted, "I can do it. No one helps me." Then he added in sudden gloom, in Spanish: "' 'Tis bitter at the end of life to walk alone and sad.' " I forget the Spanish, but the lines began "Es amargo." They are by Melendez, whom he loved and often quoted.

Lunch at Whiteley's. November 10.—Hudson, who seemed exceptionally well and actually made no complaints, did his best to destroy my temporary forgetfulness of ill-health by insisting that I looked very well. He then told us about the books he was sending to the working-men's library at Lelant, of which, I believe, he was a kind of founder. He wanted to slay the railway people for their charges, and once more urged N. and myself to let the flat and live elsewhere than in town. No hotels, of course: he couldn't stand them: never could: damnable places! The truth is that he wanted us to come to Penzance as he had done in October.

"Wherever I settle I go about the house and make friends with everyone in it and then in the village. But I don't think I shall stay where I have always stayed in Penzance. The landlady's niece has gone to Cardiff to live with her brother and his wife. She was the only one I really liked there."

"Why did she leave?" asked N. "Wasn't her aunt devoted to her?"

"Yes, in her own way."

"Perhaps she will return now you are going there again," I suggested.

"No, she says she won't. She's at peace now, even if she is separated from most of her friends and relatives."

He always attached himself at once to someone wherever he went. And certainly he attached them to him. If I had time and health I should like to go about the Down country and to Hants and Wilts and Devon and Cornwall and find out all those with whom he stayed. If they would but talk of him what a book could be made of it all! Hudson from the angle of fifty English peasants would be worth doing. Men, women, and children all more or less adored him, to say nothing of animals.

After his usual fashion he interrogated me on a scientific subject, this time the degeneration of the teeth so prevalent in England. To anyone who really knew a little about a subject he listened quite patiently and always seemed eager to learn, although he for ever refused to read any purely scientific book. After finishing with dental degeneration he spoke of my last book (mere potboilers), and said that a volume of stories all humorous was never so good as a mixed bag. He showed great appreciation of my first book of stories, and then spoke of critics, rather more impatiently than usual.

"Why is it," I asked, "that critics will never treat a book for what it is, but always ask for something else? About this last book now: some of them want to know when I'm going to give them a big book. They damn this, though one's only chance of writing other stuff is to get something to go on with by a little humour."

"They don't discriminate between a man with tenpence and one with ten thousand a year," said Hudson. "Perhaps it's not their business to do so."

About the sea he said:

"Do you remember when you and I were at Shoreham on the beach, McCormick and Roudebush ran down from town, and having got more or less jolly came to where we were?"

I had forgotten about it.

"And Mac without saying a word walked straight into the sea with all his clothes on. I said, 'What are you doing? Why don't you undress?' And he replied contemptuously, 'Oh, you understand nothing!' Of course I knew what he meant. It was the joy of the sea and the longing for it that he was satisfying."

"If anyone in the world should understand that it should be you," I said. "Old H. G. Sutton got himself ridiculed by saying that he wished he and his students could sit naked for a while on the ploughed earth. You wallow in the soil."

Hudson nodded. "Of course I understood. I remember saying just the same kind of thing to a man in South America. He was a great wanderer and traveller, and came to our house one evening and talked with another man there in a very interesting way. I was too young to join in but I enjoyed the talk tremendously. But presently he got up and said he must go. Then I *did* have something to say! 'You must be mad! Night's coming on and you have a three hours' ride. Why don't you stay here?' He turned on me with, 'You're nothing but an old granny, talking about the darkness and all that as if it mattered.' Well, he was wrong and didn't in the least understand. If I had been older and bolder I should have said to him, 'I don't care a curse what happens to you, even if you break your infernal neck. I just want you to stay and go on talking because I enjoy the conversation.' As a matter of fact I didn't care for him in the least, but what he said was interesting to me."

Somehow he got upon the subject of films.

"N., have you ever seen Chaplin in *A Dog's Life?*" he asked.

"Yes," said N., who had not greatly cared for it.

Hudson seemed disappointed to hear this and kept on talking about it, telling us over again some of the story with great chuckles at the simple humour of the thing.

Soon after that we got up to go, and as usual he asked
N. if she would like some chocolates.

"This time I should prefer Turkish delight," she replied.

"Why, it's poor sickly stuff and you can't possibly like
it," he said in great surprise. As he went down through
the china department of the big store he drew her attention to some black-and-white china.

"Isn't that very pretty?" he asked.

"I don't like it at all," she replied with decision.

"Neither do I," said Hudson promptly. And he
cackled joyously.

When transcribing this light and casual talk with Hudson I have made no real alteration. There is nothing
in this conversation, it may be thought, that any intelligent
man might not say. That is true enough, but it brings
Hudson out of the realm of the ideal and puts him among
us all, a real companion of man and not always an Isaiah,
or a St. Francis, though Isaiah, no doubt, has his lighter
moments and St. Francis might have laughed in the
Rotunda as well as preached at Assisi. It was better to
be with Hudson when he growled because there was no
suet pudding than to be with perpetual saints and prophets
and those to whom the platform seems native ground. I
daresay Hudson would have been wise if a fool had come,
though his eyes would have twinkled.

This was the very last time we saw him in the big
Rotunda in Queen's Road. He went to Penzance a day
or two later.

CHAPTER XVII

A great man and a great friend—Intellect and simplicity
—Portraits and the man—Source of inspiration—
Towns and villages—Wells and the Mendips—The
Cathedral—Jackdaws and swifts—His sense of the
past—His kinship with it—Religion and philosophy
—The root of his power—Mystics and Hudson—
Popularity and dogs—Vivisection—War—Hunting
—Exmoor deer—Foxes and their earths—Hudson's
symmetry of character—His humour and simplicity.

As my task draws to an end, a task which has been melancholy and yet engrossing, since all elucidation of character has a strange charm for humanity, Hudson seems far clearer to me than when he was still living. Though none may ever analyse the deeper essence of personality I have solved many problems for myself. But personality lies in the effect of all a man's qualities, not in one or even in many. A rose is not its scent or colour, and though we take it petal by petal and describe its foliage it still remains a flower, moving us, not by single chosen aspects, but by its whole nature, our memories, and thoughts deep-hidden even beyond memory. So Hudson was more than can be put down in words. For he was not only a great man, but a great friend, and his loss has been like the setting of the sun. If I may ask anything of those who chance to read these words, it is that they should consider them in the light and fragrance of his own books, while I myself add something almost like the memory of a dead and faithful friend. For even now he is a friend to many who never saw him, and yet recognise in all he wrote a beauty with peculiar individual strangeness. It will not seem impossible for them to believe that he was such a natural man as is here depicted, though a like "naturalness" or freedom is one of the rarest things in mankind. To reach, with a discursive intellect such as Hudson's, the simplicity of a child or some noble animal is more remarkable even than his known achievements. It is possible to be great by mere rareness of character, though nothing be written, or painted, or carved, if that character influences all that come within its ambit.

It might seem that I believe this portrait not so unsuccessful as it might have been. It was begun with fervour, with some belief that my old friend could be portrayed in such manner as might at least please some. I believed that a thousand remembrances would so resolve themselves into order that others would see him as I saw him, and that if they could not hear his voice they would at least look on his picture with awakened eyes. But how monstrously vain is all this art of ours to compass the living man! The greatest artist of all does but draw a picture. He cannot put the man on canvas: it is after all but a man, one like the subject or unlike, and perhaps fine, but not the creature who sat to him. So words, too, fail. There is in them a fatality: they carry to each a meaning not the writer's. Nay, they do not carry the writer's meaning, for who, of all the most divine among them, has written what he felt? So hard it is to come to what one feels, that in the effort to bring a thought into the open it dies, as some dim creature of the woodland might perish in a pitiless sun. This very saying suggests to me how and why I and all others must fail with Hudson. He, too, was a creature of the woodland, of his own woodland, a native of Rima-land, a beautiful and benign savage who lived wonderfully wherever he wandered, and to transplant him into a page is to slay him with words that are as arrows. When a humming-bird is dead we can see a little of its colour, we can dissect its tiny body, name its feathers and its bones, and after all it is but a spoonful of coloured dust the life is out of it and cannot return. The cloud upon the mountain, serene with the colours of the dawn or sunset, is but a wreath of vapour when the day is ended or is all ablaze. So it was and is and must be with Hudson. I have plucked a feather from him and have reduced his clouds to nothing and he is not. For he is not alive and cannot be and none can draw him. That strange, very dear, and wildest of all human beings with the variety of a world in him is dead. There is little more to say. Yet something more may be said, for this chapter was written in an ancient place he loved. Unless he is seen there and in his own wild haunts who shall know him more than a very little?

Some day one of Hudson's votaries, and there will be many and faithful, may work out an itinerary for those who would seek in old English villages and towns for the sources of the master's inspiration. They will find them in many places, some known and others far from the trail. Salisbury with its widespread hamlets on the five-fingered rivers of the Wiltshire plain was one great centre of his work. Another was round the crown and glory of the Mendips, the Cathedral of Wells, with its jackdaws and swifts, under the shadow of which I wrote part of these pages. The other Wells, in Norfolk, upon whose open saltings Hudson watched for the noble and wise wild geese, I knew before he did, but in Wells, of Somerset, he was before me and it was he who drew me to it first. In such a little city, with portions of it so academically beautiful that they seem made by some idyllic painter who was wrapped in a strict convention of English beauty, Hudson was often at his best. There in other ways he equalled what he wrote of the Downs or the rude uplands of Cornwall, for the spirit of a Cathedral, or that outward aspect which shows nothing of the rivalries and jealousies that too often swirl about such places, calmed and inspired him. As I sat in the Cathedral Close and saw the jackdaws, his jackdaws, about the towers, and, far above them, the delicate sky tracery of the flight of swifts, it seemed that he was with me. By the side of the wide moat of the Bishop's Palace, so strongly walled that the episcopal house reminds one of the fierce old clergy who led men to battle in harness, he had often walked and watched the swans and their soberly clad cygnet offspring. For him they had rung the bell by which they ask for food. He had enjoyed the reflection of the flowering walls among the green weeds of those episcopal waters and, before me, had mourned the truncated yet persistent growth of the ancient elms with their decaying branches shorn from them many years ago. I cannot trace all his English wanderings. Yet these few words may some day take others to this ancient city not far from the deep gorge or cañon of Cheddar and the open spaces of the Mendips, for ever things which moved him, since among them have been found traces and proofs of ancient man. Even in the Cathedral Close he found them and found nepenthe and dipped deep into the magic past. For to him all time was one: he did not divide it into eras or diminish it by named periods. The most ancient of palæolithic men still haunted the grounds of historic bishops or abbots, while for him the uplands and thickets were yet alive with the ghosts of a vanished fauna. This sense of the past is a notable thing in many, but Hudson had it so supremely that time itself seemed to exist no more when he came into close contact with any old monument, whether it were but a barrow or tumulus or some grey record of past powers and passions and faiths. He did not when seated beside such relics lament the decay of creeds. What he lamented in contemplation was the passing and death of men who loved and fought so long ago, and, as ghosts, fiercely resented feebler tribes holding their forests and pastures. His knowledge of prehistoric life in a scientific sense was small, but he found ancient history wherever he went and re-peopled the empty wilderness or the crowded town with curious or savage spirits which seemed at times more living than any passing citizen. I myself have grieved to think that this faculty should be so lacking in me that even moments of like vision are rare, and indeed should have discredited its power in any had it not been that once, when standing by an ancient Roman tower in another country, I did for a moment so fall under its domination that I saw the flow and march of Roman legions through the grey crumbling gateway that they themselves beheld when it came white from the builder's hands. There are passages in Hudson's work which show that his vision exceeded that of many who may boast, not unjustly, of their historic insight, and it has often seemed to me that if he had but worked that vein he might have given a truer conception of ancient man than the world yet possesses. He knew what such a great anthropologist as Frazer by much labour has shown to be true, and it is that even now we are what our ancestors were, and that they reasoned and felt as we do, though we work with a fuller knowledge of nature and a greater lack of faith in our prejudices or traditions as premises in argument. And in later years he was moved, as all can guess who know his hatred of death, by a passionate resentment against the fate which in a little time should number him, too, among those who had been displaced by succeeding generations. What life the ancient dead still enjoyed was in brains like his own, and surely that was a scanty reward for many labours and a narrow paradise for men who had once inherited the earth.

Such trains of half-unconscious thought came to Hudson in all ancient precincts, once held holier than they are now, and that the grey towers of Wells had become a sanctuary for chattering jackdaws and the nests of swifts made them lovelier to him than their outward or inward meaning. Of the religion taught within those walls he took no heed; but he felt the power of a greater doctrine, to which they also bore witness, that true religion in man flowered equally and always in beauty, whether it was expressed in stone or action, in high monuments or in the lowliest human kindness. This striving for harmony was the very essence of religion that none enjoyed so perfectly as those who stood outside the armed clash and hostility of creeds, which put into words of doubtful meaning the ancient wordless emotions of mankind. If I were asked what great simple characteristic distinguished Hudson from his compeers in the study of life I should say that it was this historic vision which went beyond the purview of history and philosophy, and in a motion and tide of his whole spirit made him not only a part of it, as it is now, but a portion and parcel of the immemorial past. This was the great root of his being, a thing not to be explained, a faculty so marvellous that taken by itself it would almost justify the unconsidered idealism of those who in some lesser measure share his kinship with Nature. It has been said to me by a kindly critic that parts of this book seem to bear the character of a defence. I may have defended myself for taking a familiar view of Hudson. Some cannot bear to see a hero out of his armour; and there are many who cannot bear the truth. Not a few would expurgate all literature and life and clothe a Grecian wrestler as for some modern arena. I have even seen Montaigne fricasseed for children, and live in expectation of a purified Rabelais, though Montaigne's wisdom excuses his avowals and Rabelais' power makes intolerable jests scarcely blots upon his pages of immortal satire. Let it at least be said that here, in spite of my attempt to paint Hudson as I knew him, I saw clearly how and where his power was rooted and maintained.

In the Church of the Mystics there are many orders. I profess no profound knowledge of its hierophants, yet have scanned with curiosity something of their doctrines. It would seem strange to these mystics to place pantheists among them, as materialism attaches to the names of them all since Spinoza, and yet even he as a pantheist was a mystic, though he expressed his feeling for the universe in argument, not in open emotion and perhaps in madness. And, indeed, those mystics who professed to abhor and lose the senses were but the more sensuous, as much Catholic literature will prove. If I were to put Hudson among the mystics I should erect a new order and foundation for him. How Nature looked to Spinoza when sunk *in substantia Dei* can with difficulty be imagained, and for many of the acknowledged mystics Nature was but another name for the world, the flesh, and the devil. But Hudson argued nothing like the Dutch philosopher, and was the truer mystic because he accepted all things and was often tolerant and even pitiful to the cruel. In his higher moments the world and he were one, the flesh was a sacred and mighty instrument, and what men named the evil one was the power and passion of the instincts which drove man along his destined path. To have creeds finally silent in such a passion was mysticism, and mysticism of the greatest and noblest kind. For he who loses himself in Nature finds himself. This was the great reward of Hudson's impassioned objectivity.

It may be that much of this will seem discursive and irrelevant. But many pages were written at various times during prolonged illness as notes to be used or rejected, and I have chosen here such as seem to throw light on him as a whole man. And now I may note that in nothing did Hudson ever take an unreasoned view. Those who arraigned Nature and proposed to substitute for it a code of delicate human arrangements were obviously wasting their time and energy. He loved life and wished that others loved it enough to make it beautiful, but he took no morbid view of killing or of death in war. These things were "natural," in the accepted order of the universe, they were found everywhere, in all animals and in the great animal—man. He was thus much more sane than many who have fought to advance humanity, for among them are ever to be found those who lack judgment and make their hopes the measure of all things. It is no discredit to their sensibilities that this should be so, but it says little for their wisdom, since to excite in the unreflecting a desire for a new heaven and a new earth through immediate action is but in the end to depress those whom a calmer philosophy might have rendered permanent disciples of a good cause. Such feelings in Hudson were perhaps the soundest part of his native conservatism. He never attacked windmills or put his finger between millstones. His views of the over-peaceful, or of those who told us that the late war was one to end war, were expressed by a shrug of the shoulders. Had he not found it hard to shame women red with the blood of mating egrets? If women were so hard and cruel, was man to turn swords into reaping-hooks just because so many had died? No, war would continue till the coming of the cocklicranes. I do not pretend that he ever said this in so many words, but affirm that such was his general attitude of mind. He was not a voluble idealist, but as sane and sound a creature of this world as ever lived. There was so much to do to-day that to-morrow might look after itself. All this may stand to balance the special knowledge of many, who may judge him solely from his philanthropic side. If he was not in the narrower sense a man of science he had in many ways the wary scientific mind which cannot be taken easily with catchwords or limed by *doctrinaires*. He saw the world as some statesman might view it, and did not permit his passionate love of beauty to deny that ugliness existed.

It is always the kindest who see the native cruelty of things; and when to kindness clarity of vision is added, the possibility of doing just a little does not confirm them in the childlike belief that Elysium will result from education, an Act of Parliament, or another, and yet another, committee. If Nature was red with tooth and claw, man was part of Nature.

It would, however, give a wholly false impression if this were taken to mean that he did not suffer, at times suffer acutely, when he contemplated some of the crueller incidents of what is called sport, to which a brutal continued tradition has given sanction. Even among sportsmen he looked for something like fairplay. Man was truly a hunting animal, but since in settled and civilised countries he no longer hunted for food, but merely for the exercise of ancient instincts in the open air, he might at least "play the game" even with those he chased. On Exmoor the wild deer still exists and is still hunted, and often succeeds in escaping in the almost pathless wilderness between Dunkerry Beacon and Spanhead and between Molland and Porlock Weir, that lies on the northern coast of Somerset. But sometimes it happens that the cornered quarry takes at last to the sea. It may swim for miles, and land in safety. So far the stag has won the game. He has eluded those who desired his head and antlers as they stand upon the shore and watch him. One would think that any man or woman (there are many women in the fields) with a spark of nobility would rejoice to see the animal which has given them a wild free day upon Exmoor, bright with yellowing bracken and purple heather, escape so splendidly with his life. But that is not the way of the sportsman: he needs blood and must have it. With a boat the stag is followed and seized as he is helpless in the water. His throat is cut and he is towed to the beach. Though Hudson knew Simonsbath, the village centre of Exmoor forest, and called it in fond remembrance of the river Barle and the woods "dear Simonsbath," he had not heard of this, and when I told him he sat silent. That was his way. What could be done? And he had so much to do.

And, yet again, when the fox is hunted and all the earths he knows, or at least those that men know, are stopped against him, what happens when by chance, or by some far run beyond the hunt's usual country, he finds an earth not barred? One would say the fox has won the game in spite of the odds against him and man's cunning that matches his own, and that any with the remotest sense of fairplay would own the fact and turn homeward not unrewarded. But that seems to be asking too much of man. He has been fairly beaten and cannot bear it. Therefore he digs out the fox and carries home the brush, or maybe gives it to the nearest lady, while others, perhaps, are awarded bloody pads, so that they may long remember that on those tired feet their prey was carried many miles to a den from which they dug him as he lay panting and exhausted. Need I say what Hudson thought of this, he a very creature of the wilds and assuredly no morbid product of mere sentiment? Those who know him can guess his opinion.

As I draw to an end and look back, as a writer does look back upon what he has written, I feel that though many will be dissatisfied I have not been wholly unsuccessful. I might have made Hudson a hero and have preferred to draw him first and chiefly as a man. He possessed in calm and equal qualities all the great characteristics of mankind, and such a noble and just balance of faculties may, perhaps, justify him as heroic when compared with most. For as I take it such notable symmetry of human characteristics is rare indeed. Most men are unequal, disproportioned, overgrown on one side and atrophied upon another. They are without equilibrium, and are, as it were, truncated. We find great men without generosity, generous men who are feeble creatures: thoughtful men without energy: strong men who are but fools in action: wise men whose wisdom perishes in the study: studious men incapable of using knowledge, and merciful men who cannot teach mercy. But Hudson had these qualities in quiet possession and command, and to them added a great and general co-ordinating wisdom. If, then, I were now to declare that I think of him as a great example of what men might be if their lives permitted them to grow evenly and without distortion, I may be held in some measure to have done him justice, though many will continue to believe that greatness comes, not by an equal union of the instincts, but rather by special overgrowths, diminutions, and atrophies. That is a judgment which Hudson would have disdained, and though he was the last man in the world to consider himself a great and excellent type, I trust I have shown reason for believing it. It is only those who would live beyond the rainbow who will imagine that his faults make him less than he showed to the world. Let me say plainly that if he had not had them I could scarcely have been his friend for so many years. We cannot live with the gods, and the perpetual hero is a bore whom Samuel Butler's Chowbuk might well have thought worse than death at the stake. But Hudson was never self-conscious and was often as simple as a really simple child with a happy sense of fun. His humour was real, and a real humour is the only thing which prevents a man from being ridiculous. That is its chief task and it preserved Hudson from imagining that he was much out of the common. It is the utterly commonplace who suffer from this delusion, while the strangest of our species only learn late, if they ever learn at all, that they are not like the rest of the world. If Hudson had been asked what chiefly distinguished him, he would have replied that he thought more about birds and beasts than other people, and if it ever occurred to him that he was utterly remarkable and a genius, then I am mistaken. Like most unselfish people he probably thought he was selfish. But his regard for his own instincts was as sincere as his regard for those of animals. He hated live things in cages and preserved his own freedom jealously. Therefore I have no desire to cage him now that he is dead, and prefer to show him at liberty and alive. A death mask is a cheerful thing compared with most stories of great men, for in it we can sometimes discern living traces of powerful passions and instincts which survive even the pains of death, and are obliterated only at last by pious hands whose effacing fingers sweep away what death itself has spared.

CHAPTER XVIII

Penzance again, 1921-22—*A Hind in Richmond Park*—
His handwriting—His late return to town—His last
card—My visit to Tower House—His condition—A
consultation arranged—His last talk—Some novelists
—The sense of smell—Script of last chapter—The
Mercury—Talk about Exmoor—His death next
morning.

It was late in the autumn of 1921 that Hudson at last
got away from London and went as usual to his old
rooms in Penzance. He made many attempts to get us
to come there for part of the winter, but though anxious
to do anything in the world to please him, since I might
never see him again, it was impossible that winter for
me to leave London. His chief task during the winter
and spring months was *A Hind in Richmond Park*, with
which he progressed but slowly. He always worked
leisurely even as a young man, and his habit of writing,
as Pope did, on the backs of any odd scraps of paper,
even on envelopes, and writing in pencil, which he sometimes failed to decipher, prolonged his task unduly. His
final script of a book in the days before type-writing
grew common, was curious to behold, as he then wrote
on pages of a small notebook size. The MS. of *A Crystal
Age* was nearly two feet in thickness. Few of his MSS.
appear to remain. His script when he desired to make
it plain was legible enough, but at times he finished a
letter to me by remarking that he feared I should not

be able to read it. When I sent him something perhaps equally illegible he complained as bitterly as if he himself wrote copperplate. On the whole, during the winter and spring of 1921-22 he was fairly well, better indeed than I expected. His heart troubled him, but not in any increasing measure, so I hoped that it might go on for many years, since his general muscular condition was remarkable. He had learnt that the safe path for such as suffered from heart trouble was to do nothing which resulted in undue fatigue either of brain or body.

I looked for him in London at the end of May or June, but he kept on postponing his departure from Cornwall to a later and later date, so that at last I was obliged to leave London before he came. Nothing that he said of himself caused me any particular anxiety, and I, therefore, remained in Somersetshire, at Simonsbath and at West Chinnock, until the fourteenth of August. I shall put down here what I wrote upon the day of his death—I cannot add to it:

The Eighteenth of August.—Hudson died to-day. It is Friday, 18th August.

I want to put down clearly just what happened. We (N. and I) came back from Somersetshire on Monday. His last letter had been cheerful: there was nothing in it hinting at impending calamity. Fatigue prevented me from going to him at once, but I wrote on the Tuesday asking him to lunch with us at the old place on Friday. His answer came in a postcard on Thursday (yesterday) morning.

"Wednesday.—I can't meet you this week as I am

ill in bed since Sunday, and even if I get up I should
not come out of the house this week.—Yours,

"W. H. Hudson."

It was wholly characteristic of him not to ask me to
come to him. He knew I should come. He would not
admit to himself that he was ill enough to need help,
but he would have been surprised not to see me that
very day. I reached his gloomy house early in the afternoon. It was Friday, the 17th. After all there was nothing to alarm me in his card.

He looked up and smiled when I entered his room.
He seemed anxious but relieved. I was not relieved.
I knew too much of his condition. He had a pink cardiac
flush. Some would have said he looked well. His circulation was failing: his heart dilated. As I sat down by
his side he moved uneasily and said that he was in pain:
the precordial pain of the overloaded dilating heart. He
had tried every attitude and had even wasted his little
energy by rubbing himself with liniment. The doctor
had been there that morning.

He made no objection to my feeling his pulse. It
was feeble, threadlike, and far too slow, with the usual
irregularity of his condition. I told him to take no
more digitalis, but was in grave difficulties, for I knew
that something must be done at once, and that if I showed
the slightest sign of apprehension or haste I should work
more harm than good. When he asked me about it I
said his pulse was rather weak, and bit by bit got out
the suggestion that he should see Dr. Frederick Price,
whom he knew so well. I said that Price would no
doubt be able to relieve the pain. He raised objections.

A Harley Street man would charge untold sums for coming to Westbourne Park. Besides and besides—but I knew the notion helped him. So I rolled a cigarette and said casually that I would go out and ring up Price. I called on the local doctor, of course, but as he was not at home, took it on myself to arrange a consultation. I called up 133 Harley Street. Dr. Price was away, but I spoke to Dr. Parsons-Smith, who was doing his work. As I had once sent a patient to this physician he knew my name and agreed to come at half-past seven. I told him all I had observed and he recognised that the case was urgent.

When I returned to Hudson and said cheerfully that it was all settled he seemed much relieved. His breathing grew better: the pain was less. But the flush remained, though he talked easily and freely of a hundred things. He criticised a certain new popular book with humorous savagery. "The last was a great book compared with it, though the last half of that was absurd."

To the very end he was a great novel-reader and critic, though his critical powers failed him at times if the mere story pleased him. In spite of all his splendid imaginative work he pretended sometimes to be no judge of fiction, especially when he disliked anything done by a friend. He broke off the talk to insist on writing a cheque for the consultant. He signed it and then made an alteration which he initialled. These were his last signatures. They were written firmly and clearly.

He picked up the *Century Magazine,* which was lying on the bed, and told me that it contained his second article on the sense of smell. He wanted me to read it, and all the time I was wondering how long I dared

stay without alarming him. I came across something
on incense in the article, and told him of High Mass
which I had once seen in a Trappist Monastery. There
was an air of magic about the incense, I said. He dis-
agreed and then agreed. Presently he made a vain effort
to straighten out the tangled bed-clothes. I helped him,
and saw better than I had ever seen how huge a man
he was. Had his heart been like the rest of him he
might have lived beyond any common age. When he
was more comfortable he lay quietly and I spoke about
the loose scraps of script upon his working table, which
was at the foot of the bed.

"It's the last chapter of *A Hind in Richmond Park,*"
he said, "the one that's given me so much trouble. It's
all finished, but not put together and revised. I can't
get it done."

I looked the script over and suggested that I should
take it away and get my stepdaughter to type it out
for him. He objected that she would not be able to
read it, and besides, the chief trouble would be verbal
alterations which no one could do but himself. I did
not press him. He criticised some things of Santayana
and presently gave me the new number of the *Mercury.*
There was something about Yeats, or by Yeats, in it
which might interest me.

"Take it away with you. But bring it back. Someone
may like a complete set—some day."

Presently he said that it tired him to talk. It was
he who did the talking, but I said I would sit for a
while on the other side of the room and read. So I
took up the *Mercury* and went where he could not see
me, as there was a curtain at the foot of the bed.

I wanted to stay all night. He had no nurse. They were hard to get. But should I not do more harm than good if I did stay? If I remained till the medical consultation he might, and would, think I was anxious. I knew nothing could be worse for him. I did not read, but sat thinking what was best to do. He did not let me remain in quiet for more than five minutes.

"I can't see you, Roberts. Sit where I can see you."

During all these years we had called each other by our surnames. I moved to where he could see me and he began talking again. Thinking that I might get him to allow me to stay, I asked where the old couch was which had been at the foot of his bed. He thought of having it out there again. His idea was that if he had a nurse she might need it. Presently the thought came out.

"I can't get a nurse and I ought to have one."

Again I began to suggest that I might stay, but refrained. Now I grieve that I did not laughingly insist on doing so. But few knew him so well as I, and I felt he would see through any brave pretences that I made.

So time passed. He lay quietly for many minutes and then spoke again, asking about my holiday in what he called "beloved old Simonsbath," that central village of wild Exmoor that I knew so well from Sherdon Water to Pinkworthy Pond, where the Barle rises. He had stayed there once: its wildness and its birds remained a memory. As I stood up at last by his bedside he asked about my own health. It was not what it might be, I told him.

"You *look* well, at any rate," he insisted. He hated

to think that anyone could be ill, just as he regretted to see a friend grow grey.

Two years before this in Penzance he had asked me to serve as his executor. Now I wished I knew who his lawyer was and could not ask him. I am glad I was not made an executor. I know that to-day, this eighteenth of August. For I found his will this morning.

I picked up Salt's *Seventy Years with Savages*. For some reason he spoke of it as being "out of date": the English were not quite such savages as they had been. I put the book down and said casually:

"Shall I come in to-morrow?"

He replied with his old quaint independence, tinged as I knew with the desire to believe that his illness was not serious: "Of course, if you'd like to."

I like to think, and indeed do believe, that my being able to go did, in fact, help him. Still in his voice there was an undertone as though he said, "Yes, do." I cannot put it down in words. Some would say he was often ungracious. I have seen him hide deep affection under the transparent cover of indifference, even of rudeness, long, long years ago.

His Scotch housekeeper came into the room then and her coming helped me to go. She spoke about making the bed for him. It was what I called, in sea-language, a "Hurrah's nest." So I took his hand, that big kindly hand, and held it for a moment but no longer. He looked so splendid, kind, and anxious, and ready, just a little, a very little, to cling not only to life but to one who loved him. As I reached the door I turned and said:

"Of course Naomi sent her love to you."

"My love to her."

Those were the last words I heard him speak.

This morning a telegram came for me. N. brought it to my working-room. She knew and I knew. Hudson had died early this very day. His housekeeper asked me to come. I knew she would be in distress. Who would not that knew him? She can speak to that, and so can many, very many. He wasn't only good and kind to birds. I reached the house before noon and went up to his room.

I found him "sleeping." He lay comfortably upon his right side with his hands as one puts them in easy sleep, the natural attitude of happy rest. Now his face was very pale and quietly noble: without a smile but without any sign of fear or pain. He seemed so big, so strong, a giant among men. Though he was over eighty, there were big, loose muscles on his arms and on his great hands which would write no more and would never finish that last chapter upon art as the result of the splendid surplus energy in man as colour is in the birds.

At four o'clock in the morning his housekeeper had risen (not many would have risen, or shall I say that for him many would have risen?) and brought him a cup of tea. The night had not been too weary, for they had spoken helpfully to him, and now he said that he felt drowsy. She thought that he needed sleep, and as she turned to leave him, to her great surprise he put out his hand and said, "Good-bye." He was very sleepy and seemed to mean no more than just what the words implied, and yet it was strange in one who never made demonstrations. She went away about her work, and at eight o'clock sent up her little girl to him with his letters. The child came back to say that Mr. Hudson was asleep. Her mother knew what that meant.

I stayed with him a long while. Presently they would bury him. Such a man! Such a beautiful big savage and genius—to be buried as we bury! I wished to take him out upon the open pampa, with a long wide view beyond the sight of man even on horseback, with the great clear sky above. So I would have digged a grave and put him there to rest in his blanket just as he had fallen asleep, without disturbing his attitude of quiet peace.

To have the wild winds sing about him and the wilder beasts crop herbage from his lonely grave, while noble-voiced birds trumpeted high choruses above one who loved them—that is the grave I would have chosen for him.

It was not to be. His other friend and I straightened his limbs at last and I laid his hands, yet warm, upon his breast.

INDEX